THE HOLY WEB

CHURCH AND THE NEW UNIVERSE STORY

Cletus Wessels, O.P.

ORBIS BOOKS

Maryknoll, New York 10545

Third Printing, April 2001

The Catholic Foreign Mission Society of America (Maryknoll) recruits and trains people for overseas missionary service. Through Orbis Books, Maryknoll aims to foster the international dialogue that is essential to mission. The books published, however, reflect the opinions of their authors and are not meant to represent the official position of the Society. To obtain more information about Maryknoll and Orbis Books, please visit our website at www.maryknoll.org.

Library of Congress Cataloging-in-Publication Data

Wessels, Cletus.
   The holy web : church and the new universe story / Cletus Wessels.
     p. cm.
   Includes bibliographical references and index.
   ISBN 1-57075-302-4 (pbk.)
    1. Religion and science. 2. Cosmology. 3. Creation. 4. Ecclesiology. I. Title.

BL240.2.W46 2000
230'2—dc21

                         99-462325

CONTENTS

PREFACE

The seed for this book was planted in the early 1980s when, as a staff member of a retreat center, I developed a workshop entitled simply, "New Paradigm." I still have the rough, handwritten outline for that original workshop. The outline has topics crossed out and added, notes scrawled up, down, and sideways, and cryptic page numbers from unknown books. The most notable thing in looking at this outline is at once how similar it is to the final outline of this book and how different it is. It is similar in the way that an acorn is similar in its genetic coding to an oak tree, and it is as different as the oak tree is from the acorn.

This should not be surprising because, since the seed was planted, many things have changed in society and in my own awareness of issues within the church. Over the last two decades, I have presented this material on the new paradigm in countless workshops, classrooms, and retreats; I have pruned and fertilized this youthful paradigm of the church during nine years as a pastor in a city parish; and I have recently had the opportunity to spend two years in research and writing, leading to the more mature ideas contained here, in what has become *The Holy Web: Church and the New Universe Story.*

The purpose of this work is to present a new vision that integrates the tradition of the Christian church with contemporary cosmology and the universe story. There is a need for such a new paradigm because, as Chet Raymo points out in his book *Skeptics and True Believers,* "Today we have a scientific story of creation, but we have not learned how to connect the new story to our search for spiritual fulfillment . . . and we have not integrated the story into our lives as believers and seekers" (p. 127–128). Such an integration, I maintain, is essential both for the Christian church and for all those searching for spiritual fulfillment.

There is also a deeper purpose. This is not a book that simply sets out to prove its thesis or to impart new information to the reader. Its purpose is to help the reader discover and intuit more deeply the new story of the universe and the possibilities for a new vision of the church flowing from that story. This new paradigm will offer an exciting vision of the church in a challenging and digestible fashion. I have attempted to write it in a style that will help the reader think in new ways demanded by new realities and new ideas. For this reason I will often share stories from my own journey in a way that can draw the reader into the process.

I invite readers of this book to an in-depth discussion of a new paradigm of the church emerging from the tremendous knowledge explosion of the last 150 years and the development of a new understanding of creation never before imagined. My goal is to provide a work that is both readable and challenging—one that will encourage educated Christians to reexamine the scientific worldview and to integrate their experience of church with this new cosmology. I hope too, that professional theologians will benefit from entering into dialogue with this new paradigm of church, and that, building on the issues and ideas that this book addresses, they might do their own serious research on new ways to articulate a vision of the Christian church.

I write out of my experience as a Roman Catholic, but over the years I have been involved at some depth with other Christian churches and with various ecumenical dialogues. It is my hope that this book will speak to a broad spectrum of educated Christians. We all share the same Bible and struggle to search for its deeper meaning in a culture vastly different from the one in which the Bible was written. All Christian churches emerged in a religious culture founded on a biblical creation story and a patriarchal society, both of which now need to be reinterpreted in the light of a new creation story and the rise of feminism in our world. Each church will come to this process from a different viewpoint and out of a different church structure. We all, however, must face the necessity of developing a new vision of the church rooted in our biblical and ecclesial traditions and moving us forward into the twenty-first century.

A new paradigm often challenges our current use of language. This will demand first of all that we look more deeply into the way we typically use words, such as *infallibility*. When people hear the word infallibility they think of the pope with the unilateral power to define Christian doctrines, which must then be believed and accepted by all Catholics, putting an end to all discussion. This is a stereotype. As the word infallibility is used in Chapter 6, it means a process that takes place within the entire Christian community in the common search for the living truth of the gospel under the guidance of God's Spirit. The pope, as the bishop of Rome, may in special circumstances define a doctrine that is already the common belief of the people, but this definition is always couched in human words and, as such, is open to an ongoing process of fuller understanding and unfolding.

Second, at times a new paradigm requires new language to articulate the perception of a new reality, such as the *holarchical* church—a term introduced in Chapter 5. Over the years, as I have experienced the changing structures of our earth, our society, and our church, I have become convinced that we must develop new terminology to articulate the new theories about the way in which organizations function. Our current language is often inadequate. For example, the organizational structures of many Christian churches are based on a hierarchical and patriarchal model, whereas contemporary research calls for emerging models based on self-organization, mutuality, and interdependence. It is my belief that such models cannot be couched in hierarchical language nor in distinctions such as that between clergy and laity. As we will see in Chapter 5, these new models can be articulated more adequately in terms of the new language of *holarchy.*

Third, even common words, such as the word *holy* used in the title of this book, will take on a new depth of meaning in the light of the new universe story. For me at times, and perhaps for other people, the word holy is ambiguous and flat; it can be pious and churchy, and occasionally rigid and unchanging. These connotations of the word holy just do not fit with my sense of "the holy web." In this book, holy describes the reality of goodness, truth, and wholeness within the universe whose inner source is God. To be a creature emerging from the inner presence of the holy God is to *be holy.* And human holiness is found in our very being as well as in our conscious awareness of and our integration with this dynamic power of God within ourselves. Holiness is not something we do or practice or merit, but it is something we experience as a dimension of the universe. Thus, in this book, when we use the phrase *holy web,* we are describing the web of relationships found in the entire universe. When we talk about a galaxy or the Earth or the church as a web of relationships, we are describing these realities as *part of* the holy web.

All the biblical quotations in this book are my own translations. I have tried to use language that does not exclude but does maintain the sense of the original texts. This is not always possible because the original texts arose within a patriarchal culture.

I am not primarily a research theologian. I am much more a teacher, a preacher, and a seeker of wisdom. I am a provocateur who tries to stimulate people by presenting ideas that are soundly based yet invite fuller research by others. I am a storyteller who wants to serve as a guide into the mysteries of the universe and the God who unfolds in the universe. I am a reconciler who seeks unity in the deepest realities of faith and reason. I am a deeply committed Christian whose life has been molded by the Christian tradition at its best; yet I am also a restless Christian, always looking for the surprising novelty of God. I hope that this book—through providing a synthesis of science and theology—will open up for readers a new way of looking at the church and a positive vision of the church for the new millennium.

For me the development of this new synthesis of the church and the universe story has been in itself an example of a self-organizing system founded on mutuality and interdependence. As you will discover in the many stories in this book, the new paradigm gradually took on a life of its own. Throughout much of my life I have been prepared to enter into this process through natural inclination, education, life experiences, and ministry settings. Unexpected books or surprising new friends or insights from movies or plays continually nudged me along. Synchronicity, an integral part of the self-organizing principle, was a constant companion. Feedback and questioning from students, workshop participants, and retreatants continually called me into the deeper mysteries of life, and parishioners guided me into a deeper awareness of the meaning of the church.

The Dominican family were my teachers and mentors, my support and nourishment, my friends and, at times, my critics. My Dominican province gave me the opportunity to spend two years of "leisure" for research and writing. The provincial leadership team was supportive of my work, and several of my Dominican brothers read the manuscript at various times and offered their comments.

During the time I was actually writing the book, I had the opportunity to share each chapter with the First Friday Group, twelve faithful people who met on the first Friday of each month for a period of two years. Their comments and suggestions were invaluable. Finally, I express my appreciation to a friend who read and edited the entire manuscript as it came to life, and to a special friend whose support and companionship helped me through the many ups and downs of giving birth to a new paradigm.

The power and presence of God is clearly present for me in the experience of the self-organizing principle flowing from trust and synchronicity; in the mutuality of family, friends, teachers, students, critics, and supporters; and in the interdependence of the holy web of relationships throughout the entire universe, and especially in my little corner of the world.

PART I

A NEW PARADIGM

The deepest crises experienced by any society are those moments of change when the story becomes inadequate for meeting the survival demands of a present situation. Such, it seems to me, is the situation we must deal with in this late twentieth century. We are confused at present because our historical situation has changed so profoundly. Our story, too, has changed. We no longer know its meaning or how to benefit from its guidance.[1]

The winds of change that currently buffet the structure of both society and the church also threaten their future survival because our story is no longer adequate. As a Christian community and as a global community, we are in the midst of a deep crisis and a turning point in the history of the human race. New directions as well as new visions and symbols are emerging, and these can be best brought together and integrated within a new paradigm of the church. This need is examined in Chapter 1.

The discovery of a new creation story over the last 150 years also calls for a new paradigm of the church. This story raises serious questions about the relationship, as we now perceive it, between the earth and humans. Are we to be the conquerors and rulers of the earth, or can we live in harmony within the community of species? In this new story we are called to embrace the presence of chaos, darkness, and the shadow side of this beautiful Earth and to articulate the images of God found in the new story.

Next, Chapter 2 presents a brief overview of the story of the human from childhood to adolescence to the possible emergence of adulthood. The overall purpose of the chapter is to introduce the reader to some of the basic principles of the universe that will later be more fully developed and used to articulate the characteristics of the new paradigm.

---

[1] Berry, Thomas, *The Dream of the Earth,* San Francisco, Sierra Club Books, 1988, p. xi.

1

THE NEED

THE WINDS OF CHANGE

Once, while visiting in Kentucky, I saw a large barn used for making and storing whiskey. The construction was very elaborate with storage bins, intricate support systems, many walls and floors tied together by struts and beams. The barn was being torn down, and a local resident commented that it would take about as many years to dismantle the barn as it did to build it because of the intricacies of its structure. Two weeks later I returned to find the entire building in shambles. The local resident explained that a strong wind (*ruah*/spirit) came up and accomplished in minutes what might have taken years. What are the strong winds that threaten to dismantle the Roman Catholic Church, and, perhaps, the whole Christian establishment?

The winds of *intellectual and cultural change* are stronger than most people realize. In the last 150 years, our way of thinking and our way of seeing the world have changed profoundly. In 1850, people thought the world was five or six thousand years old based on biblical computations; now people generally believe the world is about fifteen billion years old and the human race has been on earth for several million years. In 1850, the speed of travel and communication was very limited; now we travel thousands of miles an hour through weightless space and have instantaneous global communication.

Freud and Darwin have challenged our assumptions about what it means to be human, and molecular biology and nuclear physics leave us breathless as we try to keep pace with the meaning of our bodily make-up and our physical universe. The computer culture is making a profound impact on our way of working and living; we live in a virtual world of technoculture. The bombs that destroyed Hiroshima and Nagasaki destroyed not only the population of two cities but our whole concept of the morality of war.

The global village is smaller than we thought, whirling in a universe infinitely larger and older than we thought. The human person is vastly more

3

complex than we thought; society is more economically, culturally, and ethnically stratified and yet more interdependent than we thought. These powerful intellectual and cultural winds rattle the timbers of the Roman Catholic Church, whose traditional structure is based on a radically different worldview.

The winds of *ecumenism* have shaken the security of the Roman Catholic Church. In the 1950s we thought we were safe within the boundaries of the "one true church." Individual Protestants might be saved, but this was in spite of their religion rather than because of it; most non-Christians were out of sight and out of mind. Then the Second Vatican Council comes along and tells us that we Roman Catholics bear some of the responsibility for the divisions, and that other churches separated from Rome (notice they are called *churches*) possess some of the same salvific elements found in the Roman Catholic Church—the sacred Scriptures, belief in God and in Jesus as Savior, baptism, the presence of the Holy Spirit, spiritual gifts, prayer, worship, and ministry.[1] Official dialogues among Christian churches indicate that many of our most strident disagreements are in fact diverse ways of articulating the same basic reality and legitimate differences in theology rather than schismatic divergences in faith.

Beyond this, many people are beginning to experience the presence of God within the world's great non-Christian religions. It seems impossible to maintain that God's revelatory and salvific presence has not been experienced over the more than two-million-year history of the human race and among the many billions of non-Christians inhabiting our earth. It raises the question of the specificity of Christianity in the midst of the universality of salvation. The walls of the "one true church" begin to buckle in the wind and even break apart.

Another strong and influential wind is found in the new awareness not only of the value but the necessity of reexamining our faith and theology from the perspective of *women's experience*. Christianity is rooted in a patriarchal culture that undervalues the place of women in society and in the church. The feminist critique calls us to look at the world, at society, and at the church from the viewpoint of women's experience, one that has been ignored or repressed over the centuries. As Joan Chittister points out, "The woman question is not going to go away no matter how clearly the church says it must. There is another voice to be heard now, rich in experience, full of questions and very different in its values, goals and perceptions."[2] This viewpoint brings a new richness to Christian faith and life as it claims full equality before God for all women and men.

> As women name themselves in power, responsibility, freedom, and mutual relatedness, and affirm themselves as embodied, self-tran-

---

[1] Cf. Vatican II, *Lumen Gentium,* #15; *Unitatis Redintegratio,* #3, #19–23.

[2] Chittister, Joan, "Pentecost Papacy Would Listen to Women," in *National Catholic Reporter,* October 10, 1997.

scending persons broken by sin and yet renewed by amazing grace, new ownership of the gift of the female self as *imago Dei, imago Christi* is transacted.[3]

Finally, the most frightening wind or spirit blowing in the institutional church comes from within its own walls. The whole *myth*[4] *of the hierarchical structure* of the Roman Catholic Church seems to be crumbling. This breakdown is expressed very starkly in the book entitled *Pontiff*. It points out that Giovanni Battista Montini (Paul VI) was

> elected in 1963 to be the spiritual leader of the largest church in the world and the bearer of awesome titles, offices and power which, in theory, can reach out from this bedroom in a fifteenth-century Vatican palace and directly affect the lives of 740 million baptized Roman Catholics. In reality, he reigns over a restless church which increasingly pays little more than lip service to his teachings. Many Catholics flout his now-famous encyclical *Humanae Vitae* (*On Human Life*) by continuing to practice birth control; women want to be priests, priests wish to marry, bishops desire to be regional popes, theologians claim a teaching authority even more absolute than the powers vested in the body of the tired and frail old man in the brass bed which faces the closed shutters.[5]

There have always been prophetic and/or rebellious people in the church, and they have been dealt with through excommunication, suspension, or other canonical sanctions. Such methods worked in a predominantly Catholic culture in which most of the educated people were clergy, but they are not effective today.

Despite the discipline of the church, many Catholics use so-called artificial means of responsible parenthood and consider it an act of virtue. Some divorced and remarried Catholics continue to receive the sacraments, often with the tacit or even explicit approval of their clergy. Especially women seem to be the objects of disciplinary action. Sister Agnes Monsour is told to resign as a director of social services in Michigan or leave her religious congregation; she continues as director and remains a "nun in her heart." The difference today is that people who disagree, instead of leaving the church, often become more active because they believe that *they are the church*.

---

[3] Johnson, Elizabeth, *She Who Is: The Mystery of God in Feminist Discourse*, New York, Crossroad, 1994, p. 75.

[4] The word *myth* does not imply something that is false or simply the product of imagination, rather it is a way of interpreting our common experience of reality. "All men [and women] need, then, some more or less coherent set of implicit assumptions, symbolic meanings, characteristic configurations, and explicit beliefs that help them to organize and guide their lives; and we call this need a need for myth." Keniston, Kenneth, *The Uncommitted*, New York, Dell, 1970, p. 273.

[5] Thomas, Gordon, and Max Morgan-Witts, *Pontiff*, Garden City, NY, Doubleday, 1983, pp. 19–20.

These women refuse to go away. The church, they are saying, is theirs as much as anyone's. Authority may push them or even define them, but it cannot destroy either them or their ideas of what being the church means, for they no longer recognize authority in ways they once did.[6]

Perhaps the pressures on the institutional church are greater than at any time in history—greater than in the age of martyrs because martyrdom forged a deep sense of purpose and bonding among the faithful; greater than during the Dark Ages because there remained at that time a strong sense of tradition and holiness, especially in the great monasteries; greater than through the age of the Reformation because the reformers either left or were forced out of the institution leaving behind a united, if besieged, ecclesiastical fortress. Today pressures come from within the church itself, pressures that might dismantle the church from within.

Challenged from within and buffeted by the winds of social change and ecumenism, the church is crumbling under the stress and crises of the times. It is becoming clear, however, that stress within any open system is an opportunity for transformation, and crisis can be the beginning of a new period of growth and development. If the wind that is dismantling the structure of the church is truly the breath of God, then instead of destruction there will be a new Pentecost, a new heaven and a new earth. This new beginning calls for a new paradigm; we need to look more deeply into the meaning of a paradigm shift.

A PARADIGM SHIFT

People tend to find meaning in life and work by trying to integrate the multitude of facts, ideas, and interpretations that bombard them. This integration can take place in the depths of the personality in terms of various symbol systems and mythologies. When such integration takes place at a more conscious and reflective level it is frequently called a *paradigm*. Symbol systems, mythologies, and paradigms are social realities that surround us, enter into us and shape us throughout our lives. They are not fully under our rational control, and we tamper with them only when forced to do so and at considerable social and personal risk.

Sometimes, however, new experiences and information, new consciousness and understanding challenge the meaning of our life and work; new facts, ideas, and interpretations lead to the disintegration of our worldview. We feel like a potted plant that has been uprooted, unable to find food or water, or like a parachutist free-falling without knowing where she will land. The profound social, scientific, and religious changes of the last one hundred or so years need to be dealt with or we will remain uprooted and

[6]Beifuss, Joan Turner, "Feminists Are Clarifying Old Values," in *National Catholic Reporter,* December 23, 1983.

free-falling. Thus the question: How does a paradigm shift take place? How do we adjust when we get new and conflicting information?

The first possibility can be called *change by exception,* which is not so much a basic change in our ideas but a realization and a toleration of exceptions to the norm. For example, the authorities within the Catholic Church get new and conflicting information about contraception. Their first response is to reaffirm the condemnation of contraception but to tolerate certain exceptions for pastoral reasons.

Among many Catholics the new and conflicting information led to *incremental change.* Gradually people absorbed new values about responsible parenthood until bit by bit the time was reached when the majority of Catholics now do not see contraception as intrinsically evil. They have in fact undergone an incremental change, but they remain uneasy because this view is difficult to integrate with their acceptance of the teaching authority of the church.

A third kind of change is called *pendulum change,* when people swing from one extreme to another. It does not actually involve a transformation of ideas and a new integration, but a sense of dualism, of either-or, of giving up one position for its opposite—the youthful anti-establishment radical becomes the middle-aged corporate conservative, clericalism becomes congregationalism, and possibly back again.

All of these attempts to deal with conflicting information are inadequate because they are short-term, superficial approaches to issues that require both a profound transformation and a new integration of our symbol systems and mythologies. In a word, it is a *paradigm shift,* the fourth dimension of change, that is needed for the church to make sense to contemporary Christians and for the church to carry out its mission to and with contemporary society.

The characteristics of a paradigm and of paradigm shifts were articulated by Thomas Kuhn in his classic work *The Structure of Scientific Revolutions.*[7] As we begin to discover and articulate a new paradigm of the church, several important aspects of a paradigm shift should be kept in mind.

1. A paradigm shift may seem to some to be radical and sudden, but in fact the shift is the result of a gradual process that takes place over several decades or even centuries. Frequently the issues leading to a new order of things are present for a long time but only recognized at a time of crisis when the sudden shift takes place.
2. A paradigm shift is not fully rational or conscious. "This discovery of a new pattern transcends explanation. The shift is qualitative, sudden, the result of neurological processes too rapid and complex to be traced by

[7] Kuhn, Thomas S., *The Structure of Scientific Revolutions,* Chicago, University of Chicago Press, 1970.

the conscious mind. Although logical explanations can be laid out up to a point, the seeing of a pattern is not sequential but all-at-once."[8]

3. For this reason a new paradigm is like a simple grasp of reality that in Aristotelian logic is not subject to proof—you either see it or you don't. It arises from personal and communal experiences that lead to a new apprehension of reality. As Kuhn reminds us, "The competition between paradigms is not the sort of battle that can be resolved by proofs."[9]

4. Because a new paradigm is a new apprehension of reality, it requires new terminology. Thus the characteristics of the new paradigm of the church described in this book are couched in a language that is consciously different from that used in most discussions of the church. The purpose is not to confuse but to open up and articulate a new and unexplored wilderness.

5. No paradigm exhausts the truth of the reality it tries to integrate. It is important to be modest about our expectations. "In paradigm change we realize that our previous views were only part of the picture—and that what we know now is only part of what we'll know later. . . . Each insight widens the road, making the next stage of travel, the next opening, easier."[10] No definitive paradigm of the church is being proposed. This is only an attempt to help a pilgrim people find more meaning and direction for their life and ministry.

Any paradigm of the church is a commonly accepted pattern or model that allows people to form a community and live their lives in comparative harmony and stability. The teachings and moral precepts of the church as well as its external structure and sacramental system fit together like a puzzle to form a recognizable picture. We begin to absorb the paradigm from our baptism, it is reinforced in the family and in the Christian educational system, and it becomes second nature as we live it out as adults. Such paradigms are seen as good and even as necessary for the church because without a shared pattern or model chaos results.

And yet there are times when we need to move out of our "zone of comfort" into chaos. At those moments a profound transformation and a new integration are essential precisely because the very existence of chaos is the beginning of a paradigm shift. In fact, in recent years, physicists have begun to see paradigm shifts in a more profound way as part of the very make-up of the whole of creation. Ilya Prigogine and Isabelle Stengers, in their work *Order Out of Chaos*, present a new model of the way transformation takes place, which they call a *dissipative structure*.

---

[8] Ferguson, Marilyn, *The Aquarian Conspiracy,* New York, St. Martin's Press, 1980, p. 42.

[9] Kuhn, *The Structure of Scientific Revolutions*, p. 148.

[10] Ferguson, *The Aquarian Conspiracy,* p. 72.

In far-from-equilibrium conditions we may have transformation from disorder, from thermal chaos, into order. New dynamic states of matter may originate, states that reflect the interaction of a given system with its surroundings. We have called these new structures *dissipative structures* to emphasize the constructive role of dissipative processes in their formation.[11]

Some years ago I was attending a major conference in the east. For one of the presentations, about 200 people assembled in a large, narrow room. As the people gathered they were uneasy about the configuration of the room. The speaker's lectern was at the far end of the space, quite a distance from many participants, and all the chairs were turned to face that end. When the speaker and the introducer arrived, uneasiness gave way to some mumbling. Someone called out to the introducer, "The arrangement in this room is not satisfactory." He responded by soothing the questioner. As he started to make his introduction, someone from another section of the audience shouted, "This set-up won't work!" Some heads nodded in agreement, and some people agreed verbally. Things were getting unruly. As the speaker stepped up to the lectern, another person interrupted him and said, "We can't see, we're too far away and dispersed!" Another person took the microphone and said, "Let's each one turn our chairs sideways and reshape this room!" Someone grabbed the lectern and took it to the side of the room, everyone turned their chairs, the speaker followed with the microphone, and the whole group settled down for an excellent presentation.

This experience illustrates very well the dynamics of a dissipative structure. At first there was uneasiness in the room—the system needed an adjustment. The situation gradually became more serious as people began to mumble, and there was an increase in the negative feelings in the room. The introducer tried to smooth out the fluctuations in the system. When someone verbally articulated the problem, it perturbed the entire room. More people became agitated as the system tried to hold itself together. Then suddenly the entire shape of the room was transformed, and the participants entered into the process with new energy, and a paradigm shift took place!

Compare this experience with the following description of a dissipative structure.

> The continuous movement of energy through the system results in fluctuations; if they are minor, the system damps them and they do not alter its structural integrity. But if the fluctuations reach a critical size, they "perturb" the system. They increase the number of novel interactions within it. They shake it up. The elements of the old pattern come into contact with each other in new ways and

---

[11] Prigogine, Ilya, and Isabelle Stengers, *Order Out of Chaos*, New York, Bantam Books, 1984, p. 12.

make new connections. *The parts reorganize into a new whole. The system escapes into a higher order.*[12]

Margaret Wheately describes dissipative structures in a similar way when discussing the relationship between the new science and leadership in society.

> Disequilibrium is the necessary condition for a system's growth. He (Prigogine) called these systems *dissipative structures* because they dissipate their energy in order to recreate themselves into new forms of organization. Faced with amplifying levels of disturbance, these systems possess innate properties to reconfigure themselves so that they can deal with the new information. For this reason, they are frequently called self-organizing or self-renewing systems.[13]

As Alvin Toffler tells us, the dynamics of a dissipative structure can be applied to society and to politics.

> For this sweeping synthesis [*Order Out of Chaos*], as I have suggested, has strong social and even political overtones. Just as the Newtonian model gave rise to analogies in politics, diplomacy, and other spheres seemingly remote from science, so, too, does the Prigoginian model lend itself to analogical extension.[14]

It is my contention that these dynamics can be extended to religion and to the structure of the church as well in such a way that the winds of change will not destroy the church, as they did the storage barn in Kentucky, but they will transform the church.

The need for a paradigm shift becomes apparent when the old paradigm, which once provided harmony and stability, is now the source of cacophony and conflict. New experiences and new discoveries raise new problems and new questions with which the old paradigm is incapable of dealing. The energy of the institutional church is dissipated in trying to ignore or distract people from an awareness of new issues, in trying to silence or repress those who articulate and act out new models, and in trying to dampen the inevitable transformation of the church by taking refuge in authoritarian tactics. Such tactics can be effective for minor disturbances and for a short time, but "any time a perturbation is greater than the society's ability to 'damp' or repress it, the social organization will (a) be destroyed, or (b) give way to a new order."[15]

---

[12] Ferguson, *The Aquarian Conspiracy*, pp. 164–165.

[13] Wheatley, Margaret J., *Leadership and the New Science,* San Francisco, Berrett-Koehler Publishers, 1994, p. 88.

[14] Toffler, Alvin, "Forward: Science and Change," in Prigogine and Stengers, *Order Out of Chaos*, p. xxiii.

[15] Ferguson, *The Aquarian Conspiracy*, p. 166.

I deeply believe that under the guidance of the Spirit of God the church will be transformed, and the old order will give way to a new order. Out of our contemporary chaos will come creativity. Christianity over the centuries has been called to meet the challenges of previous moments of death and new life, just as Jesus did. The question we now face is whether we are willing to let go and face death in order to rise to new life.

> We are compelled to assert what seems initially to be an outrageous claim: a radically new future demands the destruction and death of the old reality. It is from the dying seeds that new life sprouts forth. Destruction becomes a precondition for reconstruction; disintegration undergirds reintegration; Calvary is a prerequisite for resurrection.[16]

Where then can we look for a "story," a set of "symbols," a guiding "wisdom" that will enable us to unravel the mystery of God's presence among us and to renew the structures of the church for the next millennium? How can we discover a new paradigm gradually emerging within our lives and our church? It is the thesis of this work that the source for the new paradigm will be found, not only in the stories, symbols, and wisdom of biblical and Christian tradition, but in the new creation story, the symbols of the universe, and the wisdom of the earth. Further it is my hope and expectation that these two sources will mutually enrich one another. And so, on to the New Creation Story!

---

[16] O'Murchu, Diarmuid, *Quantum Theology*, New York, Crossroad, 1997, p. 181.

2
_____

THE NEW CREATION STORY

_____

We are in trouble just now because we do not have a good story.
We are in between stories. The old story, the account of how the
world came to be and how we fit into it, is no longer effective.
Yet we have not learned the new story.[1]

THE DISCOVERY OF A NEW STORY

Foundational to every human culture is a creation story.[2] Such stories are
often very imaginative, involving cosmic events that ground all the culture's
social norms and religious rituals. Listen to this story and its water imagery.

> In the beginning, there was only water and the water animals that
> lived in it. Then a woman fell from a torn place in the sky. She was
> a divine woman, full of power. Two loons flying over the water saw
> her falling. They flew under her, close together, making a pillow for
> her to sit on. The loons held her up and cried for help. They could
> be heard for a long way as they called for other animals to come.
> The snapping turtle came to help. The loons put the woman on the
> turtle's back. Then the turtle called all the other animals to aid in
> saving the divine woman's life.
>
> The animals decided the woman needed earth to live on. Turtle
> said, "Dive down in the water and bring up some earth." So they
> did that, those animals. A beaver went down. A muskrat went
> down. Others stayed down too long, and they died. Each time, Tur-
> tle looked inside their mouths when they came up, but there was no
> earth to be found. Toad went under the water. He stayed too long,
> and he nearly died. But when Turtle looked inside Toad's mouth, he
> found a little earth. The woman took it and put it all around on

_____

[1] Berry, Thomas, *The Dream of the Earth*, San Francisco, Sierra Club Books, 1988, p. 123.

[2] One way of gaining knowledge of this new story is to consult works such as the following:
The Dream of the Earth by Thomas Berry, *The Hidden Heart of the Cosmos* by Brian
Swimme, and *The Universe Story* by Brian Swimme and Thomas Berry.

13

Turtle's shell. That was the start of the earth. Dry land grew until it formed a country, then another country, and all the earth. To this day, Turtle holds up the earth.[3]

This story is taken from the Huron culture of Native Americans who lived in the St. Laurence Valley. Water and water animals were basic to their way of life. Thus their creation story focuses on water as the life ambience of the people, and it describes how the coming of the earth is the result of the efforts of the water animals. Turtle, an amphibious animal, is a central figure in the story and its broad back becomes the foundation of the earth. Thus, the imagery of the story flows from the immediate sense experience of the people.

Here is a story from a West African tribe, where the air is so clear and the sun so bright that the heaven seems very close to the earth. Once again the content and imagery of the story flow from the way the people experience creation with their senses.

In the beginning, God was Wul-bar-I. God Wulbari was the blue heaven—spread out not five feet above the mother, earth. The God was very upset. There was not enough space between Him and the earth. The man who lived on earth kept bumping his head against the God. It didn't seem to bother the man, but it surely bothered Wulbari.

An old woman was making food outside her hut. Her stirring pole kept knocking and poking Wulbari. The smoke from her cooking fires got into His eyes. "I'll rise up a bit," thought Wulbari. And so He lifted the blue of His heavenly self just a little higher.

"There," He thought, "that's better." But still, being so close to women and men, Wulbari was useful. He became a perfect towel for everybody. And the people used Him to wipe their dirty hands. . . . Wulbari moved up higher and higher until He was out of the way of everyone.[4]

Creation stories vary greatly across tribes and cultures, but they always deal with the basic issue of the origins of all things and the relationships between the gods and the people, and the social relationships within the family and tribe. Sense perceptions are the principal source of our self-awareness as individuals and as a culture, whether it be the experience of living near water or of living where the blue sky is too close. Whatever is in our minds and hearts comes through our senses. As a people we experience the world around us, our interaction with the world, and the mystery that is the

---

[3] "The Woman Who Fell from the Sky," in *In the Beginning: Creations Stories from around the World,* as told by Virginia Hamilton, New York, Harcourt Brace Jovanovich, 1988, pp. 59–60.

[4] "Wulbari the Creator," in *In the Beginning,* pp. 53–54.

source of it all, and then we tell stories. This sense perception and self-awareness is the basic source of our creation stories and our cosmology.

Foundational to the cosmology of the Western world up to the time of Copernicus and Galileo was the biblical creation story. It fit in well with the way Western culture experienced the world, and it provided an answer to the basic issues of our human lives. The following is a brief summary of the major aspects of the story of creation as perceived by Jewish-Christian tradition and as seen through the mechanistic and materialistic eyes of Western culture:

1. The source of all creatures was a transcendent God who created all things by the power of his Word. This creative act took place "in the beginning" about five thousand years ago, and it was completed all at once. Creation was a one-time event.
2. The man was created in a unique way in the image and likeness of God. The man was the crowning point of all creation and was given power to "name" all creatures and to "be fertile and multiply; fill the earth and subdue it" (Gen. 1:28).
3. There is a deep sense that creation is good and that the whole of creation is very good.
4. The story of the temptation and fall of Adam and Eve was the source of a fatal flaw in nature and in man. This original sin carries with it the need for redemption, which can come only from God and, for Christians, through the redeeming death and resurrection of Jesus the Christ.
5. This creation story takes place within a clear historical framework—from bliss to bliss. In the beginning God created the heavens and the earth and placed the man in its midst in a state of original bliss and happiness. Then came the fall and the long history of pain and sorrow where "By the sweat of your face shall you get bread to eat, until you return to the ground, from which you were taken" (Gen. 3:19). At the appointed time came Jesus of Nazareth who was to save the people from their sins. He is the redeemer who promises salvation for all and who will come again in glory. He will build a new heaven and a new earth and will come again to restore the man to original bliss.

This story of creation contains some profound insights into the human and its relationship to the rest of creation and to God, insights that retain their value even in our day. It is couched in mythical language based on the knowledge that flows from a limited sense perception, and thus it provides only a limited vision of creation, of human life, and of God. The new creation story, as we will see, does not negate the biblical story, but it deepens its theological content and provides a balance for its cultural and theological limitations.

In the past sixty-five years, through the use of powerful telescopes and our ability to probe the inner dynamics of the atom, we have transcended the limitations of our senses, and this has given us a new perception of the world around us. We see new dimensions in the time/space continuum of the earth and the universe, such as a universe that is not five thousand years old but fifteen billion years old, a Milky Way with billions of stars, and atoms with a dynamic inner force previously unknown and now capable of destroying the earth. This raises new questions about the adequacy of the stories and cosmologies that have grounded our contemporary society. We have a new vision of outer space and inner space, and this new vision challenges our old story, our old culture, our old spirituality, and our old institutions, including the church.

Outer Space. The new vision of outer space is best illustrated by the oft-repeated story of Einstein and the discovery of the expanding universe. In the early 1900s, the commonly accepted scientific description of the universe was that of a vast and fixed place, an infinite space that contained galaxies, stars and planets, all moving in unchanging orbits. For centuries the *immutable* movements of the heavenly bodies had been plotted and mapped and viewed with awe. On November 22, 1914, Albert Einstein was working with his mathematical field equations concerning the universe.

> Einstein was stunned into bafflement by what he was seeing. Through these symbols the universe whispered that it was expanding in all directions. No one in three centuries of modern scientific work had imagined such a possibility. All his life Einstein had assumed the universe was an unchanging infinite space. Now he was confronted with the idea that space was expanding in every direction. This was not a minor modification. This was an idea that, if true, would shatter the world-view of everyone, Einstein included.[5]

Such a revelation was too overwhelming and revolutionary; it challenged all of the perceptions of past cultures and religions as well as the current scientific community. Einstein "doctored" his equations so that the story of the unchanging universe was left intact. It was only later in the 1920s that the astronomer Edwin Hubble invited Einstein to use the Mount Palomar telescope and to see with his own eyes that distant galaxies were in fact moving away from each other.

> Einstein became convinced that the old idea of the universe as a fixed, unchanging macrocosm, the old idea that the universe was simply a giant box, was wrong. Only when Einstein saw with his own eyes the galaxies expanding away from us did he realize that his original insight concerning a dynamic expanding universe was in fact truth.[6]

---

[5] Swimme, Brian, *The Hidden Heart of the Cosmos*, Maryknoll, NY, Orbis Books, 1996, pp. 71–72.

[6] Swimme, *The Hidden Heart of the Cosmos*, p. 73.

And if the universe is expanding, it must be expanding from some beginning point. The universe had a birth place and a birth time. Today as we prepare to enter the twenty-first century, we see a whole new story of a universe that flashed forth into existence some fifteen billion years ago. It is a universe that, as we perceive it today, came into existence not "all at once" but in a time development sequence unfolding from within as billions of galaxies and stars. Ten billion years ago, in the great violent collapse of a star, there was a surprising twist of events: the supernova. The supernova is simultaneously a profound self-destruction and, out of its collapse, an exuberant creativity setting a pattern for the future story of our solar system and our earth. Out of chaos comes creativity.

Five billion years ago our sun composed of hydrogen and helium was born and later became a supernova seeding all the elements of our solar system. Four-and-a-half billion years ago spinning around the sun was a disc of the original subcloud just large enough to resist the cosmic rays from the sun. A cold remnant of the subcloud, a hanger-on, a residue, a swirling disc of elements, gave birth in time to Mercury, Venus, Earth, Mars, Jupiter, Saturn, Uranus, Neptune, and Pluto. The planets were formed, and the solar system took shape as a community.

The earth was a privileged planet with its size producing a gravitational and electromagnetic balance, and its position with respect to the sun enabling it to establish a temperature range in which complex molecules could be formed. Out of these seemingly random conditions came the earth's stupendous creativity over the next four billion years that brought forth all the beauty of its land, its plants, and its animals. And then between two and three million years ago, the earth became conscious in the human.

Truly a new creation story!

Inner Space.   The use of the telescope led to the discovery of the expanding universe and the time development unfolding of our earth. During the same period, new technology enabled physicists to enter into the inner space of the material world. Atoms and molecules, which were thought to be the elementary building blocks of the material world, were found to be made up of electrons, protons, and neutrons. But this was only a beginning understanding of the astounding character of matter.

> Even the subatomic particles—the electrons and the protons and neutrons in the nucleus—were nothing like the solid objects of classical physics. These subatomic units of matter are very abstract entities which have a dual aspect. Depending on how we look at them, they appear sometimes as particles, sometimes as waves; and this dual nature is also exhibited by light, which can take the form of electromagnetic waves or particles.[7]

---

[7] Capra, Fritjof, *The Turning Point,* New York, Bantam Books, 1983, p. 78.

It became clear that things are not always what they seem. A rock, a diamond, and a steel girder, each seeming so solid and unchanging, are composed, deeply within, of dynamic and interrelated particles and waves. The material objects around us may seem passive and inert, but when we magnify such a "dead" piece of stone or metal, we see that it is full of activity. It is in a continuous dancing and vibrating motion whose rhythmic movements are determined by self-organizing patterns.

The universe not only has a profound inner space, but there is also a penetrating interrelationship among all its dimensions and aspects, a web of relationships, that can be described as organic, holistic, and ecological.

> In modern physics, the image of the universe as a machine has been transcended by a view of it as one indivisible, dynamic whole whose parts are essentially interrelated and can be understood only as patterns of a cosmic process. At the subatomic level the interrelations and interactions between the parts of the whole are more fundamental than the parts themselves. There is motion but there are, ultimately, no moving objects; there is activity but there are no actors; there are no dancers, there is only the dance.[8]

Out of these and many other discoveries has come a new story of creation. As Fritjof Capra says, "What we need, then, is a new 'paradigm'—a new vision of reality; a fundamental change in our thoughts, perceptions and values."[9]

This new creation story in its basic outline is generally accepted today by physicists and scientists, and it is based on extensive exploration and data. It is also gradually becoming part of our ordinary life. Recently, when looking for a birthday card, I found a Hallmark card with a background of galaxies and stars surrounding the following text:

> If you're feeling your age today, just put it in perspective. Imagine how all your years and experience stack up against the history of the universe. Think about the stars so far away—their light has taken millions of years to reach our eyes. Think of the moons being born . . . mountains forming . . . and all the incredible things that ever grew, gradually filling the land and sea with life. Remember that you are among the youngest and newest of everything that is. Remember, too, that one of the most important things that ever happened on earth for me is you. (Hallmark Card)

But, as Thomas Berry points out, this story also impacts human life in a very profound way. "Although as yet unrealized, this scientific account of the universe is the greatest religious, moral, and spiritual event that has

---

[8] Capra, *The Turning Point,* pp. 91–92.

[9] Capra, *The Turning Point,* p. 16.

taken place in these centuries. It is the supreme humanistic and spiritual as well as the supreme scientific event."[10] It is important to discuss some of the deeper dimensions of this supreme scientific event as it impacts human life and our relationship to the earth.

THE RELATIONSHIP BETWEEN THE EARTH AND THE HUMAN: WHO RULES THE ROOST?

Possibly we will have the sense to begin a new century by renewing our membership in the Animal Kingdom.[11]

As I watched the opening scene of the movie *The Lion King*, I was immediately drawn into the action. All the animals excitedly rush through the forest. As they gather expectantly the Lion King stands with great dignity on a large outcropping of stone high above all the animals. Then the elderly wisdom figure arrives and is shown the newborn future king. The newborn king is anointed and carried to the outcropping, held high for all to see. The sunlight breaks through and the assembly cheers. The zebra, the elephants, and the giraffes bow down before the future king. We, the audience, experience the thrill of the presence of this powerful and wise king and his son, Simba, on their throne in the midst of the forest.

But wait a moment, something is wrong here! In creation is the lion really the king of the beasts? Does the lion really rule over other creatures and govern the other species? Is this kingly power really passed on to the next male offspring? Or, is not the lion simply one among many members of the community of species? Despite its courage and strength, does not the lion struggle like other members of the community for food and shelter?

What I saw portrayed in the movie was a projection onto the lion king of an image of ourselves, the human, as the king of creation. Seeing ourselves as the ruler of creation we expect that the whole of creation should cheer us and obey us. In the same way we set up a whole series of power relations among humans—one group must be king and ruler, male over female, rich over poor, white over people of color, clergy over laity. And as Capra points out, all this is based on the image of a male God.

> The view of man as dominating nature and woman, and the belief in the superior role of the rational mind, have been supported and encouraged by the Judeo-Christian tradition, which adheres to the image of a male god, personification of supreme wisdom and source of ultimate power, who rules the world from above by imposing his divine law on it.[12]

---

[10] Berry, *The Dream of the Earth*, p. 98.

[11] Kingsolver, Barbara, *High Tide in Tucson*, New York, Harper Perennial, 1995, p. 10.

[12] Capra, *The Turning Point*, p. 41.

In order to experience more deeply the reality of our culture's belief that the human rules the roost I have gathered some excerpts from a book entitled *Ishmael*, by Daniel Quinn.[13] These excerpts are arranged in a six-act play and the two characters in the play are the Teacher (T) and the Student (S). As you read this play, you might say it aloud to reinforce the content.

Who Rules the Roost

Act One

T "Everyone in your culture knows this. The pinnacle was reached in man. Man is the climax of the whole cosmic drama of creation."

S "Yes."

T "When man finally appeared, creation came to an end, because its objective had been reached. There was nothing left to create."

S "That seems to be the unspoken assumption."

T "It's certainly not always unspoken. The religions of your culture aren't reticent about it. Man is the end product of creation. Man is the creature for whom all the rest was made: this world, this solar system, this galaxy, the universe itself."

S "True."

Act Two

T "Along about the middle of your story, the focus of attention shifted from the universe at large to this one planet. Why?"

S "Because this one planet was destined to be the birthplace of man."

T "Of course. As you tell it, the birth of man was a central—indeed *the* central event—in the history of the cosmos itself. From the birth of man on, the rest of the universe ceases to be of interest, ceases to participate in the unfolding drama. For this, the earth alone is sufficient; it is the birthplace and home of man, and that's its meaning. The Takers regard the world as a sort of human life-support system, as a machine designed to produce and sustain human life."

S "Yes, that's so."

T "Supposing there is a divine agency behind creation, what can you tell me about the gods' intentions?"

S "Well, basically, what they had in mind when they started out was man. They made the universe so that our galaxy could be in it. They made the galaxy so that our solar system could be in it. They made our solar system so that our planet could be in it. And they made our planet so that we could be in it. The whole thing was made so that man would have a hunk of dirt to stand on."

---

[13] Quinn, Daniel, *Ishmael: An Adventure of the Mind and Spirit,* New York, Bantam Turner, 1992, pp. 57, 59, 60, 61, 71–73, 80, 81.

T "And this is generally how it's understood in your culture—at least
    by those who assume that the universe is an expression of divine in-
    tentions."

S "Yes."

T "Obviously, since the entire universe was made so that man could
    be made, man must be a creature of enormous importance to the
    gods. But this part of the story gives no hint of their intentions to-
    ward him. They must have some special destiny in mind for him,
    but that's not revealed here."

S "True."

Act Three

T "All right. That's the premise of your story: *The world was made
    for man.*"

S "I can't quite grasp it. I mean, I can't quite see why it's a premise."

T "The people of your culture *made* it a premise—*took* it as a prem-
    ise. They said: *what if* the world was made for *us?*"

S "Okay. Keep going."

T "Think of the consequences of taking that as your premise: If the
    world was made for you, *then what?*"

S "Okay, I see what you mean I think. If the world was made for us
    then it *belongs* to us and we can do what we damn well please with
    it."

T "Exactly. That's what's been happening here for the past ten thou-
    sand years; you've been doing what you damn well please with the
    world. And of course you mean to go right on doing what you
    damn well please with it, because the whole damn thing *belongs to
    you.*"

Act Four

T "And it is at this point that we begin to see where man fits into the
    divine scheme. The gods didn't mean to leave the world a jungle,
    did they?"

S "You mean in our mythology? Certainly not."

T "So: without man, the world was unfinished, was just nature, red
    in tooth and claw. It was in chaos, in a state of primeval anarchy."

S "That's right. That's it exactly."

T "So it needed what?"

S "It needed someone to come in and . . . straighten it out. Someone
    to put it in order."

T "And what sort of person is it who straightens things out? What
    sort of person takes anarchy in hand and puts it in order?"

S "Well . . . a ruler. A king."

T "Of course. The world needed a ruler. It needed man."

S "Yes."

T "So now we have a clearer idea what this story is all about: *The world was made for man, and man was made to rule it.*"

Act Five

T "The world would not meekly submit to man's rule, so he had to do what to it?"

S "What do you mean?"

T "If the king comes to a city that will not submit to his rule, what does he have to do?"

S "He has to conquer it."

T "Of course. In order to make himself the ruler of the world, man first had to conquer it."

S "Good lord." [nearly leaping up out of his chair while striking his brow and all the rest]

T "Yes?"

S "You hear this fifty times a day. You can turn on the radio or the television and hear it every hour. Man is conquering the deserts, man is conquering the oceans, man is conquering the atom, man is conquering the elements, man is conquering outer space."

Act Six

S "The problem is that man's conquest of the world has itself devastated the world. And in spite of all the mastery we've attained, we don't have enough mastery to *stop* devastating the world—or to repair the devastation we've already wrought. . . . Only one thing can save us. We have to *increase* our mastery of the world. All this damage has come about through our conquest of the world, but we have to *go on* conquering it until our rule is *absolute*. Then, when we're in complete *control*, everything will be fine. . . . And that's where it stands right now. We have to carry the conquest forward. And carrying it forward is either going to destroy the world or turn it into a paradise—into the paradise it was meant to be under human rule. . . . And if we manage to do this—if we finally manage to make ourselves the absolute rulers of the world—then nothing can stop us. Then we move into the *Star Trek* era. Man moves out into space to conquer and rule the entire universe. And that may be the ultimate destiny of man: to conquer and rule the entire universe. That's how wonderful man is."

The End

Our cultural experience and the conventional wisdom of our society are dramatized in this little play. "Man" is supposed to rule the roost, to be the lion king, to conquer the earth and maybe even the universe. This "wisdom" leads to a cosmology based on human consumption and consumerism. Brian Swimme describes it in stark language:

It's a simple cosmology, told with great effect and delivered a billion times each day not only to Americans of course but to nearly everyone in the planetary reach of the ad: *humans exist to work at jobs, to earn money, to get stuff.* . . . The ultimate meaning for human existence is getting all this stuff. That's paradise. And the meaning of the Earth? Premanufactured consumer stuff.[14]

But what has happened to the earth under human rule and the cosmology of consumerism?

Through human presence the forests of the earth are destroyed. Fertile soils become toxic and then wash away in the rain or blow away in the wind. Mountains of human-derived waste grow ever higher. Wetlands are filled in. Each year approximately ten thousand species disappear forever. Even the ozone layer above the earth is depleted. Such disturbance in the natural world coexists with all those ethnic, political, and religious tensions that pervade the human realm. Endemic poverty is pervasive in the Third World, while in the industrial world people drown in their own consumption patterns. Population increase threatens all efforts at improvement.[15]

We have been taught by our culture and our religion that the human is primary and the earth is derivative. It is now imperative that we rediscover that the earth is primary and the human is derivative. The human is a latecomer in the unfolding of the earth—only two or three million years compared to the four billion years of the earth. The human is totally dependent on the earth for its origins and for its continued existence. Trees can get along very well without humans, but humans cannot exist without trees.

We humans must begin to see ourselves as members of a community of earth species, and as such, mutually dependent on the whole community. As Diarmuid O'Murchu says:

We humans are not the masters of creation; we are participators in a co-creative process that is much greater than us and probably quite capable of getting along without us (as happened for almost fifteen billion years before our species evolved). If we are to influence global and planetary life, we'll do it in cooperative interaction rather than in competitive strife. Our interrelationship with life—at both the micro and macro levels—is a learning process of mutual interdependence, and not that of exploitation, combat, and warfare, a lethal process which is almost certain to destroy us in the end.[16]

---

[14] Swimme, *The Hidden Heart of the Cosmos*, p. 18.

[15] Berry, *The Dream of the Earth*, p. 36.

[16] O'Murchu, Diarmuid, *Quantum Theology*, New York, Crossroad, 1997, p. 33.

If we are to become participators in the creative process, the earth must be seen as the source of all that we are and have. We will see the earth as our Mother who nurtures and sustains all her creatures. We will learn to live in tune with the rhythms of the earth as a child in the womb is not only nourished by its mother, but lives in rhythm with the heartbeat of its mother. We will look upon the created world as part of ourselves with a subject-to-subject relationship to all creatures.

As we look to the future we should not think in terms of some romantic return to the "noble savage." We have gone beyond any looking backward and must begin to look forward to ways in which we can use our scientific knowledge and our technology, not to rule the earth, but to live with the earth. Rather, we will listen to the music of the earth community, learn to dance with the rhythms of the earth, and to use our intelligence to foster the community of species.

> The time has come to lower our voices, to cease imposing our mechanistic patterns on the biological processes of the earth, to resist the impulse to control, to command, to force, to oppress, and to begin quite humbly to follow the guidance of the larger community on which all life depends. Our fulfillment is not in our isolated human grandeur, but in our intimacy with the larger earth community, for this is also the larger dimension of our being. Our human destiny is integral with the destiny of the earth.[17]

It is clear that the earth is the source of all that we have in human life, and that the earth will continue to unfold in an open-ended time development sequence. The future of human evolution calls us to either be cocreators in that unfolding or be left behind in the memory of the earth, and it also calls us to embrace the chaos, darkness, and shadow side of our universe.

CHAOS, DARKNESS, AND THE SHADOW SIDE

> Within the old paradigm, chaos was considered to be evil, disruptive, dangerous; it threatened the status quo of our patriarchal value system, and threatened our powers as the managers of a hierarchical, orderly system. Within this paradigm, there was no room for deviation, differences, disagreements. The shadow side was totally suppressed. Our linear mindset was neat and orderly, but so much out of touch with personal and planetary reality.[18]

There is an ancient story about a king and queen who had a beautiful daughter eagerly sought after by many suitors. The royal parents decided that the successful suitor would have to undergo many trials before winning the hand of the princess. Many young men tried and failed, until one day a

---

[17] Berry, *The Dream of the Earth*, p. xiv.

[18] O'Murchu, *Quantum Theology*, p. 129–130.

stranger appeared. He successfully underwent all the trials (the original telling of the story goes on and on in describing each trial in great detail), and the beautiful princess was betrothed to the stranger and the wedding was planned. There was great excitement in the castle as the wedding day approached. All the surrounding neighborhood was invited, and a great feast was prepared. On the day of the wedding ceremony, the stranger and the beautiful princess, still veiled as was the custom, came before the bishop and were duly united in matrimony.

After the celebration and the feast, the newly married couple retired to the bridal chamber. The princess removed her veil and, lo and behold, she was the most ugly person imaginable—a crooked nose, beady eyes, fangs for teeth, hair like a floor mop, and a blotched face. The princess explained to her husband, now shocked beyond belief, that she was under a spell. He had a choice—she could be beautiful by day and ugly at night, or she could be beautiful at night and ugly by day. He did not want the court to know the truth of his ugly wife, so he chose to have her beautiful by day and ugly at night.

She was so ugly that on the first night in bed the stranger, in his disappointment, just turned his back to her. The next day, as the partying continued, the stranger was complimented on his beautiful new bride, but at night he once more turned away from this ugly woman. As the days went along the stranger began to see the goodness and virtue of his wife, and one night in bed he turned to her and embraced her. And the spell was broken! She became the beautiful princess, and, of course, they lived happily ever after.

This ancient story contains some profound wisdom—in order to obtain the beautiful we must embrace the ugly. The new creation story tells us not only about the beauty of the earth but also what appears to be the ugliness, the chaos, the darkness, and the shadow side of creation. We, as humans, often seek to deny the ugliness within our lives and in the earth community. We try to conquer the earth in order to do away with all ugliness, pain, discomfort, suffering, and sickness, and in the process we never realize the deeper goodness and beauty within our lives and in the earth community. Only by embracing the chaos, the darkness, and the shadow side can we break the spell and find the beauty of ourselves and our world. "Evolution is an unfolding filled with another kind of eccentricity: the clash of disorder, destruction and extinction."[19]

The ancient Greek philosophers described the four elements as earth, air, fire, and water. Everything in creation is composed of these elements, and this gave the world its balance and beauty. But at the same time these four elements are the source of most of our natural disasters—earthquakes, tornadoes, fires, and floods. In a way, the philosophers were saying that within the very make-up of creation are the seeds of disaster, and without these violent events the world would not have the same balance and beauty.

---

[19] Nogar, Raymond J., *The Lord of the Absurd*, New York, Herder and Herder, 1972, p. 144.

Our more recent understanding of the earth, based on our new science, also paints a picture of destruction and chaos.

> Enhanced by modern chemical analysis and radioactive carbon-14 dating techniques, there seems to be the beginning of a consensus that every twenty-six to thirty million years our planet suffers a fate a thousand times worse than if all the world's nuclear arsenals exploded at once.
>
> These periodic catastrophes result in terrible mass extinctions that annihilate 50 to 90 percent of ecologically and genetically diverse global species within intervals of five hundred thousand to three million years. Explosions and catastrophes have been as normal to Gaia's development as fistfights in a Brooklyn schoolyard, and they occur almost as frequently.[20]

The violent dimensions of earth, air, fire, and water, and the earth's periodic catastrophes are all examples of order coming out of chaos. The chaos and apparent violence in the universe seems to produce, not ultimate destruction, but a new order, an evolutionary leap, new life from death.

> Judging from the progression of the fossil record and confirmed by the extraordinary diversity of natural development today, anywhere from 10 to 50 percent of the visible biota survives and eventually thrives from even the worst cataclysms. The global ecosystem invariably regenerates quickly and to a higher level of complexity, usually in less time than a hundred thousand years. Though this may seem like an eternity in terms of human civilization, to a life form thirty-five-hundred-million years old, one hundred millennia is, at most, a long afternoon.[21]

On a more theoretical level this dynamic process has been articulated at great length by Ilya Prigogine and Isabelle Stengers in their work *Order Out of Chaos*. Prigogine states his basic thesis in a text already quoted in Chapter 1:

> In far-from-equilibrium conditions we may have transformation from disorder, from thermal chaos, into order. New dynamic states of matter may originate, states that reflect the interaction of a given system with its surroundings. We have called these new structures *dissipative structures* to emphasize the constructive role of dissipative processes in their formation.[22]

---

[20] Joseph, Lawrence E., *Gaia: The Growth of an Idea*, New York, St. Martin's Press, 1990, p. 104.

[21] Joseph, *Gaia: The Growth of an Idea*, pp. 203–204.

[22] Prigogine, Ilya, and Isabelle Stengers, *Order Out of Chaos*, New York, Bantam Books, 1984, p. 12.

In a similar way, our human lives and our human relationships are often deepened by chaos and darkness. The slow dying process of a grandmother can bring a family together at a new level of love and caring. The darkness of the apparent breakup of a loving relationship can call the lovers to an unanticipated depth of mutuality and friendship. The shadow of a dysfunctional family can often lead its members to heroic efforts to overcome the pain and to learn new ways of relating. The whole concept of finding the beauty by embracing the ugly is also foundational to our Christian tradition. In the words of Jesus,

> Amen, Amen, I say to you, unless a grain of wheat fall into the ground and dies, it remains just a grain of wheat; but if it dies, it produces much fruit. Whoever loves his life loses it, and whoever hates his life in this world will preserve it for eternal life.   (Jn. 12:24–25)

There is a very serious question to be dealt with in connection with chaos, darkness, and the shadow side. We all know that humans are subject to chaos and darkness, and that there is a shadow side within each of us. But what about the human violence that seems to be so much a part of our human family and its history? Is this something that we just have to accept and embrace? Is this human violence just part of our nature? Are human violence and the apparent violence in the earth community one and the same? What are the differences?

The apparent violence in nature, such as a pride of lions stalking and killing prey and the bloody battles between species found in nature films, must be seen as part of a wider community interaction. For example, in nature a predator will never destroy the entire species of its prey or the entire species of its competitor. The tensions always found within the community of species ultimately lead to an overall balance. For example, an eagle has very acute eyesight so that it can see a mouse scurrying through the field, and the field mouse can run very quickly so that it can avoid its eagle predator. The outcome is a natural balance between these two species. This is a simple example of the very complex dynamic among the members of an ecological community.

This "violence" in nature, which flows from the inner instinct of the community of species, most often redounds to the welfare of the whole. Some years ago there was a major fire in Yellowstone National Park that did extensive damage to the forest land. People were very concerned about the damage to the park and its living species, but over the next few years the ashes from the fire acted as fertilizer and enabled the renewed growth of some of the plants native to the area. The return of this plant life also brought about the return of other animal species, and thus out of the chaos of fire came a renewed environment. The earth is like a living organism that can bring life out of apparent death, creativity out of apparent destruction.

On the other hand, some human "violence," such as our use of other living creatures for food, flows from our participation in the community of species of which we are members. As part of the community of species, the human, like other living things, can take from the fruit of the earth what is necessary for survival. However, this "taking" is not unlimited because we also must respect the needs and rights of other species. For example, the native peoples would frequently have rituals after the hunt, thanking the animals for providing the necessities of life, and promising to kill only what was needed and use it well.

True human violence flows from our personal choices that are destructive to our personal relationships, to human societies, other individuals, and nature. Human violence is contrary to the evolutionary drive of the earth because it often upsets the ecological balance by destroying species, polluting the water supply, and wasting natural resources. Human violence does not respect the dignity of other species and other humans. It often results in systemic violence, which is so evident in our society and on our city streets, and it often breaks out in warfare, which is the most organized and destructive form of human violence.

Human violence is also self-destructive, going contrary to the basic reality of human life and creation, because it is rooted in our human desire for power and control as well as our will to conquer the earth and to be the Lion King. As people are caught up in a spiral of power, the effort to control results in a greater loss of control. The personal, systemic, and ecological violence in our society, as well as the apex of violence in modern warfare, will lead to a life in which "love one another" becomes "destroy one another."

In the story of *Ishmael*, the Teacher describes the situation in our society and the impact of our violence on our own lives.

> The people of your culture cling with fanatical tenacity to the specialness of man. They want desperately to perceive a vast gulf between man and the rest of creation. This mythology of human superiority justifies their doing whatever they please to the world, just the way Hitler's mythology of Aryan superiority justified his doing whatever he pleased with Europe. But in the end this mythology is not deeply satisfying. The Takers are a profoundly lonely people. The world for them is enemy territory, and they live in it like an army of occupation, alienated and isolated by their extraordinary specialness.[23]

It is necessary for us, as humans, to embrace the chaos, darkness, and the shadow side if we are to find new life. But it is equally necessary for us to continue the effort to root out the personal, systemic, and ecological violence in our midst. What will be the source of our redemption from chaos and violence? The new story of creation teaches us that the universe has an inner self-organizing and self-healing power that enables it to bring order

---

[23] Quinn, *Ishmael*, p. 146. Quinn often uses exclusive language, perhaps in an attempt to dramatize the assumed superiority of the human.

out of chaos, light out of darkness, and clarity to the shadow. The redemptive power of the Creator God is built into the very substance of the universe and will unfold within the dynamics of the universe. "Redemption is planetary (and global) as well as personal. Redemption is about reclaiming the darkness, nothingness, and chaos of our world, and celebrating the negative potential for new life and wholeness."[24]

The redemptive power of God within the universe is personalized, for us as Christians, in the story of Jesus and in his life-giving death and resurrection. As Jesus began his public life, he saw the evil and violence in the society in which he lived. He saw it as contrary to his deep experience of God as a loving Mother, who wishes to shelter her children under her wings. He challenged the systemic oppression of the poor and the outcasts, and he invited his followers and the religious leaders of the times to follow a new ethic of compassion for the poor, the universality of God's love, and the call to love one another. He, himself, by his commitment to the law of love, was caught up in the violence of his society. By embracing the violence of capital punishment and the ugliness of death on a cross, Jesus, through his resurrection, became a symbol of the redemptive power of God within the universe and a source of new life for all people.

> History, then, has a capacity for being changed from within; and for the Christian the incarnation is the seed of radical change, of the new. It introduces into the process of time a new future, so that the future of death and oblivion which has been bequeathed to the historical process by distorted and confused human freedom is challenged by a radical alternative: life instead of death.[25]

IMAGES OF GOD

As part of the youth confirmation process at the parish in which I worked, we participated in the "cosmic walk." This was a ritual experience similar to the stations of the cross except that in the cosmic walk, each "station" was one of the major events in the story of the universe beginning with the flashing forth of the universe fifteen billion years ago. Then the group proceded to walk along a path lighting a candle at each of the stations that were spaced out in relation to the time development sequence of the story.

A large candle was lit at the original flashing forth and acted as the source of light for the candles at each of the stations leading up to the present day. At the end of the cosmic walk, I asked the group, "Why do we carry the large candle from the beginning throughout the entire story of the universe?" There was a period of silence. Then one young adult answered, "Because God was present within creation from the beginning and through-

---

[24] O'Murchu, *Quantum Theology,* p. 136.

[25] Hall, Douglas John, *God and Human Suffering,* Minneapolis, MN, Augsburg Publishing House, 1986, p. 111.

out all creation." A new image of God! Rather than being the transcendent Creator who brings forth the universe by a word, God is within the creative process itself.

For many of us our image of God as we grew up was someone, usually male, who was beyond us. He was a God who made us and loved us, who sometimes judged us, rewarded us, or punished us. God was someone to whom we prayed and from whom we asked for various gifts and graces. We saw God through Jesus, the Word of God, and this Jesus, through his death on the cross, redeemed us from sin and brought us salvation. For many of us, the presence of Jesus in the tabernacle was a significant sign of God's presence in our lives, especially for those of us who remember Forty Hours Devotion. But in all these manifestations, God is imaged as somehow being "out there," whether as creator and Father, or in Jesus as suffering savior, or as a friend really present in the Blessed Sacrament.

When I was a Dominican novice over fifty years ago, I had a profound personal experience. While sitting in the chapel praying before the crucifix, praying to God "out there," I had a deep sense that God came around and sat with me. God was "on my side"; God was within me. This sense of God's immediate presence was deepened during my theological studies. I remember reading in the *Summa* of St. Thomas Aquinas about the fact that "God was more present to me than I was to myself." Later I was intrigued by the teaching of St. Thomas about the indwelling of the Trinity within me, and the words of Jesus as found in the Gospel of John became central to my spirituality: "Whoever loves me will keep my word, and my Father will love her, and we will come to him and make our dwelling with him" (Jn. 14:23).

This sense of a divine presence has been deepened immeasurably by the awareness of the new creation story. The flashing forth of the universe led to a process in which the latent potential present at the beginning is gradually unfolding over billions of years—the millions of galaxies, the Milky Way, our own galaxy, our solar system, and finally our planet earth. The latent potential of the earth has gradually unfolded over millions of years and led to the vast array of riches and beauty of our living earth. In the last two to three million years, the human emerged and the earth became conscious. *And this entire process is actually the unfolding presence of God within the entire universe at every moment.*

This story of creation gives a new perspective to our images of God. In our traditional Jewish-Christian story, God is seen as a transcendent Creator who brings forth each dimension of the earth by a word, "Let there be light. . . ." The new story sees God as intimately present before and within the flashing forth and continuous unfolding of the universe. This does not mean that God *is* creation or is *identified* with creation as is taught in pantheism. Rather, God is the creative force in the universe and a dynamic presence within every nook and cranny of creation.

Recently Pope John Paul II released a statement indicating that, for Catholics, the theory of evolution was tenable provided that the immediate creation of the human soul is maintained. What does this mean? It seems to mean that the evolutionary process can explain the development of the universe and even the human body, but at the moment of conception there is a need to posit the immediate intervention by God to account for the human soul. However, the new creation story does not see God as an extrinsic agent intervening in the unfolding of the universe but as an inner power and as the immediate creator of all things. In that sense the new creation story does maintain the immediate creation of the soul and of human consciousness. However, this story goes further to posit the immediate creation by God not only of the human soul but of all that exists in outer space, galaxies, stars, our sun and our earth, and in inner space, the electrons and protons and quarks and waves and particles. What a wonderful sense of our loving God's immediacy and presence in all we are and in all we know and in all we do!

Another personal experience might help us to see this new perspective. In our Christian tradition and liturgy we often talk about heaven. We pray to God in heaven, and we all look forward to going to heaven. In our funeral liturgies we sing about the angels leading us into paradise. But where is heaven in our ordinary imaging? Most likely it is somewhere beyond the skies because that is the highest thing we can imagine. In the cosmology of the Jewish-Christian tradition the heavens are always "above." In reality, however, heaven is wherever God is. And where is God? God is everywhere, and in the new creation story, God is intimately within all things, in the stars and in the sun and even in the earth. As I have meditated on these realities, I have begun to experience the human as being born from the earth and being the consciousness of the earth. I find it as easy to pray, "Our Mother, who art within the earth," as to pray, "Our Father, who art in heaven."

Barbara Kingsolver in her novel *Animal Dreams* relates a conversation between the heroine, Codi, and her Native American lover, Loyd, that speaks about the issue of life and death.

> "Where do you think people go when they die?" Loyd asked.
> "Nowhere," I said. "I think when people die they're just dead."
> "Not heaven?"
> I looked up at the sky. It looked quite empty. "No."
> "The Pueblo story is that everybody started out underground. People and animals, everything. And then the badger dug a hole and let everybody out. They climbed out of the hole and from then on they lived on top of the ground. When they die they go back under." Loyd thought about his twin brother who had died. "I always try to think of it that way," he said. "He had a big adventure up here, and then went home."[26]

---

[26]Kingsolver, Barbara, *Animal Dreams,* New York, Harper Perennial, 1991, p. 308.

I now image God as being present within the earth out of which I and all humans have emerged. "The creative energy that makes all things possible and keeps all things in being is *within* and not outside the cosmos."[27] When I think of death these days, I imagine it as a return to Mother Earth, not the highest thing I can think of but the closest. My sense of salvation is not to depart from this earth or to enter into a purely spiritual realm, but to enter more deeply into the consciousness of the earth and into the arms of my loving Mother. Heaven is wherever God is.

As so much of our society has become alienated from nature, much of our awareness of faith is secondhand. It is derived from the outside, from teachers and preachers as well as from our biblical traditions, and we often find it difficult to experience the God within us and the God manifested in the universe around us. Thomas Berry says,

> Because our sense of the divine is so extensively derived from verbal sources, mostly through the biblical scriptures, we seldom notice how extensively we have lost contact with the revelation of the divine in nature. Yet our exalted sense of the divine itself comes from the grandeur of the universe, especially from the earth in all the splendid modes of its expression. Without such experience we would be terribly impoverished in our religious and spiritual development, even in our emotional, imaginative, and intellectual development.[28]

It is essential that we begin to derive our images of God more intimately from our direct encounter with God in the story of the universe, and we must be able to help others find this immediate experience of God in nature. Marcus Borg describes how, in his twenties, he had found it difficult to relate to God, and his uncertainty about God led him away from faith. It was an experience of God in the deep mystery of creation that changed him.

> Then in my mid-thirties I had a number of experiences of what I now recognize as "nature mysticism." In a sense they were nothing spectacular. . . . But they fundamentally changed my understanding of God, Jesus, religion, and Christianity.
>
> These experiences, besides being ecstatic, were for me *aha!* moments. They gave me a new understanding of the meaning of the word *God*. I realized that *God* does not refer to a supernatural being "out there" (which is where I had put God ever since my childhood musing about God "up in heaven"). Rather I began to see the word *God* refers to the sacred at the center of existence, the holy mystery that is all around us and within us.[29]

[27] O'Murchu, *Quantum Theology,* p. 59.

[28] Berry, *The Dream of the Earth,* pp. 80–81.

[29] Borg, Marcus J., *Meeting Jesus again for the First Time,* San Francisco, HarperSanFrancisco, 1994, p. 14.

I am convinced that some direct experience of deep mystery within creation itself is the best way to ground our spirituality and our faith. This mystery is beautifully portrayed and sung by Susan Osborn in the *Missa Gaia/Earth Mass* (Paul Winter, Earth Music Productions, 1982).

Mystery
It lives in the seed of a tree as it grows.
You hear it if you listen to the wind as it blows.
It's there in a river as it flows into the sea.
It's the sound in the soul of becoming free.

And it lives in the laughter of children at play;
It's in the blazing sun that gives light to the day;
It moves in the moon, the planets, and the stars in the sky.
It's been the mover of mountains since the beginning of time.

Oh Mystery—you are alive.
I feel you all around.
You are the fire in my heart,
You are the holy sound,
You are all of life—
It is to you that I sing.
Grant that I may feel you, always in everything.

And it lives in the waves as they crash upon the beach.
I have seen it in the gods that we have tried to reach.
I feel it in the love that I know we need so much.
I know it in your smile, my love,
When our hearts do touch.

But when I listen deep inside, I feel best of all;
Like a moon that's flowing white.
And I listen to your call,
And I know you will guide me.
I feel you like the tide
Rushing through the ocean of my heart, it's open wide.

Oh Mystery—you are alive.
I feel you all around.
You are the fire in my heart.
You are the holy sound.
You are all of life—
It is to you that I sing.
Grant that I may feel you, always in everything.
Oh grant that I may feel you, always in everything.
Oh grant that I may feel you, always in everything.
Oh grant that I may feel you, always in everything.
Oh Mystery.

Our ability to know and love and sing about the great mystery of God within the earth is part of our dignity as images of God. We can now look more deeply into the story of the human, not as rulers of creation, but as partners and cocreators with God in the continuing unfolding of the mystery that is all around us.

THE STORY OF THE HUMAN

For the first time, I became aware of my spiritual continuity and solidarity with early mankind. They were no longer "those primitive creatures"; they were "my people."[30]

Rather than imagining creation as one event with the simultaneous creation of the nonliving, the living, and the human, we now see creation in an unfinished time development sequence. The new creation story enables us to have an overview of the story of the human as part of an overall web of relationships in the broader community of species. The following gives us a sense of this time development sequence and the place of the human in the evolutionary process.

15 billion years ago	The flashing forth of the universe
5 billion years ago	The birth of the sun and the solar system
4 billion years ago	Life begins on earth
2 billion years ago	The earth's oxygen atmosphere develops
1 billion years ago	Life is drawn toward union and the first simple organisms begin to reproduce sexually
700 million years ago	The first multicellular life forms emerge and creativity expands rapidly
510 million years ago	The first fish forms with backbone emerge, protecting the earth's earliest nervous systems
395 million years ago	The first insects emerge
235 million years ago	The age of the dinosaurs
150 million years ago	The first birds take flight
114 million years ago	The first mammals appear
2.6 million years ago	**Earliest humanoid types develop**
40 thousand years ago	**Modern *Homo sapiens* emerges, developing the earliest language**
10 thousand years ago	**The beginning of agriculture and the domestication of animals**
2 thousand years ago	**The birth and ministry of Jesus of Nazareth**
2000 C.E. and beyond	**An unknown future**

[30]Nogar, *The Lord of the Absurd*, p. 28.

In order to have some perspective on this time development sequence, we can imagine that the flashing forth of the universe fifteen billion years ago is equivalent to one year of 365 days.

365 days ago January 1	The flashing forth of the universe
122 days ago September 2	The birth of the sun and the solar system
98 days ago September 24	Life begins on earth
18 days ago December 13	The first multicellular life forms emerge and creativity expands rapidly
On the last day December 31	Earliest humanoid types develop
Last 96 seconds December 31, 11:58.36	Modern *Homo sapiens* emerges, developing the earliest language
Last 21 seconds December 31, 11:59.39	The beginning of agriculture and the domestication of animals

Thus after an unimaginable period of time, on the last day, the final twenty-four hours of the story of the universe, some form of human life appeared on earth. In terms of the entire process of divine unfolding in the universe, the appearance of the human species is a very recent development, a blink of the eye relative to the vast age of our earth. As *we* perceive the story of the human from our historical perspective it does not seem like "the blink of an eye." It seems to be a long and complex story rising from the mists of prehistory and gradually becoming known in the archeological ruins left by ancient peoples and finally appearing on the pages of historical records. It is difficult to chronicle this complex story within the limitations of this work, but in very broad strokes I will attempt to paint a picture of the human story in the context of the unfolding of the story of the earth. I will include some of the major characters and colors of that story.

The story will be presented as a play in three acts: Act One, Childhood, from the beginning of human history two to three million years ago to the agricultural revolution; Act Two, Adolescence, from 10,000 years ago until the present; Act Three, Adulthood, beginning now and leading into the new millennium.

ACT ONE: THE CONCEPTION, BIRTH, AND CHILDHOOD OF THE HUMAN

In its beginning, and in its early development, the human was so frail, so unimpressive, a creature hardly worth the attention of the other animals in the forest. But these early humans were on a path that would in time explode with unexpectedly significant new power, a power of consciousness whereby Earth, and the universe as a whole, turned back and reflected on itself.[31]

Prior to the introduction of modern technology, the conception of a child was an event that took place within the dark mystery of the womb. Nothing was known clearly of its origins and its early growth. The history and life of our earliest forerunners, called *hominids,* who came before the birth of the human race, is also shrouded in the dark mystery of the past. We have only the merest hint of its presence based on some footprints and the earliest skull discovered in Africa. The following is a delightful description of hominids by Brian Swimme and Thomas Berry.

> The hominids were distinguished by their increased brain size and by their capacity for walking in an upright posture, although they still spent time in trees, as is indicated by the length and muscular quality of their arms relative to their shorter legs. They lived now mostly in the savannas, the grasslands of the region.
>
> Such was the situation some four million years ago when a young female hominid, now designated as "Lucy," lived in southern Ethiopia. Her brain capacity, between four hundred and five hundred cubic centimeters, was slightly greater than that of the chimpanzee. In diet, Lucy and the other hominids apparently were vegetarians; neither Lucy nor any of the others left behind any evidence of implements for hunting or dissecting, or of bones discarded after eating.[32]

Homo Habilis: *2.6 Million Years Ago.* The fetus in the womb develops and begins to take on the bodily shape of a human, with arms and legs, heartbeat, and brain functioning. Likewise, there is evidence that human evolution began about 2.6 million years ago when the African climate changed to drought and the lakes shrank and the forest thinned out to savannah, and our ancestors were not well adapted to such conditions. In dealing with these climatic changes *Homo habilis,* formerly a tree dweller, had to adapt to becoming a forager on the ground. "In a parched African landscape like Omo, man first put his foot to the ground. . . . Two million years ago, the first ancestor of man walked with a foot which is almost indistinguishable from the foot of modern man."[33] The human appears in its species identity possessing skills in working with stone, skills that manifest not only a sense of utility but also an emerging feeling for esthetic beauty.

---

[31] Swimme, Brian and Thomas Berry, *The Universe Story,* San Francisco, HarperSanFrancisco, 1992, p. 143.

[32] Swimme and Berry, *The Universe Story,* p. 145.

[33] Bronowski, Jacob, *The Ascent of Man,* Boston, Little, Brown, 1973, p. 28. Bronowski wrote at a time when inclusive language was not commonly used when speaking of the human race.

Homo Erectus: *1.5 Million Years Ago.*   *Homo erectus* appeared first in Africa, and later accomplished the first migration from Africa throughout Asia and southern and western Europe. During this period, we can recognize a clear ancestor of *Homo sapiens* in the increase of brain capacity, the use of stones and primitive tools, the use of animal skins for clothing, and especially the use of fire.

> Control of fire gave the human a sense of power as well as an increased sense of human identity in distinction from other living beings. With the fire in the hearth a communing with mythic powers takes place, social unity is experienced, a context for reflection on the awesome aspects of existence is established.[34]

***Archaic* Homo Sapiens:** *120,000 Years Ago.*   Perhaps the appearance of archaic *Homo sapiens,* the human species that succeeded these other forms and from which all contemporary humans are descended, might be compared to the birth of a child. During the time of the Neanderthals there was a continuing migration into a wide area of Europe, and these peoples exhibited an amazing ability to adapt to varied geographical terrain and environmental conditions. The Neanderthals used fire extensively, and they were not only food gatherers but also hunters as is evidenced by animal remains in their living sites. These people also give evidence of a spiritual consciousness with elaborate burial rites. They experienced the need to relate to the all-pervasive spiritual powers within the world and to seek the psychic support needed by the human mode of consciousness. "To obtain this support, to invoke that numinous presence perceived as the origin, support, and final destiny of all that exists, humans from the earliest times engaged in symbolic rituals, often with sacrificial aspects."[35]

***Modern* Homo Sapiens:** *40,000 Years Ago.*   This period was a time of continuing migration, with the human reaching the Americas and Australia. The last advance of the Ice Ages was in process throughout the Northern Hemisphere with many species retreating south and later returning to flourish in the north. Humans survived the Ice Ages because their mental flexibility recognized climatic changes, adapted to those changes, and developed functional community living. Much as is the case with growing children, collaboration and socialization became necessary. One example is found in the shift of their hunting strategy from stalking larger animals to following herds of smaller animals. The people had to work together and learn to anticipate and even to adopt the habits of the hunted.

Upon their arrival in the region of modern Europe, these peoples, called the Cro-Magnon, manifested an artistic and inventive genius unknown in earlier peoples.

---

[34] Swimme and Berry, *The Universe Story,* p. 149.

[35] Swimme and Berry, *The Universe Story,* p. 153.

Since these artistic abilities were associated with a new capacity for the understanding and use of spoken language, we are meeting here not simply with another change in methods of stone working or the processing of some physical material but with a transformation of human consciousness on a scale and with a dramatic impact such as we seldom encounter in this narrative of our emergent human development.[36]

Throughout the Paleolithic period, hunting and gathering were the basic life support systems of the people, implying a knowledge of and a dependence on other species, and a need to be in tune with the earth and its creatures. More and more highly developed tools and implements, as well as the use of fire, show a specifically human mode of adaptation to its place in the community of species. These new ways of living, as well as the continual presence of danger and the fear of the unknown, called for new social relationships, the building of family groupings, collaborative hunting, shared housing, and communal rituals. The artistic and ritualistic genius of both early and later *Homo sapiens* is evidence of the experience of the deep mystery contained within the earth. This was the unfolding of a spiritual consciousness and reverence for Gaia, the Earth Mother.

The human was a species in its childhood (1) depending on the earth for food, clothing and shelter; (2) its education flowing from a deep and dynamic interaction with the other creatures of the earth; (3) developing a social awareness to fend off danger and to reap the benefits of a communal relationship with the earth; and (4) possessing a sense of awe and even worship for Mother Earth and a need to express these feelings in art and ritual.

The story of the Garden of Paradise in Genesis may be a romanticized expression of the collective human memory of the story of its childhood. The coming of agriculture and the domestication of animals is the beginning of a new era, a period of adolescence when the human experiences the attractiveness of the earth and the desire to be like God, knowing good and evil. The human becomes aware of its own nakedness and the need to earn its bread by the sweat of the brow.

ACT TWO: THE ADOLESCENCE OF THE HUMAN

Human history is divided into two unequal parts. The first is the biological evolution of the human that includes all the steps that lead us from our hominid ancestors to modern *Homo sapiens* over a period of two million years. The second is its cultural history that includes the movement of civilization that takes us from our hunting and gathering Paleolithic ancestors beginning about twelve thousand years ago until today. And the cultural evolution, once it began in earnest, developed at least a hundred times faster than the biological evolution.

---

[36] Swimme and Berry, *The Universe Story*, p. 156.

"It is extraordinary to think that only in the last twelve thousand years has civilization, as we understand it, taken off. There must have been an extraordinary explosion about 10,000 B.C.E.—and there was."[37] And that explosion was the agricultural revolution, the domestication of animals, and the change from a nomadic culture to the Neolithic village. "If the first distinctive human relation with the planet Earth was the inauguration of tool-using processes, the second was the invention of horticulture and the domestication of animals within the context of the Neolithic village."[38]

> The active intrusion by humans into the functioning of the life forces of the Earth until this time had been minimal, limited mostly in the effects that hunting was having on the animal world. Now there was a more active involvement with the vegetative world first through selection of plants for adoption and then through the breaking of the soil and the planting processes with a digging stick and then the hoe and eventually with the plow.[39]

Swimme and Berry describe the Neolithic village in terms that seem romantic but are based on substantial archeological evidence.

> In reality the Neolithic village has been the exciting context of immense creativity. It was as peaceful a period as humans would ever know. In Neolithic Old Europe, for instance, we find little evidence of warfare instruments or fortifications prior to the Bronze Age; walls and weapons were the exception rather than the rule. In the social order it was a period of community intimacy and apparently the widespread sharing in decision making.[40]

With the coming of agriculture, domestication, and the early village some ten thousand years ago, the human took on a new relationship with the earth. There were now efforts to interfere with the natural world, both animal and plant, in order to provide a more stable life and to feed a more stable and growing village population. Even though this new relationship had some negative effects on the regions it impacted, in the larger perspective the damage was sustainable. We can describe the impact of this revolution as follows.

Relation to Nature. The easy and childlike Paleolithic identity of the human with the functioning of the natural world began to change into a more conscious understanding and adjustment to the natural systems whereby humans themselves had come into being. Humans were searching

---

[37] Bronowski, *The Ascent of Man*, p. 60.

[38] Swimme and Berry, *The Universe Story*, p. 164.

[39] Swimme and Berry, *The Universe Story*, p. 164.

[40] Swimme and Berry, *The Universe Story*, p. 175.

for new ways to relate to nature that would be increasingly beneficial to the human.

The Role of Women.   Most likely women discovered three of the great inventions of the Neolithic village: horticulture, pottery making, and weaving. The domestication of animals, such as sheep, goats, cows and pigs, was also probably the outcome of women's close relationship to harvesting, cooking, and feeding. Thus in the arts, in clothing, and in the care of domestic animals, women were clearly present in a primary role.

Images of God.   The universe itself was experienced primarily in its inexhaustible fecundity and thus primarily identified through the image of woman. Thousands of female images have been discovered in Neolithic villages, indicating the role of women in society and in the religious expressions of the people in terms of a feminine deity.

> The intimate association of the peaceful goddess with the early earth-based religions ritually integrated with the seasonal rise and decline of the vegetative cycle has been so enduring that the Neolithic village continued this primordial devotion as a subculture, even after the warring male sky deities took over control of the various societies as a ruling class with an entirely different ethos from that of the peoples over whom they ruled.[41]

Between 8000 and 3000 B.C.E. the revolution begun at the end of the last Ice Age continued in the development and spread of the Neolithic village. At the same time these cultural forces were pressing forward to the development of classical urban civilizations often called the horticultural-based city-centered mode of the human. The remnants of these cultural changes can be seen in many human populations, and it is often found in the history of Israel as recorded in the Hebrew Scriptures. The story of the conflict between Abel, a keeper of the flocks, and Cain, a tiller of the soil, reflects the conflicts among various civilizations. The rise of the Davidic kingship is also indicative of the changes in society from prophetic leadership to the judges to a king, who in Israel became the representative of God, the King. These cultural and social changes led to the development of a patriarchal culture and the transition from the female Goddess to the male God.

About 10,000 years ago the human entered into its adolescence. As the peoples of the earth moved toward the development of an agricultural way of life and the domestication of animals, the human began to see itself as able to control the earth and its fruits. The use of fire and the power of words helped the human to establish its species identity, and, much like an adolescent searching for identity, this "clarity of species identity tended toward isolating the human within itself over against the nonhuman compo-

---

[41] Swimme and Berry, *The Universe Story,* pp. 175–176.

nents of the larger Earth community."[42] This was a time of mental and ego development, and the power issues of adolescence led to the growth of a patriarchal society and a patriarchal God.

With the coming of the scientific and technological age, in the last few centuries and especially among those people from the Western world, the human could begin to manipulate the earth without regard for the impact of such manipulation on the rest of creation. Excitement, novelty, and self-gratification became central issues in our society as it does in the experience of adolescence. These developments gave rise to an economic system that has gradually become the controlling factor in our relationship with the earth. In the name of economic progress, the impact of such a system on the earth and on the human was neglected or ignored. The gap between the rich and the poor, between rich nations and poor nations, continued to grow and plant the seeds of violence, war, pollution, and destruction.

> If we don't grow up—soon—we may abort the human evolutionary journey. Our adolescent immaturity, with physical and mental development out of balance with spiritual development, has us on the brink of a "teenage suicide." The short view, and the self-centered view, of adolescent vision has brought us dangerously close to killing ourselves—either suddenly in a nuclear holocaust, or slowly by maiming our life-support systems. For human evolution to continue into health and wholeness, physical and mental development must now be matched with spiritual maturity.[43]

In the midst of all the historical and cultural changes among peoples and nations, the past remains present for us. As we move forward into the unknown we cannot shake the dust from the feet of our historical journey, nor can we ignore the values of our many ancestors that have become foundational to our lives. Ishmael, whom we quoted above in the six-act play, sees the agricultural revolution as one of those ongoing events that is still part of our lives.

> So you see that your agricultural revolution is not an event like the Trojan War, isolated in the distant past and without direct relevance to your lives today. The work begun by those neolithic farmers in the Near East has been carried forward from one generation to the next without a single break, right into the present moment. It's the foundation of your vast civilization today in exactly the same way that it was the foundation of the very first farming village.[44]

As we step back and examine the adolescent phase of our story as humans, we can glimpse both its positive and its negative impact on the ma-

---

[42] Swimme and Berry, *The Universe Story,* p. 178.

[43] Keck, L. Robert, *Sacred Eyes,* Boulder, CO, Synergy Associates, 1992, p. 6.

[44] Quinn, *Ishmael,* p. 153.

ture development of the human. The agricultural revolution, the development of the horticultural-based city-centered mode of the human, and the more recent scientific and industrial revolutions have, indeed, brought many wonderful benefits to the human family. There are, however, two interrelated negative outcomes from this period of human adolescence: (1) the rise of our patriarchal society and the male domination of women and (2) the domination of nature with its devastation of the earth and of the environment. Both of these realities will be treated more at length in Chapter 3 in the section "The Earth as Womb or Tomb."

ACT THREE: ADULTHOOD

The following is an analogy offered by a friend in which he compares an adolescent's moving into adulthood with the call for the human species to move into adulthood. It seems to describe some of the feelings of our current situation.

> The emergence from adolescence is often incomplete. Some never quite emerge at all. Others embrace the responsibilities of adulthood and put their emotions and hormones in order. But most are still susceptible to being drawn back into the maelstrom—triggered by an event, a relationship, a discovery, or a failure of the structure they have built for themselves. That failure may be a lay-off by their company, a spouse that leaves for another, a church that turns a deaf ear on their cry for help.
>
> As a child, we accept the world for what it is and ourselves as special within that world. As adolescents, we question who we are and try to resolve that question by making the world satisfy our appetites. And as adults? Do we perhaps come to realize that we are the world? And that appetites, like other natural forces, have their place but that place is not one of control? Do we begin to understand that, like a good provider, we care for others first, then satisfy our needs? And that the order—first those in our care, then ourselves—extends to all species and all of nature? Is adulthood humankind as caretakers? Or is that too exalted a role? Does being caretaker, in our minds, require that we shape as well as administer?
>
> Perhaps, like most adolescents, we don't yet know what adulthood means. And, unfortunately, we have no models. Perhaps, like so many children we will become adults only when crisis forces us to, and then only if we are lucky enough to survive. I confess to being very unsure of the future of humanity. And equally unsure as to whether the universe cares one way or another.

Despite all the ambiguity and uncertainty, it is time for the human to move from adolescence into adulthood. We now have a new story of creation. We have gained knowledge about the universe that leaves us in awe.

Our advanced technology has given us a new way of seeing our outer space and our inner space. It has given us the potential for a whole new relationship with the earth and with each other through our instantaneous worldwide communication and our sense of the global village.

Adulthood also calls us to a new sense of our relationship with the whole of creation. We are no longer called to conquer the earth or to rule over our fellow creatures. The evolutionary process calls for a new stance toward the rest of creation by recognizing the dignity and rights of the whole community of species. We are called in new ways to live out the web of relationships that surrounded our ancestors and surrounds us still.

> Because everything in our universe is interdependent, evolutionary growth is fostered not by the competitive ability of the various life forms to outwit each other (as in the Darwinian-type survival of the fittest), but by the cooperative and concerted interaction, characterized by mutual respect and a communal commitment to the advancement of all. For us humans, to let go of our adversarial and arrogant stance, over against the universe and the earth, and learn instead to befriend universal life as *subject* in relation to *subject*, is the unique and most urgent challenge of our time.[45]

Adulthood means making responsible decisions not simply for our own benefit but for the common good of all the earth and its community of species. The human has a significant role in the future evolution of our earth.

> The earth that directed itself instinctively in its former phases seems now to be entering a phase of conscious decision through its human expression. This is the ultimate daring venture for the earth, this confiding its destiny to human decision, the bestowal upon the human community of the power of life and death over its basic life systems.[46]

The earth seems to have given over its future to us and our decision-making powers, but it has not left the human without guidance.

> What is needed on our part is the capacity for listening to what the earth is telling us. As a unique organism the earth is self-directed. Our sense of the earth must be sufficiently sound so that it can support the dangerous future that is calling us. It is a decisive moment. Yet we should not feel that we alone are determining the future course of events. The future shaping of the community depends on the entire earth in the unity of its organic functioning, on its geological and biological as well as its human members.[47]

---

[45] O'Murchu, *Quantum Theology*, pp. 58–59.

[46] Berry, *The Dream of the Earth*, p. 19.

[47] Berry, *The Dream of the Earth*, p. 23.

CONCLUSION

In this chapter we have outlined the sources of the new creation story. We have challenged the notion that the human is called to "rule the roost" and to conquer creation. We have seen the importance of not denying but embracing the reality of chaos, darkness, and our shadow side. We have searched more deeply into various images of God flowing from the creation story, and we have unearthed some of the bare bones of the human story. Because the focus of this work is on the discovery of a new paradigm for the church, we can ask a crucial question at this point. As we enter into the third millennium, as the human moves toward adulthood and takes on its responsibility in deciding the future of our earth, will the church have a positive impact on the outcome of this momentous turning point of history?

Clearly, the church *can* have a role, but only if we all learn to listen to the voice of the universe story, to listen to the voice of the earth, to listen to the voice of the people, and only if the church speaks to the real concerns of the earth and of the people. The church, as a part of the holy web embracing the whole universe, will be a force for the future only if it heeds the call of Jesus, "The time is fulfilled, and the kingdom of God has come near; repent, and believe in the good news" (Mk. 1:15). The church can be a partner in this new world only if it undergoes a profound conversion and transformation, calling all people to adulthood in our common search for the presence and reign of God among us.

In the optimistic words of Brian Swimme:

> The tragedy here is that our religions would remain true to their essence if they were to think and work within the larger context of the universe. It would not mean shrinking away from the central religious truths. On the contrary, expressed within the context of the dynamics of the developing universe, the essential truths of religion would find a far vaster and more profound form. The recasting should not be a compromise nor a diminution nor a belittlement; it would be a surprising and creative fulfillment, one whose significance goes beyond today's most optimistic evaluations of the value of religion.[48]

---

[48]Swimme, *The Hidden Heart of the Cosmos*, p. 12.

PART II

CHARACTERISTICS OF A NEW PARADIGM

The church is a many splendored thing, and thus it can be understood and appropriated only by looking at its various dimensions or characteristics. There are four characteristics of the church described in this section of the book: (1) Church of the Earth, (2) Church of Deeper Consciousness, (3) Holarchical Church, and (4) Church of the World.

These characteristics are not separate or different realities but expressions of different dimensions of the same reality. They tend to be overlapping and circular with mutual interrelationships as might be expected in a quantum universe (see pages 17–18, 98–99). The Christian church is the people of God gathered to celebrate the presence of the Risen Christ and called by the Spirit to a mission of service to all creation. This church is the one reality that is being examined. Everything said about this new paradigm is an effort to articulate in story, word, and symbol our experience of this reality.

It will be helpful to compare the discussion of these four characteristics to a symphony with its musical flow from the exposition of the major theme, to its development and recapitulation, to the coda that summarizes the theme with all of its complexity. The major theme of these characteristics is *the holy web*, and this theme is first heard at the beginning of Chapter 3. There will be subthemes sounded at various times, but it is this web that is continually being exposed, developed, recapitulated, and summarized as this process spirals to a greater understanding and appropriation of the new paradigm.

As I describe these characteristics of the church, it might seem as though I am far from the topic, speculating on holons and implicate matter; sometimes it might seem as though I am losing my focus, going after the Jungian unconscious and cosmic awareness; and maybe losing my mind in discussing dissipative structures and chaos theory. However, like a good teller of stories, I hope that all these seeming digressions, blind alleys, and moments of confusion and darkness will eventually lead to a deeper understanding of the meaning of the church. A new vision will unfold from the new creation story as well as the long tradition of the church, and this vision can emerge as a new light in the darkness and a new voice crying in the wilderness.

3

CHURCH OF THE EARTH

This chapter introduces the basic question of the relationship between the earth and the church. The web of relationships as it relates to the new vision of the church is then developed in terms of three concepts from the new creation story: (1) the theory of holons, (2) the field theory, and (3) the theory of the implicate order. We will discuss the impact of the destructive power of patriarchy and the life-giving power of ecofeminism on the church. Finally, we will return to the major theme of the holy web by visioning the church as a community of disciples.

THE RELATIONSHIP OF THE CHURCH AND THE EARTH

Recent developments in the field of natural science and a deeper understanding of cosmology are leading us to a realization of our close relationship to the earth. Evidence presented in the new story of the universe paints a picture of the radical unity of all things moving forward with an inner drive toward greater complexity and fuller expression. The planet earth takes its place in the solar system with the gradual shaping of its lands and seas and atmosphere. Living creatures begin to emerge and swim and crawl and run and fly, and finally the earth has become conscious in the human.

> The law of complexity-consciousness reveals that ever more intricate physical combinations, as can be traced in the evolution of the brain, yield ever more powerful forms of spirit. Matter alive with energy, evolves to spirit. While distinctive, human intelligence and creativity rise out of the very nature of the universe, which is itself intelligent and creative. In other words, human spirit is the cosmos come to consciousness.[1]

The church as a gathering of humans called to serve the whole of creation is a Church of the Earth because humans are completely earthbound creatures. The human has the same chemical composition as the earth—

---

[1]Johnson, Elizabeth, *Women, Earth, and Creator Spirit,* New York, Paulist Press, 1993, p. 37.

71 percent salt water and 92 elements—and, as we have learned from the effects of toxic wastes, whatever happens to the earth, the air, and the water happens to humanity. "When we destroy or deny any part of the earth, we deny and destroy part of our own essence. We are from the earth and of the earth. What we do to the earth we do to ourselves."[2] Thus our image of how the world comes into existence and the relationship of the earth to the human, our cosmology, is deepened and given a new direction by the new creation story. Thomas Berry explains it in these words:

> Humans in their totality are born of the earth. We are earthlings. The earth is our origin, our nourishment, our support, our guide. Our spirituality itself is earth-derived. If there is no spirituality in the earth then there is no spirituality in humans. Humans are a dimension of the earth.[3]

The idea of a transcendent God who created the human over against the earth can be misleading. It tends to make the goal of human life domination and control over the earth and our return to God a process of transcending and separating ourselves from nature and the earth. Creation, however, is more than this. The Creator God is found unfolding within the very developmental processes of the planet earth itself, and we can find ourselves and God by a return to the earth from which we emerged.

Aspects of this deeper cosmology are also found in the Jewish scriptures in the creation stories of Genesis. The Hebrew word usually translated "man" in our English Bibles is *adam*. This word, as used most frequently in Genesis, Chapters 1 and 2, is not gender-specific, and hence it does not mean a male of the species nor is it used as a proper name. It is probably a generic term signifying humankind. Moreover, *adam* seems to be derived from the Hebrew word *adamah*, meaning "earth," and it could appropriately be translated as "earthling." In a public lecture Phyllis Trible, a well-known biblical scholar, suggested that we might translate the word *adam* as "undifferentiated earth creature."

Thus the deeper sense of the biblical story of the creation of the human is highlighted by translating it as follows:

> God created the earthling in God's own image,
> In the image of God was the earthling created,
> Male and female God created them.   (Gen. 1:27)

> The Lord God formed the earthling (*adam*)
> From the dust of the earth (*adamah*) and
> Breathed into its nostrils the breath of life,
> And the earthling became a living being.   (Gen. 2:7)

---

[2] Mische, Patricia, "Towards a Global Spirituality," in *The Whole Earth Papers*, No. 16, 1982, p. 6.

[3] Berry, Thomas, "The Spirituality of the Earth," in *The Whole Earth Papers*, No. 16, 1982, p. 43.

Even the Genesis story proclaims that the *human is the earth become conscious.*

As the Genesis story progresses, we are presented with the story of God's command and the disobedience of Adam and Eve. This was the Hebrew attempt to deal with the issue of the presence of evil in a world created as good by God. It is clear that the wedge between the human and the earth, and between the human and God, is the result not of God's creative plan but the result of the free choice and failure of the earthling. *Adam* becomes alienated from *adamah*. Because the man ate from the forbidden tree, God says:

> . . . Cursed be the ground [*adamah*] because of you,
> In toil shall you eat its yield all the days of your life,
> Thorns and thistles shall it bring forth to you,
> as you eat of the plants of the field.
> By the sweat of your face shall you get bread to eat,
> Until you return to the ground [*adamah*],
> From which you were taken,
> You are dirt, and to dirt you shall return.   (Gen. 3:17–19)

This alienation from God, from the earth, and from ourselves is the continuing struggle of humankind. In God's plan how does reconciliation take place? Many religions throughout human history taught that, in order to be reconciled and find union with God, it was necessary to reject the things of the earth and to be freed from our bodily corruption. In the Christian story the opposite happens! We do not have to leave aside the earth to find God but, in Jesus, God comes to us in a new and special way. The redemptive power of God, as we have seen in Chapter 2, is already present in creation, and this power is embodied in Jesus who is an earthling like us. "The Word became flesh and made his dwelling among us" (Jn. 1:14). "God was reconciling the world to himself in Christ" (2 Cor. 5:19). In Jesus, God identifies with the earthling and becomes one like us in all but sin, which is our alienation; Jesus is the new Adam.

In Romans 5:12–21, Paul explicitly raises the issue of the relationship and contrast between Adam and Christ. Through one man, Adam, death and condemnation comes to all; and through one man, Jesus Christ, life and justification comes to all. Through the disobedience of one man, many were made sinners; through the obedience of one man, many will be made righteous.

What does the word "man" signify in this passage? Is it gender-specific, implying maleness? Does it refer merely to the historical figures of Adam and Jesus? Or is there a deeper meaning? In our context, and in the context of reconciliation in Chapter 5 of Romans, the word "man" harkens back to the concept of Adam as the earthling (*adam*). The force of the analogy is that the alienation resulting from the disobedience of the earthling can be reversed only by the obedience of an earthling. Jesus is the new earthling (*adam*) through whom we are reconciled to God, to the earth, and to ourselves. Our salvation comes from an earthling like ourselves.

In his first letter to the Corinthians, Paul seems to contradict this interpretation by positing an even more radical disjunction between the first Adam and the second Adam.

> The first man, being from the earth, is earthly by nature,
> The second man is from heaven.
> As this earthly man was, so are we on earth,
> and as the heavenly man is, so are we in heaven.
> And we, who have been modeled on the earthly man,
> Will be modeled on the heavenly man.
>
> (1 Cor. 15:47–49)

However, the context of this letter is different from that of the letter to the Romans. Here Paul is trying to explain the mystery of the resurrection of the dead, and its meaning for Jesus and for ourselves (vs. 35). The contrast is between the perishable and the imperishable, between dishonor and glory, between weakness and power. To be raised from the dead is to be transformed, to be sown a physical body and raised a spiritual body.

These images should not be interpreted in terms of a dualism between body and soul or matter and spirit. The physical is not destroyed by the spiritual but transformed by it. The resurrection of the body is a transformation of the whole human person by the power of the Spirit, restoring in a new way the imperishability, glory, and power promised by God.

Paul also tried to explain the mystery of the resurrection by an analogy between the earthly man and the heavenly man. The contrast here also should not be interpreted as a dualism between heaven and earth. In the resurrection, the earthly is not destroyed by the heavenly but transformed by it. The contrast is between the earthly as expressing the negative dimensions of the human such as disobedience, sinfulness, and death and the heavenly as expressing the positive dimensions of the human such as obedience, justification, and life that come from the Spirit.

All the negative connotations of the earthly are wiped away by the resurrection. Jesus is like Adam in being an earthling, but Jesus is an earthling renewed by the power of the Spirit. Far from removing the human from its earthbound character, the Risen Christ empowers us to embrace the human and the earthly, confident that it has been transformed by the presence of the life-giving Spirit.

The earth is our home; it is the source of our life and power. The earthly has been transformed by Jesus and the Resurrection into the locus of grace and salvation. In Adam, a child of the earth, we as humans are the earth become conscious, and through Jesus, a child of the earth, we as believers become the Church of the Earth.

The question of the relationship between the earth and the human is also clarified in the biblical figure of Wisdom/Sophia, and this figure offers a unique way of speaking about the mystery of creation and of God in a female symbol.

> The biblical depiction of Wisdom is itself consistently female, casting her as sister, mother, female beloved, chef and hostess, preacher, judge, liberator, establisher of justice, and a myriad of other female roles wherein she symbolizes transcendent power ordering and delighting in the world. She pervades the world, both nature and human beings, interacting with them all to lure them along the right path to life.[4]

There is much that could be said about Wisdom/Sophia, and extensive treatments of this image are available.[5] At this point I want to highlight the relationship of Wisdom to her role in creation, revelation, and salvation.

In Creation.   Sophia is sometimes portrayed as being made by God before the creation of the world, and she is present with God before all other things. She is the source of life and of all creatures on earth and in the heavens. Listen, she speaks:

> The Lord begot me as the firstborn, the forerunner of God's prodigies of long ago; from of old I was poured forth, at the first, before the earth. When there were no depths I was brought forth, when there were no fountains or springs of water; before the mountains were settled into place, before the hills, I was brought forth; while yet the earth and the fields were not made, nor the first clods of the world. When God established the heavens I was there, when God marked out the vault over the face of the deep; when God made firm the skies above and fixed fast the foundations of the earth; when God set for the sea its limit, so that the waters should not transgress the command. Then was I beside God as the artisan, and I was God's delight day by day, playing before God all the while, playing on the surface of the earth; and I found delight in the children of the earth.   (Prov. 9:22–31)

In Revelation.   Sophia is often portrayed as a teacher and preacher of wisdom, and then in a deeper sense she is the source of wisdom.

> For Sophia is instructor in the understanding of God, the selector of God's works. And if riches be a desirable possession in life, what is more rich than Wisdom, who produces all things? And if prudence ren-

---

[4] Johnson, Elizabeth, *She Who Is: The Mystery of God in Feminist Theological Discourse,* New York, Crossroad, 1994, p. 87.

[5] Johnson, *She Who Is*; Denis Edwards, *Jesus the Wisdom of God: An Ecological Theology,* Maryknoll, NY, Orbis Books, 1995; Anne Clifford, "Creation," in *Systematic Theology: Roman Catholic Perspectives,* Minneapolis, MN, Augsburg Press, 1991, Vol. 1, pp. 195–247.

ders service, who in the world is a better craftsman than she? Or if one loves justice, the fruits of her works are virtues; for she teaches moderation and prudence, justice and fortitude, and nothing in life is more useful.   (Wis. 8:4–7)

Then Sophia speaks again:

So now, O children, listen to me; instruction and wisdom do not reject! Happy those who obey me, and happy those who keep my ways, happy those watching daily at my gates, waiting at my doorposts; the one who finds me finds life, and wins favor from the Lord.   (Prov. 8:32–36)

In Salvation.   Although salvation is not so frequently seen as connected to Sophia, the books of wisdom literature clearly give a central place to the saving role of Wisdom in the history of Israel. The following are some examples among many.

Send her [Wisdom] forth from your holy heavens and from your glorious throne dispatch her that she may be with me and work with me, that I may know what is your pleasure, . . . and thus were the paths of those on earth made straight, and people learned what was your pleasure, and were saved by Wisdom.   (Wis. 9:10, 18)

She [Wisdom] preserved the first-formed father of the world [Adam] when he alone had been created; and she raised him up from his fall, and gave him power to rule all things. . . . When on his account the earth was flooded, Wisdom again saved it, piloting the just man [Noah] on frailest wood. . . . Wisdom delivered from tribulations those who served her. . . . She did not abandon the just man [Joseph] when he was sold, but delivered him from sin.   (Wis. 10:1–2, 4, 9, 13)

For Wisdom will enter your heart, knowledge will please your soul, discretion will watch over you, understanding will guard you; saving you from the ways of evil, from those of perverse speech.   (Prov. 2:10–12)

In many ways this feminine figure of Wisdom echoes many of the dimensions of the new creation story. God's Wisdom is identified with the wisdom of the earth. Sophia is the spotless mirror of the power of God and the image of God's goodness. She penetrates and pervades all things. She is the inner unfolding of creation, the source of God's self-revelation and the saving power bringing about the renewal of all things. The following passage gives a picture of the beauty, depth, and complexity of the role of Wisdom.

For Wisdom is mobile beyond all motion, and she penetrates and pervades all things by reason of her purity. For she is an aura of the might of God and a pure effusion of the glory of the almighty; therefore nought that is sullied enters into her. For she is the refulgence of eternal light, the spotless mirror of the power of God, the image of God's goodness. And she, who is one, can do all things, and renews everything while herself is perduring. And passing into holy souls from age to age, she produces friends of God and prophets. For there is nought God loves, be it not one who dwells with Wisdom. For she is fairer than the sun and surpasses every constellation of the stars. Compared to light, she takes precedence; for that, indeed, night supplants, but wickedness prevails not over Wisdom. Indeed, she reaches from end to end mightily and governs all things well.   (Wis. 7:24–8:1)

While typing this text from the Book of Wisdom, I was reminded of the figure of Gaia, the ancient Mother Goddess that has returned in more recent years as the symbol of the earth as a living organism, the embodiment of Wisdom.[6] The following are three characteristics of the ancient ideas of the earth:

First, the Earth is the oldest goddess, supporter and nurturer of her children, human and nonhuman, and therefore entitled to respect and worship. Environmental problems are seen as a result of the failure of human beings to worship the Earth and her unwritten laws.

Second, the Earth is a living being of whom humans are only a part. Right relationship with the Earth means that the total organism is in good health; so environmental problems are seen as illness, as a failure on the part of the organism to interact supportively with the others.

Third, Earth is seen as responsive to human care or the lack of it, giving rich returns to those who treat her well and punishing those who are lazy or who weary her by trying to wrest from her what she is not ready to give. Environmental problems are seen as the revenge of the Earth on those who fail either through ignorance or greed, to practice well the art of the attentive tender of the land.[7]

In their struggle to explain their belief in the role of the Risen Christ in creation, revelation, and salvation, the early Christian community found the figure of Sophia/Wisdom as an appropriate vehicle.[8] The language they used reflects the language from the Wisdom literature, and in the following texts that language will be italicized. In Paul's letter to the Colossians we find

---

[6] Joseph, Lawrence E., *Gaia: The Growth of an Idea*, New York, St. Martin's Press, 1990, p. 30. "Fundamentally, the Gaia Hypothesis finds the Earth to be more like a life form than an inanimate sphere, adjusting to internal and external changes much as an organism might react to threats and opportunities in the environment."

[7] J. Donald Hughes, "Mother Gaia: An Ancient View of Earth," in *Proceedings of "Is the Earth a Living Organism?" Symposium at Amherst College, Audubon Expedition Institute, Spring 1986*, 34–4, as quoted in Joseph, *Gaia*, p. 199.

[8] For an excellent presentation of the relationship of Jesus and Sophia see Johnson, *She Who Is*, pp. 150–169.

what was probably an early Christian hymn taken up into the letter from its liturgical use.

> He [Christ] is the *image of the invisible God*, the *firstborn of all creation*. For in him *were created all things in heaven and on earth*, the visible and the invisible, whether thrones or dominions or principalities or powers; *all things were created through him* and for him. He is *before all things, and in him all things hold together*. He [Christ] is the head of the body, the church. He is the beginning, *the firstborn* from the dead, that in all things he himself might be preeminent. For in him *all the fullness was pleased to dwell*, and through him to reconcile all things for him, making peace by the blood of the cross, whether those on earth or those in heaven.   (Col. 1:15–20; emphasis added)

In this text the hymn ties in a reference to the role of Wisdom in creation with the role of the Risen Christ as head of his Body, the church, in salvation and reconciliation. The role of Christ as God's mediator in revelation is also tied into the Wisdom tradition in the Letter to the Hebrews.

> In times past, God spoke in partial and various ways to our ancestors through the prophets; in these last days, God spoke to us through a son, whom God made heir of all things and through whom he *created the universe*, who is *the refulgence of God's glory*, the *very imprint of God's being*, and who *sustains all things* by God's mighty word.
> (Heb. 1:1–3; emphasis added)

Finally, in the prologue to the Gospel of John we find a fuller exposition of the Wisdom theme in terms of the Word of God, who is with God in the beginning, from whom all things came to be, who became flesh and pitched his tent among us, from whose fullness we have all received, who is the source of grace and truth, and who reveals to us the unseen God (Jn. 1:1–18).

We, as humans, are the children of Wisdom/Sophia, the divine source of creation, revelation, and salvation, and we, as Christian believers, find in the Risen Christ, Wisdom incarnate, the divine mediator and model of creation, revelation, and salvation. We are all children of Wisdom, and we are intimately bound up with the earth. We are a Church of the Earth. We are called to live out the profound unity of all peoples in the earth and in Wisdom/Sophia, and the profound unity of all believers in Jesus/Sophia, the Word made flesh and the embodiment of Wisdom.

The Church of the Earth sees the Wisdom of God as the inner source of creation, the power within unfolding the marvels of the universe over fifteen billion years. In that power the human emerges as the earth becomes conscious, and in Jesus, the new earthling, there is a renewal of the earth and the human. Revelation in its deepest sense is the Wisdom of God manifested in this unfolding of the universe, the earth and the human.

Consequently, we are invited to move toward a new revelatory horizon. It is new in terms of recent theological reflection, but very old in terms of our human, spiritual unfolding. It suggests that the creation itself is the *primary* revelation, of which the various disclosures of the major religions are particular expressions offered in the specific context of a certain historical and cultural milieu.[9]

We find God revealed to us in every dimension of the universe and especially in the earth become conscious, and we find God revealed to us, as Christians, in a more significant way in the Risen Christ, the eternal Word made flesh. The power of God within the universe is also the fundamental source of the healing of the universe as seen in creative energy of an exploding supernova, in the new life from the ravages of a forest fire, and in the restoration of a lake found dead from pollution. That salvific power of God was manifested in the death and resurrection of Jesus, the new earthling, and it becomes the source of healing, reconciliation, and liberation for all humankind.

THE WEB OF RELATIONSHIPS

Over the years I have experienced and studied the earth from many points of view: first, as a high school and college student dealing with basic science, then as a graduate student of Thomistic philosophy and theology, and later as a professor of theology. As I look back, the most significant and recurrent theme is the web of relationships within the universe and the earth. This is becoming a very common starting point for many people. The following quotations from many different sources are indicative of how deeply this sense of relationality impacts the way we think and the extent to which it has become a major principle of the new science.

> The conception of the universe as an interconnected web of relations is one of the two major themes that recur throughout modern physics. The other theme is the realization that the cosmic web is intrinsically dynamic.[10]

> But isolation and alienation are profoundly false states of mind. We were born out of the Earth Community and its infinite creativity and delight and adventure. Our natural state is intimacy within the encompassing community. Our natural genetic inheritance presents us with the possibility of forming deeply bonded relationships throughout all ten million species of life as well as throughout the nonliving components of the universe.[11]

---

[9] O'Murchu, David, *Quantum Theology,* New York, Crossroad, 1997, p. 74.

[10] Capra, Fritjof, *The Turning Point,* New York, Bantam Books, 1983, p. 87.

[11] Swimme, Brian, *The Hidden Heart of the Cosmos,* Maryknoll, NY, Orbis Books, 1996, p. 34.

We need to be open to fundamental shifts of mind. It's about a shift from seeing a world made up of things to seeing a world that's open and primarily made up of relationships.[12]

Some of us saw the world through the eyes of modern physics: an interconnected web of relationships, with all matter constantly in motion and fundamentally open. Therefore, the future was not fixed. The world was full of possibilities for change and creativity.[13]

We live in a relationship of mutual influence with the other subjects in the earth community; we do influence them and they do influence us. This interrelationship is so profound, so thorough, and so pervasive that we usually do not see it.[14]

But something much deeper is at stake, a conviction that is resurfacing in the emerging consciousness of our time, namely, *we are our relationships*. What we are as individuals, and what we will become in the future, is determined by the quality of our interdependence on others—humans and nonhumans alike.[15]

Woven into our lives is the very fire from the stars and the genes from the sea creatures, and everyone, utterly everyone, is kin in the radiant tapestry of being. This relationship is not external or extrinsic to who we are, but wells up as the defining truth from our deepest being.[16]

In order to understand the dynamic web of relationships that is so central to the universe and that will impact our understanding of the Church of the Earth, we will weave together three different threads: (1) the theory of holons, (2) the field theory, and (3) the theory of the implicate order.

THE THEORY OF HOLONS

Throughout the centuries, philosophers have searched out the depth of reality, and, as a budding scientist and philosopher, I was led through that search. History teaches us that some thinkers proposed that all reality was composed of individual "atoms," others suggested the four elements (earth, air, fire, and water), and others came up with "matter" and "form" as the intrinsic meaning of reality. Modern theorists believed that the more recent discovery of the atomic elements gave us the ultimate building block of all

[12] Senge, Peter, "Introduction," in Joseph Jaworski, *Synchronicity: The Inner Path of Leadership*, San Francisco, Berrett-Koehler Publishers, 1996, p. 10.

[13] Jaworski, Joseph, *Synchronicity: The Inner Path of Leadership*, San Francisco, Berrett-Koehler Publishers, 1996, p. 160.

[14] McFague, Sallie, *Super, Natural Christians*, Minneapolis, MN, Fortress Press, 1997, p. 153.

[15] O'Murchu, *Quantum Theology*, p. 83.

[16] Johnson, *Women, Earth, and Creator Spirit*, p. 39.

reality. Then the atom was smashed, and the various subatomic particles and waves took over, for a while, the role as the ultimate reality.

And now a new twist on this search for the ultimate in reality is found in the theory of holons, a description of the relationships that are fundamental to the universe. A holon is not a kind of matter or a particle or a wave or a process; a holon is a whole/part. The theory, as integrated and presented by Ken Wilber, is that whatever exists in the universe is a whole/part. Every whole is also a part and every part is a whole. This is true in the realms of matter, of life, and of mind. Wilber in his book *Sex, Ecology, Spirituality* expounds the theory of holons as a way of describing the web of relationships in the universe. In his introduction he says:

> This is a book about holons—about wholes that are parts of other wholes, indefinitely. Whole atoms are parts of molecules; whole molecules are parts of cells; whole cells are parts of organisms, and so on. Each *whole* is simulaneously a *part*, a whole/part, a holon. And reality is composed, not of things nor processes nor wholes nor parts, but of whole/parts, of holons. We will be looking at holons in the cosmos, in the bios, in the psyche, and in theos; and at the evolutionary thread that connects them all, unfolds them all, embraces them all, endlessly.[17]

I do not think Wilber or anyone else can actually prove the holon theory. It is too basic a premise. One of my philosophy professors said that if he saw a bird in a bush, there is no way he could prove it. He could just point to it, and you either see it or you don't. It is the same with holons. We can only point to them, describe them, and discern their patterns and capacities, and then you either perceive holons or you don't. If the theory makes sense to you in terms of your experience, you will indeed see the relevance of holons in science and in a new paradigm of the church.

Wilber contends that "holons display four fundamental capacities: self-preservation, self-adaptation, self-transcendence, and self-dissolution."[18] We will give a brief explanation of each of these four capacities using the example of hydrogen and oxygen and water.

Self-Preservation.   All holons preserve their own particular wholeness or autonomy, and all holons differ in their level of stability. Oxygen is a whole with various electrons and protons as its parts, and it seeks to maintain its own individuality. But oxygen tends to be unstable and easily combines with other elements to form a new holon such as water. On the other hand, water, as a holon, maintains its wholeness and autonomy with much greater stability. Thus a holon often exists by virtue of its interlinking relationships, but it is not defined by its role as a part. Its intrinsic form, or

---

[17] Wilber, Ken, *Sex, Ecology, Spirituality: The Spirit of Evolution,* Boston, Shambhala, 1995, p. viii.

[18] Wilber, *Sex, Ecology, Spirituality,* p. 40.

pattern, or structure is what defines oxygen, not its relationship to hydrogen or water.

Self-Adaptation.   A holon functions not only as a self-preserving whole but also as a part of a larger whole, and in its capacity as a part it must adapt or accommodate itself to other holons. Hydrogen is a whole, but it is also a part when combined with oxygen to make water. As a part, it needs to adapt to its relationship with oxygen and with the new holon of water. Another example is that of two autonomous people who enter marriage and thus form a new social holon. They are defined as wholes in their autonomous selves, but in their role as parts of a marriage they are called to fit into and adapt to a new environment.

Thus self-preservation and self-adaptation can set up two opposed tendencies in a holon.

> We can just as well think of these two opposed tendencies as a holon's *agency* and *communion*. Its agency—its self-asserting, self-preserving, assimilating tendencies—expresses its *wholeness*, its relative autonomy; whereas its communion—its participatory, bonding, joining tendencies—expresses its *partness*, its relationship to something larger.[19]

Self-Transcendence.   When different wholes come together to form a new and different whole, there is some sort of creative twist on what has gone before. When hydrogen and oxygen come together to form water, something radically new emerges. Two gases come together to form a liquid. When two people come together in marriage, the whole is something new and creative, and the character of the new holon cannot be predicted on the simple basis of the character of the two people. Self-transcendence introduces a vertical dimension to our sense of a holon, one that cuts at a right angle to the horizontal relationship between self-preservation and self-adaptation.

> Self-transcendence is simply a system's capacity to reach beyond the given and introduce some measure of novelty, a capacity without which, it is quite certain, evolution would never, and could never, have even gotten started. Self-transcendence, which leaves no corner of the universe untouched (or evolution would have *no point* of departure), means nothing more—and nothing less—than that the universe has an intrinsic capacity to go beyond what went before.[20]

Self-Dissolution.   Just as holons are capable of building up through transformation and self-transcendence, they are able to break down. Water can break into its component parts of oxygen and hydrogen, and marriage can break down because of various conflicts, struggles, and loss of cohesion.

---

[19] Wilber, *Sex, Ecology, Spirituality,* p. 41.

[20] Wilber, *Sex, Ecology, Spirituality,* p. 44.

The general direction of evolution and of human society leads to self-transcendence, but the reality of self-dissolution is also an integral part of nature and society.

Wilber concludes his discussion of the four capacities of holons by saying, "Preserve or accommodate, transcend or dissolve—the four very different pulls on each and every holon in the Kosmos."[21] (See schema below.)

Because of the self-transcendent capacity of holons, it is evident that holons *emerge*—first atoms, then molecules, and then cells. Wilber goes on to explain that somehow, as holons emerge, there is something new, surprising, and indeterminate about the outcome. "The emergent holons are in some sense novel; they possess properties and qualities that cannot be strictly and totally deduced from their components; and therefore they, and their descriptions, cannot be reduced without remainder to their component parts."[22]

CAPACITIES OF HOLONS

SELF-TRANSCENDENCE

Self-transcendence is a transformation that results in something novel and emergent—different wholes have come together to form a new and different whole. There is some sort of creative twist on what has gone before.

SELF-PRESERVATION

All holons display some capacity to preserve their individuality, to preserve their own particular wholeness or autonomy.

SELF-ADAPTATION

A holon functions not only as a self-preserving whole but also as a part of a larger whole, and in its capacity as a part it must adapt or accommodate itself to other holons.

SELF-DISSOLUTION

Holons that are built up through vertical self-transcendence can also break down. Not surprisingly, when holons "dissolve" or "come unglued," they tend to do so along the same vertical sequence in which they were built up.

---

[21] Wilber, *Sex, Ecology, Spirituality,* p. 46.

[22] Wilber, *Sex, Ecology, Spirituality,* pp. 46–47.

Without knowing it would be so ahead of time, there would be no way to predict from a study of hydrogen and oxygen that when combined the new holon would emerge as water. We can never know what a holon will do next, but we do know that in some way the emergent holon will be of a higher or deeper level. This is true because the new holon is a new whole containing within itself its constituent parts leading to a series of increasing whole/parts.

> Organisms contain cells, but not vice versa; cells contain molecules, but not vice versa; molecules contain atoms, but not vice versa. And it is that *not vice versa*, at *each* stage, that constitutes unavoidable asymmetry and hierarchy (holarchy). Each deeper or higher holon embraces its junior predecessors and then *adds* its own new and more encompassing pattern or wholeness.[23]

Many modern scientists describe the emergence of an unpredictable yet higher or deeper level of holons as an hierarchical order. The following is a typical example:

> Reality, in the modern conception, appears as a tremendous hierarchical order of organized entities, leading, in a superposition of many levels, from physical and chemical to biological and sociological systems. Such hierarchical structure and combination into systems of ever higher order, is characteristic of reality as a whole and is of fundamental importance especially in biology, psychology and sociology.[24]

Many Christians who are suspicious of the hierarchical structure of the church will be uncomfortable with the notion that hierarchy is characteristic of reality as a whole. Wilber points out that there is nothing intrinsically wrong with hierarchy, but in society and institutional religion we often find *pathological hierarchy*. Thus he prefers to use the word *holarchy* and to say that holons emerge holarchically. "It is for these reasons that Koestler, after noting that all hierarchies are composed of holons, or increasing orders of wholeness, pointed out that the correct word for 'hierarchy' is actually *holarchy*."[25] I, too, prefer that terminology and later I will use the concept of holarchy to critique any instances of *pathological hierarchy*.[26]

Another important dimension of the holon is what is called its *depth* and its *span*. (A more complete discussion of these concepts can be found in Chapter 6, "Church and the New Universe Story.") The number of levels that a holarchy incorporates determines its depth. For example, a cell

---

[23]Wilber, *Sex, Ecology, Spirituality*, p. 49.

[24]Bertalanffy, L. von, *General System Theory*, New York, Braziller, 1969, p. 74.

[25]Wilber, *Sex, Ecology, Spirituality*, p. 21.

[26]See Chapter 5.

has greater depth than subatomic particles because the cell incorporates a greater number of levels, such as molecules, atoms, and subatomic particles. It is a whole containing molecules, atoms, and subatomic particles. The span of a holon is determined by the number of holons at that level. Because holons with less depth are components of deeper holons, the number of holons at a given level is greater than the number of holons at a level with more depth. In the human body there are a greater number of atoms than molecules, more molecules than cells. Thus the greater the depth the less the span (cells), and the greater the span the less the depth (atoms).

This leads us to another distinction between what is more *fundamental* and what is more *significant* in reality. The less depth a holon has the more fundamental it is because it is the component of so many other holons. Atoms are more fundamental than cells because they have a greater span and are the necessary part of not only cells but a multitude of other holons. They are more fundamental; without atoms much of the beauty and depth of the earth would not exist, including the cells of the human body.

On the other hand the greater the depth of a holon the more *significant* that holon is because it possesses a greater wholeness. A living body is more significant than an atom because it contains not only atoms but molecules and cells, and organs, and so on. Thus we can say that the greater the depth of a holon, the lesser its span, and the more significant it is; the greater the span of a holon, the lesser its depth, and the more fundamental it is.

It is very important to note that holons of greater depth emerge from the more fundamental holons and cannot exist without them. For example, in building a house the lumber is more *fundamental* than the house. There are more pieces of lumber than there are houses (a greater span) and lumber is used for the roof, the walls, the floors, and the ceilings. Even though the lumber is more fundamental, the house is more *significant* than the lumber because it possesses a greater wholeness and many other parts that are not lumber.

QUALITIES OF HOLONS
DEPTH OR SPAN: FUNDAMENTAL OR SIGNIFICANT

The greater the depth, the less the span

Depth   The greater the depth, the more significant

Cells Cells Cells

Molecules Molecules Molecules Molecules

Atoms Atoms Atoms Atoms Atoms Atoms Atoms Atoms Atoms Atoms

Span

The greater the span, the less depth

The greater the span, the more fundamental

One final aspect of holons is the question of whether there is a direction in the evolutionary scheme of things. There is a growing consensus among physicists that there is. Despite some occasional setbacks and self-dissolution, there appears to be a definite direction in the process of evolution. This direction is marked by self-transcendence, creative emergence, increasing depth, and greater consciousness. The process is also described as one of increasing complexity, increasing differentiation, increasing organization, increasing relative autonomy, and increasing *telos*. We could spend time on each of these aspects of evolution, but the one that is of most relevance to our focus on the Church of the Earth is increasing *telos*.

Teleology is defined as the study of ends, goals, or purposes. More specifically, teleology maintains that events can only be adequately explained by a consideration of the ends toward which they are directed. There does seem to be a certain inner directedness exhibited by all holons, such as an acorn's inner drive to become an oak tree or the DNA and its inner code directing the development of the human body. In Aristotelian and Thomistic thought this was called the "final cause" that gave direction to each holon in moving toward and expressing its inner being. Wilber describes it in this way:

> The regime, canon, code, or deep structure of a holon acts as a magnet, an attractor, a miniature omega point, for the *actualization* of that holon in space and time. That is, the end point of the system tends to "pull" the holon's actualization (or development) in that direction, whether the system is physical, biological, or mental.[27]

We can also speak of *telos* as the omega point guiding each holon in its self-preservation, self-adaptation, and self-transcendence. "Telos—the miniature omega-point pull of the end state of a holon's regime—is, of course, rampant not only in physical systems but in the biosphere and noosphere as well."[28] Teilhard de Chardin speaks of an ultimate omega point that is the death and resurrection of Christ, and this event, which now transcends history, can be seen as the purpose of evolution and history alike. The Risen Christ, Wisdom incarnate, can be the model and goal of human life and faith. And Wilber asks an even deeper question.

> And a final Omega Point? That would imply a final Whole, and there is no such holon anywhere in manifest existence. But perhaps we can interpret it differently. Who knows, perhaps telos, perhaps Eros, moves the entire Kosmos, and God may indeed be an all embracing chaotic Attractor, acting, as Whitehead said, throughout the world by gentle persuasion toward love.[29]

---

[27] Wilber, *Sex, Ecology, Spirituality*, p. 74.

[28] Wilber, *Sex, Ecology, Spirituality*, p. 76.

[29] Wilber, *Sex, Ecology, Spirituality*, p. 78.

The Church of the Earth is a holon, a whole/part, and thus it has the four basic capacities of every holon: self-preservation, self-adaptation, self-transcendence, and self-dissolution. The church, as any holon, has a capacity for self-preservation. Everything being equal it will tend to use its energies to preserve itself and its traditions, and this is best accomplished by its internal dynamics. There is a certain stability built right into a holon, and the church is no exception as is obvious by the church's strong sense of tradition. But the church also has the capacity for self-adaptation. It can use its energies to adapt to environmental and cultural changes, and it can adapt to various ethnic and racial groups. Once again, the history of the church shows this adaptability century after century, evidenced by the profound changes in its theology and its sacramental rituals. For example, in the Middle Ages, the church adapted to the introduction of Aristotelian philosophy through the theological synthesis of Thomas Aquinas. In its sacramental rituals over the centuries the sacrament, now called reconciliation in the Catholic Church, underwent many changes from its early emphasis on public penance to a private ritual of confession to a more positive sense of reconciliation.

The church also has the capacity for self-transcendence. At times the tension between preservation and adaptation is so powerful that preservation is possible only through self-transcendence. Faced with many challenges throughout its two-thousand-year history, the church has been able to be reborn and renewed. In the so-called Dark Ages when much of civilization was collapsing, the church retained the inner core of its tradition and was reborn in the great medieval tradition. Faced with the great challenges to its very existence at the time of the Reformation and from the many papal scandals of the time, the Roman Catholic Church was able to transcend itself and find a new source of life through the reforms of the Council of Trent. On the other hand, the reformation churches can claim that their emergence at the time of the Reformation was also a creative transcendence and a new holon bringing reform and new life to the church.

But the church as a holon must also be aware of its capacity for self-dissolution. Any human organism has the potential for behavior that can be destructive to individuals and to local communities. It is possible for some local communities to dissolve themselves as Christian communities through their own self-destructive behavior. It is possible for some individuals in the church to feel that for them the life of the church has become more destructive than life-giving, and this is the case for many women at this time in history. Perhaps the gates of hell will never prevail against the church, but the church can dissolve itself within certain communities and for certain individuals.

The Church of the Earth always has the capacity for self-preservation, self-adaptation, self-transcendence, and self-dissolution, and there is always a mutual dependency between the more fundamental and the more significant. In Chapter 6 we will show how these four capacities and these mutual relations can be realized and embodied in a new paradigm of the church.

FIELD THEORY

We often experience certain forces in our lives, such as gravity, magnetism, and electricity, that are real and powerful and yet invisible. These forces draw things together and energize them. Such forces are all around us, are almost universal, and are the systems within which relationships emerge. Joseph Jaworski describes many of the characteristics of fields.

> Fields are nonmaterial regions of influence—invisible forces that structure space or behavior. The earth's gravitational field, for example, is all around us. We cannot see it, it's not a material object, but it's nevertheless real. It gives things weight and makes things full. There are also magnetic fields that underlie the functioning of our brains and bodies. . . . There are also fundamental quantum matter fields recognized by physicists—electron fields, neutron fields, and others. They are "invisible, intangible, inaudible, tasteless, and odorless," and yet in quantum theory, they are the substance of the universe. Fields are states of space, but space is full of energy and invisible structures that interconnect.[30]

Margaret Wheatley also gives us a general definition of fields.

> Space everywhere is now thought to be filled with fields, invisible, nonmaterial structures that are the basic substance of the universe. We cannot see these fields, but we do observe their effects. They have become a useful construct for explaining action-at-a-distance, for helping us understand why change occurs without the direct exertion of material "shoving" across space.[31]

These fields emerged at the very beginning of creation with the flashing forth of the universe fifteen billion years ago. They have provided the inner force for self-organization in the universe as it began to be shaped. The fields are a primary source of order and of the wholistic quality of the universe, and they are integral to the organization of all systems from atoms to galaxies. "The implications of field theory are far-reaching, not just for science and theology, but for every aspect of life. It provides a whole new perspective on how we understand life and the influences that bring about change."[32]

Fields incorporate two significant capacities of holons—self-preservation and self-adaptation. The self-organizational properties of a field are

---

[30] Jaworski, *Synchronicity,* pp. 149–150.

[31] Wheatley, Margaret J., *Leadership and the New Science,* San Francisco, Berrett-Koehler Publishers, 1994, p. 48.

[32] O'Murchu, *Quantum Theology,* p. 71.

manifested in what appears to be "memory" within the field and thus a capacity for self-preservation.

> Fields are endowed with a memory, in which the influence of the most common past types combines to increase the probability that such types will occur again. Thus, for example, the morphogenetic fields of the foxglove species are shaped by the influences from previously existing foxgloves. They represent a kind of pooled or collective memory of the species. Each member of the species is molded by these species fields, and in turn contributes to them, influencing future members of the species.[33]

At the same time fields are a source of energy that can, in fact, bring about the self-adaptation essential to the evolutionary process. This is apparent in what are called *morphogenic fields* that govern the behavior of a particular species of plant or animal life. These morphogenic fields enable a species as a whole to adapt more easily to a change in its micro-environment and a community of species to adapt more easily to a macro-environment.

> Morphogenic fields are built up through the accumulated behaviors of species' members. After part of the species has learned a behavior, such as bicycle riding, others will find it easier to learn that skill. The form resides in the morphogenic field, and when individual energy combines with it, it patterns behavior without the need for laborious learning of the skill.[34]

The field theory can also be applied to various human and social dynamics, such as group process, family therapy, and organizational leadership—the school spirit of a particular high school, the destructive dynamics of a dysfunctional family, the sense of purpose in a business organization. These are all manifestations of a social field in human relationships, and these fields impact not only the dynamics of the group but the actions of the individuals. There is a field memory that can serve to preserve and, perhaps, rigidify the group, and there is a field energy that can help group members to adapt to and perhaps transcend the group.

As a web of relationships the Church of the Earth is also a field, and it has all the positive and negative potential of a field. As a lifetime member of the church and as one who has exercised a leadership role in the church for over forty years, I have had extensive experience with this ecclesial field through years of great change and turmoil. I have experienced its power for healing as well as its power for destruction. I would like to describe these experiences, first, in terms of the relationship of the church to the larger

---

[33] O'Murchu, *Quantum Theology*, p. 69.

[34] Wheatley, *Leadership and the New Science*, p. 51.

fields of spirituality and revelation, and, second, in terms of the inner dynamics of church leadership and church symbols and rituals.

In my earlier life I saw my spirituality and my religion as more or less the same reality, even though I could not at that time articulate this view. My Catholic faith was all I needed internally, and my Catholic Church was all I needed externally as a support system. Gradually I began to perceive the tremendous spiritual power beyond the boundaries of the church and beyond the boundaries of religion, and I began to experience a spirituality hidden in the inner dynamics of the universe. Diarmuid O'Murchu captures this deeper experience: "The primitive urge to connect spiritually is innate to our human nature and, from a quantum viewpoint, it is also considered to be an intrinsic feature of universal life, manifested in the attraction and repulsion of subatomic particles."[35] The Church of the Earth must situate itself within this broader spiritual field, if it is to be authentic and meet the spiritual needs of people of the new creation story.[36]

Likewise, revelation was seen as coming from God in the Holy Scriptures through the church. All that was necessary and important for my faith was found within the Scriptures and the teaching of the church, and this gave me a sense of confidence and of peace. Later I began to ask about the more than two-million-year history of the human race before the coming of the Christian church or any other organized religion. Was there no revelation from God during this time? What about God's dynamic, inner presence over the last fifteen billion years? Was not the glory and goodness of God somehow made manifest to these millions of people? I gradually began to experience a larger field of revelation within other religions, within the long history of the human race, and at the depth of creation. Listen to O'Murchu: "And the spiritual story of humankind, unfolding over the millennia, suggests that the divine life force (God) reveals itself with a prodigious generosity of presence, power and cultural expression."[37] Once again, the Church of the Earth must situate itself within this broader field of revelation, if it is to fully articulate the beauty of God's revelation within the universe.

The two larger fields of spirituality and revelation do not deny the specific role of the Christian church in these two fields, but they call the church to see itself in the context of the larger fields and to benefit from the memory and energy of these fields.

One very powerful experience for me over the years has been the way that rituals function as a field that can impact, positively or negatively, the memory and energy field of the community of faith. Central to the life of any religion are the rituals that express symbolically the mystery of the presence of God within the community. The depth of this mystery and of our relationship to God is so powerful that words alone are inadequate. It is only

---

[35] O'Murchu, *Quantum Theology,* p. 73.

[36] See Chapter 4, "Spirituality."

[37] O'Murchu, *Quantum Theology,* p. 73.

in symbolic rituals that the community can articulate its inner life with its memory and energy field. Despite what any faith community *says* about its spirit and its purpose, its spirit and its purpose will be *felt* and *experienced* only in the midst of its rituals. In their rituals many Christian communities tend to be a field of passivity and boredom, following the rules but without much participation, rather than a field of excitement, participation, power, memory, energy, and the presence of God. There are exceptions, but they only tend to prove the rule. In the Church of the Earth, the larger fields of spirituality and revelation, the depths of our relationship to the earth, are brought to bear on our Christian traditions to bring forth rituals and symbols that can renew and build the inner life of the community.[38]

Another powerful and mostly negative experience for me is that of leadership in the Catholic Church. Leadership is a very significant dimension of any community with a major impact on its field. Leadership creates a certain "spirit" or way of functioning within the community that can use its memory to preserve and rigidify the community and frustrate the energy of the field in a climate of fear. Or leadership can use the memory and the energy of the community to adapt in new ways to its environment and to transcend its past in a new birth. There is a crisis of leadership in the Catholic Church today that is negatively affecting the life of the community. As I stated it elsewhere:

> The Catholic Church in the United States is a vibrant, educated and faith-filled community, but it also remains at times a harsh, repressive and sexist community. If we are to answer the call of God to grow up into the fullness of our humanity and to reach out in ministry to the poor and powerless of our world, then it is essential that we recognize the destructive climate of fear within the church and help the church become a community of trust.[39]

The Church of the Earth, in light of the new creation story, calls us to a new sense of leadership. The church is an energy field and a web of relationships within the holy web of the universe. It can be a field brimming with life, filled with love, motivated by compassion, serving the poor and the outcasts (in the model of Jesus, the suffering servant) only if it can become a community with servant leaders, open and honest dialogue, an atmosphere of mutual trust, and a willingness to let the future unfold in the power of God's Spirit.

THE THEORY OF THE IMPLICATE ORDER

Another strand of the holy web is discovered in the theory of the implicate order. Let's go on a journey into wholeness and the implicate order with

---

[38] See Chapter 4, "Rituals, Symbols, and Sacraments."

[39] Wessels, Cletus, "Coping with Conspiracy of Silence, Climate of Fear," *National Catholic Reporter,* January 29, 1988.

David Bohm as our guide.[40] As any good guide, he will do most of the talking, and you will have to listen carefully as we go along. We will ask questions and seek to have this great physicist clarify his theories. As the tour begins we can pose to Bohm[41] the following question: What is the value of a study of this relatively abstract notion of the implicate order?

> I would, in this connection, call attention to the general problem of fragmentation of human consciousness. . . . It is proposed there that the widespread and pervasive distinctions between people (race, nation, family, profession, etc., etc.), which are now preventing mankind from working together for the common good, and indeed, even for survival, have one of the key factors of their origin in a kind of thought that treats *things* as inherently divided, disconnected, and broken up into yet smaller constituent parts. Each part is considered to be essentially independent and self-existent.
>
> When man thinks of himself in this way, he will inevitably tend to defend the needs of his own "Ego" against those of the others; or if he identifies with a group of people of the same kind, he will defend this group in a similar way. He cannot seriously think of mankind as the basic reality, whose claims come first. . . . If he thinks of the totality as constituted of independent fragments, then that is how his mind will tend to operate, but if he can include everything coherently and harmoniously in a overall whole that is undivided, unbroken, and without a border (for every border is a division or break) then his mind will tend to move in a similar way, and from this will flow an orderly action within the whole.[42]

Bohm is searching for a way to discover the inner wholeness within all reality in order ultimately to help people find a sense of wholeness and of holiness despite the apparent fragmentation of the world. He has more to say to us:

> Men have been aware from time immemorial of this state of apparently autonomously existent fragmentation and have often projected myths of a yet earlier "golden age," before the split between man and nature and between man and man had yet taken place. Indeed, man has always been seeking wholeness—mental, physical, social, individual.

---

[40] The classic work on the implicate order is Bohm, David, *Wholeness and the Implicate Order*, New York, Routledge & Kegan Paul, 1980. There are also two conversations with David Bohm by Renee Weber in *The Holographic Paradigm and Other Paradoxes*, edited by Ken Wilber, Boulder, CO, The New Science Library, 1982, "The Enfolding—Unfolding Universe: A Conversation with David Bohm," pp. 44–104, and "The Physicist and the Mystic: Is Dialogue between Them Possible? A Conversation with David Bohm," pp. 187–214.

[41] As is the case with many authors in past years, Bohm does not use inclusive language. It is my hope that, if he were writing today, he would not use language that excludes.

[42] Bohm, *Wholeness and the Implicate Order*, p. x.

It is instructive to consider that the word "health" in English is based on an Anglo-Saxon word "hale" meaning "whole": that is, to be healthy is to be whole, which is, I think, roughly equivalent to the Hebrew "shalem." Likewise, the English "holy" is based on the same root as "whole." All of this indicates that man has sensed always that wholeness or integrity is an absolute necessity to make life worth living. Yet, over the ages, he has generally lived in fragmentation.[43]

We might ask Bohm where the study of physics and of the natural world has led him in this search for wholeness:

All this calls attention to the relevance of a new distinction between implicate and explicate order. Generally speaking, the laws of physics have thus far referred mainly to the explicate order. Indeed, it may be said that the principle function of Cartesian coordinates is just to give a clear and precise description of explicate order. Now, we are proposing that in the formulation of the laws of physics, primary relevance is to be given to the implicate order, while the explicate order is to have a secondary kind of significance.[44]

In order to understand better the meaning of the implicate and explicate order, we can think in terms of the ocean, or, rather, for me Lake Michigan. I have often camped on the eastern shore of Lake Michigan. In the morning as the sun was rising over the sand dunes I often walked along the beach and discovered what had been thrown up on the shore. There usually were small pieces of driftwood, some sea shells, refuse that had been cast overboard by boaters, and some dead fish. If there had been a storm, there were large floating logs and tree branches and occasionally the wreckage of a small boat. Each morning the lake shore was different because the lake often reclaimed much of the debris, although there were some very big logs that seemed to be there forever.

The explicate order is found in the debris that is cast up on the lake shore. It is visible and measurable, it comes forth from the depths of the lake and can return there, and while it is on the shore it is relatively stable. The implicate order is like the hidden depths of the lake out of which comes the flotsam on the shore. The lake is the source of all that unfolds on the shore and into which everything enfolds.

We need to ask our guide whether there is another analogy that might illustrate certain essential features of the implicate order. In his answer he explains a device that has become the classic analogy for the implicate order.

This device consisted of two concentric glass cylinders, with a highly viscous fluid such as glycerine between them, which is ar-

---

[43] Bohm, *Wholeness and the Implicate Order,* p. 3.

[44] Bohm, *Wholeness and the Implicate Order,* p. 150.

ranged in such a way that the outer cylinder can be turned very slowly, so that there is negligible diffusion of the viscous fluid. A droplet of insoluble ink is placed in the fluid, and the outer cylinder is then turned, with the result that the droplet is drawn out into a fine thread-like form that eventually becomes invisible. When the cylinder is turned in the opposite direction the thread-form draws back and suddenly become visible as a droplet essentially the same as the one that was there originally.[45]

In this analogy the viscous fluid is the implicate order in which the droplet of insoluble ink, the explicate order, is enfolded and then unfolded. Thus, it is Bohm's contention that the reality, which we perceive with our senses, is explicated from the deeper reality, which we cannot perceive with our senses. The universal implicate order, out of which everything unfolds, gives us the underlying sense of the wholeness and unity of all reality. This analogy to the viscous fluid, similar to the analogy to the depths of the lake, sees all things as flowing movement. The ink droplet flows and unfolds from the fluid, just as the debris on the lake shore flows and unfolds from the lake.

What can we call this new form of insight?

The new form of insight can perhaps best be called *Undivided Wholeness in Flowing Movement*. This view implies that flow is, in some sense, prior to that of the "things" that can be seen to form and dissolve in this flow. One can perhaps illustrate what is meant here by considering the "stream of consciousness." This flux of awareness is not precisely definable, and yet it is evidently prior to the definable forms of thoughts and ideas which can be seen to form and dissolve in the flux, like ripples, waves and vortices in a flowing stream. As happens with such patterns of movement in a stream some thoughts recur and persist in a more or less stable way while others are evanescent.[46]

But how does this all relate to our understanding of the web of relationships in creation?

The proposal for a new general form of insight is that all matter is of this nature; that is, there is a universal flux that cannot be defined explicitly but which can be known only implicitly, as indicated by the explicitly definable forms and shapes, some stable and some unstable, that can be abstracted from the universal flux. In this flow, mind and matter are not separate substances. Rather, they are different aspects of one whole and unbroken movement. In this way, we are able to look on all aspects of existence as not divided

---

[45] Bohm, *Wholeness and the Implicate Order,* p. 179.

[46] Bohm, *Wholeness and the Implicate Order,* p. 11.

from each other, and thus we can bring to an end the fragmentation implicit in the current attitude toward the atomic point of view, which leads us to divide everything from everything in a thorough-going way.[47]

Does this mean that everything is mushed together in this flux and there are not separate beings with their own autonomy and stability?

Nevertheless, we can comprehend that aspect of atomism which still provides a correct and valid form of insight; i.e., that in spite of the undivided wholeness in flowing movement, the various patterns that can be abstracted from it have a certain relative autonomy and stability, which is indeed provided for by the universal law of the flowing movement.[48]

In summary, David Bohm is proposing that in the formulation of the laws of physics primary relevance is to be given to the implicate order carried by the *holomovement*, whereas the explicate order with its laws is to have a secondary kind of significance. But what is this holomovement (the word comes from *holo* meaning *whole* and from *movement* meaning *flux*), and what are its characteristics?

To generalize so as to emphasize undivided wholeness, we shall say that what "carries" an implicate order is *the holomovement,* which is an unbroken and undivided totality. . . . Thus, in its totality, the holomovement is not limited to any specifiable way at all. It is not required to conform to any particular order, or to be bounded by any particular measure. Thus, *the holomovement is undefinable and immeasurable.*[49]

Bohm, here and in other places, describes the holomovement in terms reminiscent of the divine. The holomovement is undefinable and immeasurable, it is one unbroken whole, including the entire universe with all its "fields" and "particles."[50] It is the ground for the existence of everything, including ourselves, and it is an immense ocean of cosmic energy creating a sudden wave pulse from which our "universe" was born billions of years ago.[51] The holomovement is beyond space and time and yet contains within it all space and time, it is infinite insofar as it goes beyond any limits.[52]

---

[47] Bohm, *Wholeness and the Implicate Order,* p. 11.

[48] Bohm, *Wholeness and the Implicate Order,* p. 11.

[49] Bohm, *Wholeness and the Implicate Order,* p. 151.

[50] Bohm, *Wholeness and the Implicate Order,* p. 189.

[51] Bohm, *Wholeness and the Implicate Order,* pp. 191–192.

[52] Weber, "The Enfolding—Unfolding Universe," in *The Holographic Paradigm and Other Paradoxes,* Wilber, ed., pp. 56, 90–91.

There is a way in which even Bohm reaches the limits of human knowledge and he, and we ourselves, must be modest about our ability to grasp the full meaning of holomovement, much less the meaning of God. Bohm quotes Alfred Korzybski (philosopher and semanticist) as saying, "Whatever we *say* it is, it isn't." That reminds me of the saying of Thomas Aquinas in the introduction to the third question in his treatise on God where he says, "Because we cannot know what God is, but rather what God is not, we have no means for considering how God is, but rather how God is not."[53] Bohm also speaks of a wholeness that is both immanent and transcendent, a common characteristic of God, but he does so once again in a modest way because we are approaching the unknowable and the realm of the mystic.

> In any discussion of this sort, people often are led to speak of the totality, of a wholeness which is both immanent and transcendent, and which, in a religious context, is often given the name of God. The immanence means that the totality of what is, is immanent in matter; the transcendence means that this wholeness is also beyond matter.
>
> However, the totality can be described as *both* immanence and transcendence in one sense, and *neither* immanence nor transcendence in another, since it is beyond the possibility of description. Words are, after all, limited; they are merely a sign which points to an actuality that cannot be completely symbolized.[54]

Using the new science we have traced the web of relationships from holons (the whole/parts that are the fabric of the universe), to fields (those invisible sources of memory, energy, and self-organization in the universe), and finally to holomovement (the undefinable and immeasurable ocean of energy and source of all that exists).

The Church of the Earth is a holon that always has the capacity for self-preservation, self-adaptation, self-transcendence, and self-dissolution with mutual dependency between the more fundamental and the more significant. The Church of the Earth is a field and part of the holy web. This field can be one brimming with life, filled with love, motivated by compassion, serving the poor and the outcasts, only if it can become a community with servant leaders, with open and honest dialogue, an atmosphere of mutual trust, the ability to celebrate its life in vibrant rituals, and a willingness to let the future unfold in the power of the Spirit of God.

We now must hear a final word from David Bohm.

> By following science itself we have been led to a view which is compatible with the wholeness of mankind, or its holiness, if you want

---

[53] Aquinas, Thomas, *Summa Theologiae*, I, 3, Intro.

[54] Weber, Renee, "The Physicist and the Mystic," in *The Holographic Paradigm and Other Paradoxes*, Wilber, ed., pp.187–188.

to call it that. Mankind has now splintered and fragmented into countless bits, not only nations and religions and groups, but each individual is in many fragments; and this tremendous fragmentation gives rise to chaos, violence, destruction and very little hope of any real order coming about.[55]

The Church of the Earth is called to challenge this fragmentation at every level and become a profound source of the unity of our planet and the unity of the human race. Pictures of the planet earth taken from space satellites belie the artificial boundaries that separate nations and peoples. The sun and the rain, the life-supporting ecosystem of plants and animals, the scattering of seeds and the flight of wild birds, the seas and the atmosphere do not follow the dividing lines between peoples and nations. We are one planet and we live and die together. Mother Earth is the common source of life for all people. We are all earthlings, and we are all called to share in the one divine life flowing from the earth. This can be seen concretely in the fact that everyone springs from the same earth, depends on the earth for life, and returns to earth at death.

For Christians this web of relationships has a deeper dimension. Jesus is the new creation, the new earthling (*adam*), the firstborn of all creation (Col. 1:15), who emptied himself, taking the form of a servant, being born in the likeness of men (earthling) (Phil. 2:7). Jesus has broken down the dividing wall of hostility that he might create in himself one new man (*adam*) (Eph. 2:14–15). All the artificial divisions, separations and alienations that flow from the sinful human condition have been overcome in Christ. The unity of all peoples is stated clearly and unambiguously by Paul. "There is neither Jew nor Greek, there is neither slave nor free person, there is neither male nor female; for all are one in Christ Jesus" (Gal. 3:28).

This radical unity of all humans based on sharing a common creation from the earth and a common re-creation in Christ Jesus also flows over into the life of the believing community. There is no place in the Church of the Earth for divisions or discrimination based on racial or ethnic differences, based on prestige or social differences, based on sexual orientation or gender differences. No people of good will can be refused full participation in the life and ministry of the church merely because they are rich or poor, married or single, female or male, gay or straight, black or red or white or yellow or brown, capitalist or socialist. Such differences reflect the fullness of the earth, the inclusiveness of God and the richness of the life and ministry of the community that is the Church of the Earth. All that is required is that

Speaking the truth in love, we grow in every way into the one who is the head, Christ, from whom the whole body, joined and held together by

---

[55] Weber, "The Enfolding—Unfolding Universe," in *The Holographic Paradigm and Other Paradoxes*, Wilber, ed., p. 71.

every supporting ligament, with the proper functioning of each part, brings about the body's growth and builds itself up in love.

(Eph. 4:15–16)

THE EARTH AS WOMB OR TOMB

The historical mission of the present is to introduce a more integral period of earth development, a period when a mutually enhancing human-earth relationship might be established—if indeed the human is to prove itself to be a viable species on a viable planet. That the human is nonviable in its present mode of patriarchal functioning seems to be quite clear.[56]

Several years ago I taught a college course on religion and adult development. One of the students was a young woman from Kenya. She shared with me her dream, which eloquently describes the dilemma of human viability, using the image of a journey within her subconscious.

The journey was so long but also so quick. I had no time to think—to decide—to protest. I just followed. I closed my eyes.

When I opened them I was no more! Or was I? I was aware of my being alive, but where was I? I had changed! I felt like I had lost something. But what and where? I was different. I never saw that color before, and it never was so dark! Where was I? Where did that bright sun go? As I last remembered I was journeying towards him. He was so beautiful! But now, I don't recognize anything or anybody around here. I have lost my sight. What shall I do now?

After a few days of crying and mourning I decided it was a foolish pastime. I bowed my head and prayed I would find my liberty! But how? I looked around and I perceived a warmth around me that I had not paid attention to before. Oh! I knew it! I knew where I was! I was in the Earth. "O Mother Earth! What will you be for me? A WOMB OR A TOMB?" There was a rumbling, one that was the echo of another, coming from very far away. It was an answer to my question.

O Daughter! I have longed for such a long time to hold you, caress you, to be a mother to you—But you kept going, running. How could you know that my love pursued you?! Whether I will be a womb or a tomb for you depends on YOU. Don't let me hold you too tight or too long. That you must teach me. Only those that do so will find a womb in me. For those others I am an unwilling tomb. Choose life and live.

---

[56]Berry, Thomas, *The Dream of the Earth,* San Francisco, Sierra Club Books, 1988, p. 145.

PATRIARCHY AS A TOMB

Mother Earth, the source of life, will live on. She was here before the human arrived, and, if the human goes the way of the dinosaurs, she will endure and be renewed. But is the human species viable? Will the earth be a womb or a tomb for us? As we saw in Chapter 2, after two million years of childhood the human race has been in its adolescence since the agricultural revolution about 10,000 years ago. During its adolescence the human species, at least in Western culture, has been infected with a patriarchal poison that is a powerful obstacle to our ability to "choose life."[57] Once I asked a friend of mine who is both a father and a grandfather to describe some of the characteristics of adolescence. His description of adolescent sexuality gives us one insight into patriarchal culture that is destructive of personal relationships:

> Awakening sexuality is a powerful force. The adolescent becomes aware of a powerful need to couple. For men, this drive is usually quite separate from any desire to assume adulthood and start a family. It is an urge to spill seed. This need often is awakened before the adolescent boy discovers that girls are people and not just forces that awaken sexual desire. Unfortunately many men never grow beyond this state.

This common sexual awakening in adolescent boys can be seen as a "power over" the other, rather than a mutual loving relationship. Such "power over" based on our human adolescence has infected a broad spectrum of human society and leads to a social and ecological crisis of unimagined proportions. We are attempting to conquer the earth, we are squandering its resources, and we are dumping our wastes in its oceans, its atmosphere, and its bowels. We continue to destroy our topsoil, our rain forests, and our water tables. Warfare and violence stalks our earth with nation rising against nation, tribe against tribe, race against race, and neighbor against neighbor. I believe that the most pervasive poison that is eating away our society is *patriarchy* that is divisive, oppressive, and destructive.

> Culturally, it [the Agricultural Revolution] was a supreme moment of breakthrough, but also one of long-term negative and destructive repercussions. For the first time in history, we humans carved up and fragmented our world, imposing divisions and categories that in time became the basis for separate tribes, cultures, nations, and religions. The dominant patriarchal orientation was to divide and conquer, and hence the introduction of the deadliest divisive force of all: warfare. The idea of *man* being master of creation emerged

---

[57] See Chapter 11, "Patriarchy: A New Interpretation of History," in Berry, *The Dream of the Earth*, p. 149.

at this time and became ingrained in the formal religious creeds of subsequent centuries.[58]

It is not my intention to present a negative critique of the male gender or of men in general. The male gender is not internally programmed to patriarchy, and there are many men who are well aware of the dangers of patriarchy and who are working to overcome its negative impact on our society. The social institution of patriarchy, however, is so deeply ingrained in Western culture and institutional religion that most of us are not even aware of it. Yet patriarchy contradicts all that we have said about the holy web and the new universe story.

The etymology of the word *patriarchy* is simply "father-rule" over an extended family or tribal people. Most likely, as a social reality, it began very gradually prior to or at the same time as the agricultural revolution and the domestication of animals. In its origins, patriarchy may have met some of the social needs of the time, but it later developed into a negative force in the lives of many humans. "The sense of *patriarchy* has now evolved as the archetypal pattern of oppressive governance by men with little regard for the well-being or personal fulfillment of women, for the more significant human values, or for the destiny of the earth itself."[59]

Patriarchal culture is characterized by several features:

- The institutionalization of male privilege and power and the accompanying social mythology to account for it
- The hierarchy of male rulers' control over slave labor, the land, and their women
- The social and cultural inequality of men and women and the assumption that this represents the appropriate (and even God-given) pattern for all social relationships
- The formation and legitimation of vertical structures of power based on the presumed superiority and inferiority of given classes of people based on gender, race, class, ethnic origin, and sexual orientation

Patriarchy has also seeped into the inner life of the Christian church. A woman once reported her experience in church on a Sunday morning:

> I heard from the scriptures that God our Father cares for the needs of men; I heard that we must love our brothers; and I heard that it is a wonderful thing to become a son of God. These words came to us through the male ministers of the community. They stood far away from us, in front of us, and elevated above us on a raised platform that was holy space. There were no women in the holy space.

---

[58] O'Murchu, *Quantum Theology*, p. 74.
[59] Berry, *The Dream of the Earth*, p. 143.

. . . Our only access to the holy was through the benevolence of the male ruling class in the spiritual community.[60]

One evening I was watching a Russian movie and there was a scene that included a marriage ceremony. The bride and her father processed into the church and, as they approached the groom, the father held out a whip and presented it to the groom. This gesture symbolized the fact that up to this time the woman, as a daughter, was the father's property to control, even by a whip. In the future this woman, as a wife, would be the property of the husband to control, even by a whip. To this day, in wedding ceremonies, there is often the symbolic handing over of the daughter from her father to her husband, as if she were a piece of property.

Several years ago when I was pastor in a parish, I received an emergency call on the pager. When I responded, I found a man very distraught over some difficulties with his wife. He asked me, "Is it necessary for my wife to obey me since the New Testament says wives should be submissive to their husbands?" I replied, "A husband and wife are partners in a marriage, and decisions should be made together out of mutual respect for one another." He did not like my answer so he responded, "St. Paul said that the father was the head of the family, and what the Bible says is what I should do." I said to him, "Paul was living in a situation very different from ours, and mutual love and not submission provides the basis for a growthful marriage." He became quite abusive to me and said, "You are denying the Bible," and he hung up.

These are examples of the pervasive institutionalization of male privilege and power in the Christian church. It is a reality that seems natural to many people, both members of the church and outside observers. Throughout the history of the church prior to the last twenty-five years the leadership function, the teaching, preaching, and presiding roles, and the decision-making power has been limited to the male clergy. This continues today in the Roman Catholic Church. It is a system that denies the equal dignity, power, and responsibility of all human persons. As Thomas Berry says, "The rulership of men in the church, by divine determination, assured the relegation of women to subordinate status in the religious community, the denial of integral participation in religious ritual, the identification of women with seduction and moral evil."[61]

Moreover, the church is an institution that usually speaks about God using the model of the ruling male. The images and language, which the church uses, reflect the experience of men within a patriarchal system. The exclusive use of male images of God and literal patriarchal speech about God bears witness to the patriarchal character of the church. Furthermore, it justifies broader social structures of dominance/subordination and pro-

---

[60] Bozarth-Campbell, Alla, *Womanpriest: A Personal Odyssey,* New York, Paulist Press, 1978, p. 177.

[61] Berry, *The Dream of the Earth*, p. 150.

vides an androcentric worldview inimical to the genuine and equal human dignity of women.

While writing this section on patriarchy, I saw the movie *Titanic*. The opening scenes show this marvelous shining new ship from many different angles. With its great size and its phallic shape, it seemed to be a symbol of patriarchy. Like patriarchy it was the most powerful, the largest, the fastest, and the most splendid ship ever afloat, and it was believed to be unsinkable. The *Titanic* was the pride of the architect who designed it and the shipyard that built it. The ship, like patriarchy, carried people from many nations and from many social and economic classes. Their accommodations, of course, were on different levels of the ship and with a different quality of life. The gates separating the various classes of people were locked. Most importantly, the *Titanic* was unsinkable.

But sink it did. In order to make headlines by arriving in port a day early, the captain stoked the untested boilers up to full speed. There was no danger because the *Titanic* was unsinkable. It was the greatest ship afloat ready to deal with any emergency. But sink it did. An iceberg was spotted, and, despite the boast of the designers and engineers that it could outmaneuver any danger, the ship could not turn rapidly enough. The iceberg ripped a series of holes in the side of the ship, but, do not fear, it has watertight compartments. But sink it did. The damage was greater than anticipated and the ocean came pouring in to swamp the unsinkable *Titanic*. The ocean became its tomb.

And patriarchy will sink as well. The captain on the deck will call for more power, and the crew will comply because patriarchy is the most powerful, the largest, the fastest, and the most splendid ship ever afloat. But sink it will. Holes are being ripped in the metal sides of patriarchy, and its weaknesses are becoming more apparent. The only question is how much of humanity will go down with the ship? The ship does not have enough lifeboats because it is "unsinkable." Many people will be washed away as the ocean comes pouring in to swamp our "unsinkable" patriarchy.

In her dream the African woman becomes the symbol of the human race. She describes how she "was journeying toward HIM [patriarchy?]. HE was so beautiful!" Then she began to perceive how barren that journey was and how blind she had been. "But now, I don't recognize anything or anybody around here. I have lost my sight." She prayed that she would find her liberty, and she perceived a warmth around her—the embrace of Mother Earth. And Mother Earth responded to her and to us, "O Daughter! I have longed for such a long time to hold you, caress you, to be a mother to you—But you kept going, running. How could you know that my love pursued you?!" The love of Mother Earth will become the womb promising new life, but, like any child in the womb, we must be willing to let go in order to be reborn. "Don't let me hold you too tight or too long. That you must teach me. Only those that do so will find a womb in me. . . . Choose life and live."

ECOFEMINISM AS A WOMB

> I am persuaded of the truth of ecofeminism's insight that analysis of the eco-
> logical crisis does not get to the heart of the matter until it sees the connec-
> tion between exploitation of the earth and the sexist definition and
> treatment of women.[62]

Today's growing ecological movement is raising our awareness about our relationship to the earth and to one another, and it is calling us to action based on the new creation story. The feminist movement also challenges patriarchy and calls us to a new society in which the rights of all peoples will be respected. "Ecofeminism brings together these two explorations of ecology and feminism, in their full, or deep forms, and explores how male domination of women and domination of nature are interconnected, both in cultural ideology and in social structures."[63]

Most of us are comfortable with the ecological movement because clearly something must be done to save our world. Some do not agree with those who chain themselves to the trees in order to stop logging, whereas others feel that governments and corporations need to do more. Nevertheless, the desire to save the earth is growing in many parts of the world, and there are serious and difficult decisions to be made.

On the other hand many people are very uncomfortable with the feminist movement—because they just don't know how to handle it. What do feminists want? They are demanding too many changes in society. What will it be like if we don't maintain the "God-given" differences between men and women? Do women want all the power? These questions indicate that many people do not understand the basic meaning of feminism. Women are not demanding superficial social changes, nor are they denying the God-given gender differences, nor do they want all the power. Rather, feminism is a new vision based on the experience of women, an experience that has been ignored or denied throughout the centuries.

> Feminism is a new worldview. Feminism is a spirituality which
> the world and the church ignore to the peril of us all and to itself,
> as well. Feminism is not simply about femaleness. It is about an-
> other way of looking at life, about another set of values designed
> to nurture a dying globe and rescue any people too long ground
> under foot, too long ignored, unseen, invisible. Feminism is about
> a new way of thinking for both women and men who are tired of
> the carnage, sickened by the exploitation of the globe, disillu-

---

[62] Johnson, *Women, Earth, and Creator Spirit,* p. 10.

[63] Ruether, Rosemary Radford, *Gaia and God: An Ecofeminist Theology of Earth Healing,* San Francisco, HarperSanFrancisco, 1992, p. 2.

sioned by the power struggles and searching—as Ezechiel promises—for a heart of flesh in a world of stone.[64]

In brief the goal of feminism is to "accord equal dignity, power or responsibility to all human persons and/or to all baptized Christians, [because] creation in the image of God and baptism into the body of Christ ground basic human dignity and provide a new basis for radical equality in all human relationships and social arrangements."[65] Mother Earth is the common source of life for all people. We are all earthlings, and we are all called to share in the one divine life flowing from the earth and within the church.

That the church developed a patriarchal structure is not surprising because the church emerged in a society that was deeply rooted in patriarchy. But what is surprising is that in the Christian scriptures and the earliest Christian communities we find a sense of egalitarianism that is new to the world around it. The stories of the birth of Jesus gave evidence of the inclusivity of the early Christians by describing the appearance of the angels to shepherds, who were the unwashed of Jewish society, and the coming of foreign magicians bringing gifts to the newborn. Jesus, himself, attacked the Jewish holiness code that was firmly founded on a male ruling class. Jesus opened himself to all the outcasts and marginals, eating with tax collectors and befriending adulterers. Some of his close followers were women, who were the first witnesses to the resurrection. In the early Christian communities, women were leaders of house churches. And even Paul, who could be at times very exclusive, had an image of a community in which there would be no ethnic, social, or gender distinctions because all are one in Christ Jesus.

> In the light of the original gospel story . . . it becomes clear that the heart of the problem is not that Jesus was a man but that more men are not like Jesus, insofar as patriarchy defines their self-identity and relationships. Reading Scripture through feminist hermeneutics makes it possible to affirm that despite subsequent distortion something more than the subordination of women is possible, for Jesus-Sophia's story of ministry, suffering, final victory, and new community signify love, grace, and shalom for everyone equally, and for the outcast, including women most of all.[66]

Thus ecofeminism provides a way to reclaim the best of our biblical and Christian traditions and to recall us to inclusivity and equality in our Christian churches. Ecofeminism also reaffirms what we learn from the earth. A

---

[64]Chittister, Joan, "Heart of Flesh: A Feminist Spirituality for Women and Men," in *Spirituality Justice Reprint*, Call To Action, January 1998.

[65]Hilkert, Mary Catherine, *Naming Grace: Preaching and the Sacramental Imagination*, New York, Continuum, 1997, p. 171.

[66]Johnson, Elizabeth, *She Who Is: The Mystery of God in Feminist Theological Discourse*, New York, Crossroad, 1994, p. 161.

deep wholeness is found within all creation symbolized by the implicate or-der and the holomovement out of which all things emerge. There is a reali-zation that all reality is enveloped in fields that are concentric circles of un-seen but powerful sources of energy and creativity. We experience everything in the universe as being a whole/part intimately bound up with one another and dependent on each other. Ecofeminism is in tune with the earth.

> It begins to be possible to hold together in a rich synthesis all man-ners of previously dichotomous elements: not just self and other, but matter and spirit, passions and intellect, embodiedness and self-transcendence, nurturing and questing, altruism and self-affirma-tion, receptivity and activity, love and power, being and doing, private and public domains, humanity and the earth. Oppositional, either-or thinking, which is endemic to the androcentric construc-tion of reality, dissolves in a new paradigm of both-and.[67]

Ecofeminism calls us to go beyond simple "technological fixes" in order to build a new earth, a new society, and a new religion based on the princi-ple of equal dignity, rights and responsibilities for both women and men, and on the earth principle of the community of all species with their respec-tive dignity, rights and responsibilities. We are called to transformation within a new symbolic culture and a new sense of spirituality. Joan Chittis-ter gives us the following description of ecofeminism:

> Ecofeminism sees the intrinsic value and, therefore, the equal worth of all creation. It draws us beyond ourselves into the preservation of the whole universe. A commitment to the entire web of life in ecofeminism guarantees that we do not become exclusive in our movement toward inclusion. . . . Ecofeminism is the story of com-panionship, of responsibility, of accountability for life. All life.[68]

In a very deep sense we are being called to a new image of God stated in these words of Elizabeth Johnson:

> Holy Wisdom is the mother of the universe, the unoriginate, living source of all that exists. . . . Her creative, maternal love, is the gen-erating matrix of the universe, matter, spirit and embodied spirit alike. This is true not only in the case of human persons but of all living and inanimate creatures and the complex interrelationships between them that constitute "the world." All creatures are kin to one another and therefore, where spirit has reached the break-

---

[67] Johnson, *She Who Is*, p. 69.

[68] Chittister, Joan, *Heart of Flesh: A Feminist Spirituality for Women and Men*, Grand Rapids, MI, Eerdman's, 1998, p. 168.

through of human intelligence, creatively responsible for one another. All creatures are siblings from the same womb, the brood of the one Mother of the universe who dwells in the bright darkness.[69]

The Church of the Earth embraces ecofeminism with its concern for both feminism and ecology. The Church of the Earth will call for an internal change of heart and an external change of institutional structures that will include full participation in the church's various ministries for all qualified candidates. In the Church of the Earth there are no locked compartments separating genders. There is no place in the Church of the Earth for divisions or discrimination based on racial or ethnic differences, based on prestige or social differences, based on gender differences.

The Church of the Earth challenges all social structures that are in any way founded on domination and oppression, whether these be of women, or other races or nations, or different colors or cultures, or those of different economic and social standing, or sexual orientation, or different jobs. The Church of the Earth will rejoice in the beauty of the diversity among the peoples of the earth and among all species of the earth. Such differences reflect the fullness of the earth, the inclusiveness of God and the richness of the life and ministry of the community.

The Church of the Earth challenges the sources of the current ecological crisis that pits the human against the earth, and which sees the earth as ours to conquer and rule for our own benefit with no thought of the rights of the earth and our future on this planet. The Church of the Earth calls all peoples to embrace wholeness, collaboration, and creativity in tune with the community of species that is the earth. This could be the most radical call of all because

the will to dominance *over the earth* leads to a will to dominance *over other humans*, other races, other cultures, other religions. It leads not only to violations against the environment but also to violations of human rights. "Other" humans are seen as separate from self or "us" rather than as sharing one life flow.[70]

Now is the time to bring back to consciousness the image of Mother Earth as the Creator God, and to see creation as the dynamic interaction of the transcendent Word and the immanent power of God in the earth. Thus the earth could once more be the profound source of our knowledge of God, and the feminine dimension of the earth can transform our image of the earth, ourselves, and God. "Once this (new creation) story is told it immediately becomes obvious how significant the title Mother Earth really is, how

---

[69] Johnson, *She Who Is,* p. 179.

[70] Mische, "Towards a Global Spirituality," p. 6.

intimate a relationship exists, how absolute our gratitude as humans must be, how delicate our concern. Our long motherless period is coming to a close."[71]

A COMMUNITY OF DISCIPLES

The Church of the Earth as a web of relationships is a community of disciples. As Avery Dulles says, "'Church of Disciples' is precisely what Jesus undoubtedly did found."[72] Jesus founded the church not in the sense of laying out its structure but by forming a group of followers whom he chose and with whom he gradually shared his deep experience of God's presence. Jesus called his disciples aside and explained the mystery of God's plan. They followed him to Jerusalem, and, despite their many weaknesses, they stayed with Jesus through his death and beyond his resurrection. The Risen Christ opened their hearts to the meaning of the Scriptures, and the coming of the Spirit sealed the mission of this community of disciples as they went out to spread the good news.

One of the basic foundation stones of this community of disciples is that they are a community of hearers and listeners. In the Gospel of Luke, Jesus says that we should let our light shine before others and that nothing hidden will remain secret. Jesus then adds a strange ending to the passage. "Take care, then, how you hear" (Lk. 8:18). The disciple is by definition a person who is a learner and a listener, one who is willing to "hear" others, and one who is open to new and challenging things in life.

> Discipleship is the common factor uniting all Christians with one another, for no one of them is anything but a follower and a learner in relation to Jesus Christ. As disciples, all must help, using their own talents for the benefit of the rest. All are ministers, and all are ministered to. The concept of discipleship undercuts the illusion that some in the Church are lords and masters.[73]

The Christian church is a community of the disciples of Jesus. At a deeper level, however, the members of the Church of the Earth are also disciples of God and disciples of Mother Earth. This call to radical discipleship is inherent in Jesus' message. The human community must first of all be in tune with the universe and in a special way with the earth as an essential foundation to its call to become disciples of Christ. The members of the community of disciples are called to *listen* and to *hear* the Wisdom of God embodied in the earth as well as the Wisdom of God embodied in Christ.

---

[71] Berry, Thomas, "Contemplation and World Order," in *The Whole Earth Papers,* Vol. 1, No. 10, 1978, p. 45.

[72] Dulles, Avery, *A Church to Believe In: Discipleship and the Dynamics of Freedom,* New York, Crossroad, 1985, p. 8.

[73] Dulles, *A Church to Believe In,* p. 12.

As we listen to the Wisdom of God embodied in the earth, we will discover three basic principles that can guide us in forming a community of disciples, principles that have been present from the flashing forth of the universe.

1. *Diversity:* The universe and our planet earth seem to glory in diversity! Millions of galaxies with millions of kinds of stars. A solar system with not just one planet but many planets, each one radically different from the other. An earth with an overwhelming variety of species of every size, shape, color, and form. A trip to a major zoo provides a breathtaking experience of diversity. There is a constant push for the new and different, for the unusual and even for what seems to be bizarre. It is such diversity that enables the community of species to establish itself, to heal itself, to govern itself and to maintain itself in times of environmental crisis. Diversity is the essential richness of the earth.

2. *Interiority (Subjectivity):* Interiority is a characteristic of all creation, even the most seemingly passive and inert. Superficially, a rock seems to be inert and without an interior life, but beneath the surface its atomic elements and particles are a beehive of activity and energy. Plants and animals have an interior sense of awareness that often surprises us. The human level of interiority includes self-consciousness and reflective thought.

And where there is interiority there is subjectivity. Every creature is more than a thing to be used. It is a subject to be respected with rights to its own habitat and way of being. As Sally McFague says, "The ecological model of knowing rests on the assumption that the world is composed of living, changing, growing, mutually related, interdependent entities, of which human beings are one. None of these entities is a mere object; all, in different ways, are subjects."[74]

The difference between subjectivity and objectivity was illustrated for me when I toured a forest on two occasions with different nature guides. In order to show us how to identify different species of trees, the first guide ripped off a small branch so we could see the leaves—objectivity; and the other guide gently pulled a branch down lower so we could observe—subjectivity. The second guide treated the tree with due respect and care; the first did not.

In Western culture today we tend to see the earth as a "thing," an object for our exploitation, a wilderness to be conquered for the benefit of the human. In our industrial world we rarely take seriously the "earth deficit" of our economic system. We take into account the cost of mining raw materials, the cost of turning them into useful products, and the cost of marketing those products. But do we include in our plans the cost to the earth and its resources, and the cost to the community of species resulting from the pollution of air and water in the production process? Do we include the cost of

---

[74] McFague, *Super, Natural Christians,* p. 96.

dealing with the waste products both during production and following consumption? Our attitude is, these are only things destined for our use, so what does it matter? We forget about the mutual dignity and rights that are rooted in all creatures as subjects.

Although it is true that the human is the only creature in our awareness that has reflective consciousness, there is strong evidence for some level of consciousness throughout the universe. "If the capacity to deal with information, to communicate, defines a system as conscious, then the world is rich in consciousness, extending to include even those things we have classified as inanimate."[75] And where there is interiority and subjectivity, there is dignity and there are mutual rights to be respected.

3. *Communion:* Diversity and interiority can be fully realized only in a community of species, each carrying out its proper role in relationship to others. As we have seen in looking at holons, fields, and the implicate order, every reality in the universe is intimately present to every other reality and finds its fulfillment in this mutual presence. The entire evolutionary process depends on this web of relationships.

The gravitational field in which all creation is held in mutual attraction makes communion the universal basis for all reality from a galaxy to the solar system to the human family. Thomas Berry tells us, "The universality and intensity of this communion indicate its immense value. But even more evident is the fact that human survival depends so immediately and absolutely on this capacity for intimate human relationships."[76] Our continuation as a human species and a community of disciples calls us to a new vision of collaboration involving a communion of subjects with the maximum diversity.

There is a song that is often sung by children at night around the campfire, called "All God's Critters!" Listen for the diversity, subjectivity, and communion in this song.

Chorus
All God's critters got a place in the choir,
Some sing low, some sing higher,
Some sing out loud on the telephone wire, and some just clap their
    hands or paws,
or anything they got. NOW

Listen to the bass, it's the one on the bottom
Where the bull-frog croaks and
Hippopotamus moans and groans with a bit t'do,
And the old cow just goes "Moo."

---

[75] Wheatley, *Leadership and the New Science*, p. 106.

[76] Berry, *The Dream of the Earth*, p. 107.

The dogs and the cats they take up the middle,
While the honey bee hums and cricket fiddles.
The donkey brays and the pony neighs,
And the old coyote howls.

Chorus

Listen to the top where the little birds sing
On the melodies with the high notes ringing.
The hoot owl hollers over everything, and the jay bird disagrees.

Singing in the nighttime, singing in the day,
The little duck quacks, and then he's on his way.
The possum ain't got much to say, and the porcupine talks to himself.

Chorus

It's a simple song of living sung everywhere
By the ox and the fox and the grizzly bear,
The grumpy alligator, the hawk above,
The sly racoon and the turtle dove.

Chorus

All God's critters got a place in the choir,
Some sing low, some sing higher,
Some sing out loud on the telephone wire, and some just clap their
    hands or paws,
or anything they got. NOW

All God's creatures got a place in the community. Some can fly and some
can run, some are big like mountains and some are little like grains of sand.
Some live in water and some live on land, some eat meat and some eat plants.
Some are human with a rainbow of colors, some work hard and others just
think. But all God's creatures got a place in the community, all God's creatures are precious, all speak their own "language" and all are "learners."
This is the richness of a diversity of subjects living in community.

As Christians we will also be listeners and hearers of the Wisdom of
God made flesh in Christ Jesus. John Paul II unfolds the principles of diversity, subjectivity, and communion in his description of the community of
disciples.

Therefore, if we wish to keep in mind this community of the People
of God, which is so vast and so extremely differentiated, we must
see first and foremost Christ saying in a way to each member of the
community: "Follow me." It is the community of disciples, each of

whom in a different way—at times very consciously and consistently, at other times not very consciously and very consistently—is following Christ. This shows also the deeply "personal" aspect and dimension of this society.[77]

The Gospels show us in Jesus a person who is open to an all-inclusive sense of the reign of God. He eats with sinners and prostitutes, and he welcomes tax collectors and pagans. He heals the lepers and the woman with the issue of blood. He touches those who are "unclean" and heals on the Sabbath in defiance of the law. He tells stories about bringing the outcasts into the banquet when those of the establishment refuse to come, and about publicans and poor women who are found more acceptable to God than are the rich.

Jesus never treats people as objects. He becomes personally involved by sharing their lives and listening to their stories. We see personal relationships in his table fellowship with many diverse people and in his acceptance of the leper, who in the society of the time were objects of horror and outcast. We see it in his respect for questioners whether they were people honestly searching or those trying to trap him. We see it in his special loving friendship with Martha, Mary, and Lazarus. This shows the deeply personal aspect and dimension of the life of Jesus and the life of the community of disciples.

Although Jesus did not directly found a church in terms of specific structures and functions, he undoubtedly did found a *community* of disciples. The community dimension was confirmed in the story of Pentecost with its striking symbolism of wind and fire. These men and women went forth to preach the gospel and, as a result of their preaching, communities and churches emerged throughout the known world. And so, today as we struggle to discover and foster a new paradigm of the church, we must search for ways to preach the gospel and build a community of disciples with the greatest possible diversity who will treat everyone as subjects and as learners filled with a deep sense of communion in the one body of Christ.

We must strive to build a Church of the Earth as a dynamic web of relationships based on wholeness and relationality within the universe, within the earth, within the human community, and within the church.

---

[77] John Paul II, "*Redemptor Hominis,*" in *Origins,* March 4, 1979, Washington, DC, U.S. Catholic Conference, No. 21, 1979, pp. 89–90.

4

THE CHURCH OF DEEPER CONSCIOUSNESS

In the Church of Deeper Consciousness, we expand the major theme of a web of relationships in a discussion of self-awareness and wholeness as sources of deeper consciousness and in a recent theory of the quantum basis for consciousness. We trace this web through the human experience of spirituality in our ancestors, in the life of Jesus, and in the new creation story. Rituals, symbols, and sacraments are essential to both religion and spirituality insofar as they build a deeper consciousness and a stronger web of human relationships. The ritual, confessional, and ethical dimensions of performance are examined and applied to the sacraments of the church.

The title of this chapter is the result of an evolution in my own thinking, and it shows a gradual change in my own perspective. The original title (about twelve years ago) was "The Church of Higher Consciousness." This title tends to focus our attention on a transcendent God, a God Most High who calls us to let go of the earthly and seek the things that are above. Gradually, as my understanding of the new creation story developed, I began to experience, both in prayer and in study, an immanent God whose love, power, and compassion unfold from within the continuing and sometimes chaotic evolution of the universe, a God who is the inner source of all being and becoming.

These two perspectives, the transcendent and the immanent, are not in opposition to each other. They both proclaim the power and presence of God in all things and especially within human consciousness. All creatures proclaim the compassion and love of God, but humans can freely choose to respond to God with love and compassion for all creation. The view of a living and immanent God, however, calls us in a very special manner to enter into the earthly and seek the things that are within: the Church of Deeper Consciousness. Moreover, as we shall see, consciousness is an embodiment of a particular web of relationships within the human mind and a special web of relationships with reality outside of and beyond the human mind. It enables us as humans to reflect upon and respond to all of the multiple relations within and beyond us.

DEEPER CONSCIOUSNESS

We still tremble before the Self like children before the falling dark. Yet once we have dared to make our passage inside the heart, we will find that we have entered into a world in which depth leads on to the light, and there is no end to entrance.[1]

The human family has always believed in and searched for a deeper level of consciousness. Evidence for this comes from the history of ancient peoples who had their soothsayers, diviners, shamans, medicine people, and witch doctors. Eastern religions have their gurus and swamies; Islam has its imam. Within the Jewish tradition there were prophets and dreamers who were touched by God at the deepest levels of awareness. In medieval times there were various marginal groups such as witches and warlocks, alchemists and enthusiasts, all claiming to have discovered something of the deeper mysteries of human life. Likewise the mainstream of Christian spirituality, as found in monastic and religious life and in its saints and mystics, has sought for a deeper consciousness of God's presence.

Such a broad and universal consensus is also confirmed by contemporary discoveries in the areas of psychology, brain research, biofeedback, meditation, dream analysis and the human potential movement. There is a dimension of deeper consciousness that is now seen not as the suspicious realm of a few, but as a positive reality for all. Our discussion of this reality will revolve around three topics: self-awareness, wholeness, and the quantum self.

SELF-AWARENESS

One of the most ancient sayings of Christian spirituality is "know thyself." This search has deepened and broadened during the last one hundred years. Freudian psychology was able to articulate in a scientific model what many primitive, ancient, and modern cultures saw as strange and inexplicable phenomena. Freud opened to us a theory of the unconscious and our need to delve into it by the use of dreams and symbols. Freud's unconscious was often a frightening place because it contained the darker urges and the traumatic experiences of the human spirit, both of which are frequently repressed by our superego, often leading to mental or emotional illness or erratic and destructive behavior. The Freudian method of dealing with the unconscious tended to use a medical or therapeutic model that strives to bring the repressed feelings or experiences to consciousness so that they can be dealt with or dissipated.

In the years since Freud a different model has developed following Carl Jung and other depth psychologists. This model distinguishes between the personal and collective unconscious. Within the collective unconscious are

---

[1]Heilig, Gabriel Saul, "Spirituality and Manhood," in Harold Lyons Jr., *Tenderness Is Strength*, New York, Harper and Row, 1977, p. 239.

certain archetypes common to all that are expressed consciously in recurring symbols such as the Great Mother, the Maid, the Hero, and the Anima. The personal unconscious contains not only repressed feelings and experiences but more importantly the latent potentiality of the human person. Rooted in the unconscious is everything that the person is capable of becoming individually or collectively.

Thus depth psychology approaches the unconscious using a developmental model searching for the principle of human potential at the depths of the person and freeing it to reach its fullest actualization. This is called by Ira Progoff the "psyche" that he describes as "the directive principle in the human being which guides its growth from the moment of conception forward."[2]

The psyche is like a seed that contains within itself potentially all that the plant can be as it develops toward maturity. It is similar to the genetic coding that directs first the growth of the embryo and then the physical characteristics that gradually develop over the years. Deep within us is a seed, a psychic coding that contains in potentiality all that the self is and can become. The emergence of this genetic and psychic coding is a reflection of the emergence of all of creation from the first flashing forth of the universe fifteen billion years ago.

Self-awareness is the process of discovering and trusting the depths of our collective and individual unconscious, opening up the potential for growth within us and finding ways to realize this potentiality in our lives. Self-awareness is also a deeper understanding of the web of relationships that is essential to our individual, social, and spiritual lives, and finding in these relationships the source of both our inner lives as individuals and our outer lives in society.

But most of us are like a young priest in his early thirties named Peter[3] who came to see me about some personal and vocational issues. He announced that in recent years he had become aware of the fact that he had no significant relationship with God and no prayer life. He wanted to come to the retreat center in which I was working and spend several months dealing with the personal issues that were affecting his work as a priest. We met together at least one hour each day for the next three months.

As we talked over the next few weeks, it became clear that he had no sense of his own selfhood. Throughout his life Peter had lived almost entirely out of the expectations of others. His early education was determined by his parents, and his choice of career as a priest flowed from what his family and friends thought he should do and be. Once on the vocational track, Peter merely walked along the path of least resistance. His teachers and the stereotypical demands of his seminary education became the direc-

---

[2] Progoff, Ira, *The Symbolic and the Real,* New York, McGraw-Hill, 1973, p. 73.

[3] This story is based upon a real experience that has been combined with several other personal histories.

tive principles of his career and his personal relations. He was the fully *heteronomous* person living up to the expectations of others but lacking any sense of self-awareness.

Heteronomy, meaning "other-directed," describes a person whose life is based on the external demands of family, friends, society, and church. During childhood and often throughout life, we all need to relate to the environment and the expectations of those around us, but in heteronomy these expectations become the sole or primary motive in life resulting in a profound loss of self-awareness. Such was the case with Peter in his pursuance of a priestly vocation. How could Peter be helped to find himself? He seemed unwilling or unable to articulate his inner feelings or share any inward experiences that might open up the self. His life was so determined from the outside that his responses lacked spontaneity and creativity.

The breakthrough came when we began to discuss his friends and what, if any, meaning they had for him. He had four close friends who were very different in background and character. As we probed the reasons for his friendship with each person, Peter was able gradually to identify different feelings and experiences that bound him to these four people. Then one morning Peter arrived with a big smile. He had discovered that the qualities found in each of these relationships might be and actually were mirror images of the qualities of his own inner self. An awareness of the web of relationships led him to an embryonic self-awareness. For the first time in his adult life he ever so gently began to experience his true self.

With excitement he began to enter the treasure of his inner personality. He began to remember some of his dreams and to discover a recurrent image of a house, which was beautifully landscaped and well furnished, but empty of people. He became aware of an image in his dreams of a spring that was capped and could not flow. The potentiality within him began to unfold, and he started to write poetry that expressed his deeper consciousness. He rediscovered a talent for woodcarving. Creativity and imagination began to flow, and his house began to be alive with people. He was discovering the self and tapping the unconscious that would eventually lead him to a sense of *autonomy.*

The *autonomous,* meaning "self-directed," person is one who is able to go beyond the false self of the expectations of others (heteronomy) and to rise to the new life of an awareness and trust of inner being. This new life brings with it a feeling of freedom, a liberation to become who we are, and an openness to the future with whatever it may bring. Peter discovered that, although dealing with his personal and vocational issues is the work of a lifetime, the power and resources were within him. This gave him a tremendous sense of freedom and autonomy.

Self-awareness does not end with autonomy. One night Peter woke with a sense of anxiety and fear. The discovery of self is exciting, but it is also frightening. We enter a depth dimension leading to a new level of mystery and transcendence. The experience of self takes us beyond our self. As Peter awoke he began to pray. For the first time in many years he experienced a deeper Self, a mysterious indescribable presence that he could touch but not explain, and he prayed.

When Peter first came he claimed he had no relationship with God, most likely because he had no real relationship with himself. Later as he discovered his own self and became more autonomous, he was led beyond himself to become a *theonomous* person. *Theonomy,* meaning "God-directed," enables a person to experience a deep relationship with God and to reach out to others in new ways. The external web of relationships now becomes an opportunity for new life and for deeper relations with the people in our lives and with the whole of creation. But Peter now also realized that the movement from heteronomy to autonomy to theonomy is not a one-time journey. He could not finish one stage and move on to the next. Rather this process is an ongoing, dynamic, and ever-growing spiral curling back on itself seeking new depths of consciousness.

The paradox of the human person is that awareness of the psyche helps us to find the transcendent within us.

> By its very nature, therefore, the functioning of the psyche tends to have a connective effect. As it brings about an experience of meaning within the person, it awakens in the finite being a sensitivity to the infinite. It leads to the realization that since this sensitivity is possible it must be that somewhere in the depths of the finite person there lies a capacity to perceive some of the meanings implicit in the infinite.[4]

We find divinity at the depth of our humanity. Deeper consciousness leads us from heteronomy to autonomy and opens us to theonomy, to an awareness of that which is beyond us, to love of God and love of neighbor, to a deeper concern for all creation.

> A new understanding of *self* is discovered, one that has little resemblance to ego, self-ishness, self-lessness. There are multiple dimensions of self; a newly integrated sense of oneself as an individual . . . a linkage with others as if they are oneself . . . and the merger with a Self yet more universal and primary.[5]

This should not be surprising. The earthling is created in the image and likeness of God (Gen. 1:26). In some mysterious way we share in the life of God because in God we live and move and have our being (Acts 17:28). The reign of God is like a seed that grows from within (Matt. 13), and the new law is written on the heart (Jer. 31:33).

The Church of Deeper Consciousness is a gathering of people who will foster this process of self-awareness, who will encourage people in the con-

---

[4] Progoff, *The Symbolic and the Real,* p. 81.

[5] Ferguson, Marilyn, *The Aquarian Conspiracy,* New York, St. Martin's Press, 1980, p. 98.

tinuing journey from heteronomy to autonomy to theonomy, who will support each other in the exciting and fearful entrance into the individual and collective unconscious.

WHOLENESS

As a person deepens her sense of self-awareness there is also an experience of more than one "self" within. An inner multiplicity of dimensions of the personality is part of self-discovery. We may be husband and lover, tennis pro and mother, artist and academic, Dr. Jekyll and Mr. Hyde, musician and clown, priest and professor. We discover that none of these "selves" exhausts the fullness of our individuality because at the deepest level we touch the mystery of wholeness and the presence of God.

The self is the sum of all the divergent forces, energies, and qualities that live within us and make us who we are—unique individuals. The self is the balanced, harmonious, symmetrical unity at the very center of one's being, which each of us senses within. But we rarely experience the self with our conscious mind; we rarely have that sense of unity and wholeness. We feel ourselves usually as a chaotic mass of conflicting desires, values, ideals, and possibilities, some conscious and some unconscious, pulling us in many directions. The search for wholeness is the attempt to discover the divergent forces, energies, and qualities within us, to claim them for ourselves, and to integrate them into our functioning lives.

One dimension of wholeness is the search for gender identity. A young woman or a young man during adolescence and early adulthood is concerned with questions of identity—who am I?—and this includes the question of gender identity—who am I as a woman or as a man? How can I develop those characteristics of being masculine or feminine as called forth by societal expectations? This search for gender identity and the specific societal roles related to it is part of the ordinary developmental process. However, it often involves an imbalance with a young man focusing on the stereotypical male qualities and repressing the stereotypical female qualities and the young woman focusing on the stereotypical female qualities and repressing the stereotypical masculine qualities. This can lead to a one-dimensional sense of gender identity.

There are several unhealthy ways to respond to the development of a one-dimensional gender identity. One way is to deny the repressed dimension of the personality and to take refuge in the stereotypical image of the "macho warrior" or the "earth mother." Such a resolution of the issue of gender identity is one of the most serious obstacles to deeper consciousness and personal development. It impedes communication and intimacy, and it boxes people into destructive behavior patterns. Denial is a dead end calling for more and more repressive measures until the self becomes weighted down and immobilized under its own one-sidedness.

Another unhealthy response is to project a romanticized image of masculinity or femininity on another person or even at times on a social group.

For example, a man who does not name and claim the feminine dimension within himself will tend to "fall in love" with another on whom he projects an idealized and even divinized image of the feminine. The object of this projection might be a woman as friend or lover, it might be a church or social group, or it might be a religious figure such as Mary, the Mother of Jesus. A woman who does not name and claim the masculine dimension within herself will tend to "fall in awe" before another on whom she projects an idealized and even divinized image of the masculine. The object of this projection might be a man as friend or lover, it might be a religious or social leader, or it might be the patriarchal image of God.

Projection is also a dead end. We eventually find that the idealized man or woman with whom we fall in love or fall in awe is a flesh and blood person with ordinary human weaknesses and failings. We find that our church or social group in its imperfections and humanness cannot support the divinized image of the feminine or masculine, and we find that a purely patriarchal God is an inadequate representation of the fullness of the divinity. We are left with a feeling of emptiness at our loss of wholeness only to continue the fruitless search for the idealized other.

The solution is to search for wholeness within our inner selves. I once had a dream that I was sitting on the side of a swimming pool. There was a couple swimming in the pool. I noticed that the woman was pushing the man under the water. He struggled to get away, but she held him under water until he sank to the bottom of the pool. I jumped into the water, grabbed him and pulled him up on the side of the pool.

I shared this dream with a friend of mine, and he asked me if I had recently been "put down" by a woman. As I pondered this dream, it became clear that this was not the symbol of an outer struggle with another, but an inner struggle taking place within me in terms of my gender identity. It was necessary for me to dive into the pool, my deeper consciousness, and retrieve my true self with any and all of my stereotypical masculine and feminine qualities. We can only find true gender identity and wholeness when we become fully aware of our true self with all its dimensions.

> When one side of human nature grows out of balance with the other, it becomes a tyranny in the soul. . . . But the unconscious will not tolerate this kind of imbalance; we have already learned that the greatest force in the psychic universe is the demand for completion, for wholeness, for balance.[6]

Another dimension of wholeness that has emerged from recent research on the brain provides evidence that the two hemispheres of the brain function in different but complementary fashions. The left brain is more verbal, logical, and linear, whereas the right brain is more symbolic, imaginative, and creative. The left brain organizes and analyzes, and it sees things as in-

---

[6] Johnson, Robert A., *We: Understanding the Psychology of Romantic Love*, San Francisco, Harper and Row, 1983, p. 23.

dependent particles in competition. The right brain transforms and synthesizes, and it sees things as interconnected wholes in collaboration.

The modern scientific and technological society is built on a largely left brain model of the world and of the mind giving priority to the verbal, logical, and linear while minimizing the symbolic, imaginative, and creative. The Cartesian and Newtonian worldview is a mechanistic model of particles moving in space and time following definite laws with predictable outcomes. Other fields of human endeavor such as biology, psychology, health care, and economics have followed the lead of physics in emphasizing the linear, the mechanistic, the rational, and the scientific, bringing to society marvelous progress in science, business, and technology. Left brain thinking has become dominant. But these developments are being challenged by new discoveries that call for the balance provided by the right brain's emphasis on relationships and symbolic thinking.

> In contrast to the mechanistic Cartesian view of the world, the world view emerging from modern physics can be characterized by words like organic, holistic, and ecological. It might also be called a systems view, in the sense of a general systems theory. The universe is no longer seen as a machine, made up of a multitude of objects, but has to be pictured as one indivisible, dynamic whole whose parts are essentially interrelated and can be understood only as patterns of a cosmic process.[7]

A very descriptive image of right and left brain wholeness is found in the legend of Tristan and Isault. As a young man Tristan learns to fight with the sword and to play the harp. The sword is a symbol of the left brain—sharp, cutting, potentially destructive—and the harp is a symbol of the right brain—melodic, feeling, potentially healing. On one occasion Tristan becomes the hero by using the sword to defend his king against the invaders, but he is wounded in the battle. Now his sword is useless for it cannot bring healing and save his life. He lays down his sword and takes up the harp. He sets out in a small boat on the uncharted sea (the unconscious) gently playing the harp and finds the source of healing that restores his wholeness.

We are learning to recognize this need for wholeness in the lives of individuals and societies, but, what is even more important, we are beginning to experience whole brain consciousness as greater than the sum of its parts. Using both the sword and the harp, the verbal *and* symbolic, the rational *and* the feeling, the linear *and* the circular, the logical *and* the creative opens us to new levels of awareness and transformation.

The wholeness that comes from the inner marriage of the masculine and feminine within us and from the interconnectedness of the left and right brain are only two examples of the potential for wholeness in human life. These examples can illustrate the basic dialogical structure of the human,

---

[7] Capra, Fritjof, *The Turning Point*, New York, Bantam Books, 1983, pp. 77–78.

and they can serve as catalysts for further developments in the search for wholeness. These examples also illustrate the need to overcome the many dualistic, either/or patterns in our lives and to embrace the web of relationships found in all of reality. Overcoming dualism and embracing relationality can become a quantum leap into the fullness of being human, an appreciation of the infinite potential of each person, the richness of personal and social diversity, and the deeper consciousness of our wholeness.

Unless it is short-circuited by a lack of courage or a lack of vision, the dialectical journey toward wholeness leads us to a "conscious attunement to the sacred source of life. At the deepest part of every and all being is the sacred."[8] This journey becomes a pilgrimage to the shrine of God within us, and we experience the power and presence of God giving us the fullness of life. As Clement of Alexandria, a second-century pope and theologian, puts it, "For knowledge of man is the beginning of wholeness, but knowledge of God is perfect wholeness."

The Church of Deeper Consciousness is a gathering of people who will foster the journey toward wholeness for all people. The Church of Deeper Consciousness will foster and embody the full development of all dimensions of the human—the feminine and the masculine, the rational and the feeling, the creative and the logical—the whole dialogic of human personhood so that all can grow up into the fullness of Christ and of God.

THE QUANTUM SELF

Chemically, we are no different from the rest of creation. Our elements are among the most common in the universe—a few pennies' worth of atoms. Yet we are anything but commonplace. Each of us is intensely conscious of being unique. Out of ordinary substance, a self has somehow arisen. There is no greater mystery than this: the genesis of self.[9]

A book by Danah Zohar, *The Quantum Self: Human Nature and Consciousness Defined by the New Physics,* attempts to analyze human personhood and human conciousness—the self—in terms of quantum reality. It is a fascinating search, and it will help us to understand more deeply both the conflicting dimensions of the self as well as the "internal causality" that underpins our wholeness. *The Quantum Self* also raises the profound questions of the origins of human consciousness and the possibility of finding God at the depths of quantum reality. The ideas in this work are complicated, creative, and captivating.

Zohar's purpose is to consider the possibility that

Consciousness, like matter, emerges from the world of quantum events; that the two though wholly different from each other, have

---

[8] Mische, Patricia, "Towards a Global Spirituality," in *The Whole Earth Papers,* No. 16, p. 4.

[9] Raymo, Chet, *Skeptics and True Believers: The Exhilarating Connection between Science and Religion,* New York, Walker and Company, 1998, pp. 180–181.

a common "mother" in quantum reality. If so, our thought patterns—and beyond that, our relationships to ourselves, to others, and to the world at large—might in some ways be explained by, and in other ways mirror, the same laws and behavior patterns that govern the world of electrons and photons.[10]

If, in fact, consciousness emerges from quantum events—if our thought patterns mirror the same patterns that govern the world of electrons and protons—then, in knowing nature, we can come to know ourselves, and, in knowing ourselves, we can come to know nature. This reaffirms a major premise of this book that the universe, and in a special way the earth, is the primary source of our knowledge of self and our knowledge of God. If quantum reality is the source of roses and sequoia trees, of bees and birds, as well as ourselves, it deepens the web of relationships among all creatures, and supports a mutual dependency within all creation.

The word *quantum*, though frequently used, is difficult to define. Perhaps in a way it is more easily intuited in metaphorical terms. With patience we will gradually begin to have a sense of the meaning of quantum reality.

Diarmuid O'Murchu describes *quanta* and *quantum reality* as follows:

In the 1920s the German physicist Max Planck postulated that all radiation (whether light or heat) is not emitted continuously, but appears in the form of energy packets. Einstein called these energy packets "quanta" and recognized them as fundamental aspects of nature. The most fascinating thing about these quanta is that one could never say for sure whether they were particles or waves of energy, whether they could be said to exist at definite times and places or whether they tended to exist as probability waves.[11]

This description seems almost like a magician's words—now you see it, now you don't. *Quantum energy* is now a wave, now a particle, and we don't know where it is or when it is. Given our Newtonian ideas of cause and effect this all seems to be beyond our comprehension. We will let Zohar explain it further.

The most revolutionary, and for our purposes the most important statement that quantum physics makes about the nature of matter, and perhaps being itself, follows from its description of the wave/particle duality—the assertion that all being at the subatomic level can be described equally well either as solid particles, like so many minute billiard balls, or as waves, like undulations of the surface of the sea.[12]

---

[10] Zohar, Danah, *The Quantum Self: Human Nature and Consciousness Defined by the New Physics*, New York, Quill/William Morrow, 1990, p. 23.

[11] O'Murchu, Diarmuid, *Quantum Theology*, New York, Crossroad, 1997, p. 27.

[12] Zohar, *The Quantum Self*, p. 25.

So far, so good. Quantum energy can be seen as either a wave or a particle, but the magic gets even more complex. According to Zohar "both the wavelike and the particlelike aspects of being must be considered when trying to understand the nature of things, and that it is the duality itself that is most basic. Quantum 'stuff' is essentially, *both* wavelike and particlelike, simultaneously."[13]

Quantum stuff is not *either* wavelike *or* particlelike but it is *both* wavelike *and* particlelike *simultaneously*. Moreover, there is strong evidence for the relationality and the interaction among things at the quantum level dependent on whether a system is more or less in a "particle" or a "wave" state. Particles are more like separate individuals; they are antisocial; they are the self-preservation capacity of holons. Waves are more correlated and behave more like a group; they love parties. They are the self-adaptation capacity of holons. This powerful relationality of all things flowing from the wave dimension of matter can profoundly impact our vision of reality. Quantum physics tells us that there is a deep interrelationship among things and events reminiscent of our discussion of the "dynamic web of relationships" in Chapter 3.

The quantum view of consciousness can also give us a new sense of the web of relationships that can also be described as *internal causality*. When Newtonian billiard balls are bouncing around on a table they do have a kind of relationship to each other, but it is an *external* relation. When electrons are bouncing around in a box they relate in an entirely different way. Their wave aspects interfere with each other and overlap. They "merge, drawing the electrons into an existential relationship where their actual inner qualities—their masses, charges, and spins as well as their positions and momenta—become indistinguishable from the relationship among them."[14] This brings about a deeper relationship called *internal causality*.

This is evident in the case of the intimacy of lovers. Zohar explains that "in intimacy, I and you appear to influence *each other*; we seem to 'get inside' each other and change each other *from within* in such a way that 'I' and 'you' become a 'we.' This 'we' that we experience is not just 'I *and* you'; it is a new thing in itself, a new unity."[15] In other words, two lovers are changed internally by their love and, in a real sense, become a new being, a new holon with its own unique characteristics. Sometimes this new reality is expressed by a couple's taking a new name that is different from either of their previous names. Sometimes this new holon becomes enfleshed in a child born of this intimacy, or in giving birth to a life-enhancing project or theory.

Our human consciousness seems to involve a "self," an internal unity, an underlying personhood that integrates the various dimensions of con-

---

[13] Zohar, *The Quantum Self*, p. 25.

[14] Zohar, *The Quantum Self*, p. 99.

[15] Zohar, *The Quantum Self*, p. 128.

sciousness and keeps us from splintering into many disparate parts as happens with persons who are very distracted or are mentally ill. What is the connection between quantum reality and an integrated human consciousness? The following personal story will help to answer that question.

> When I was in high school, every day at four o'clock something happened that so intrigued me that I would sometimes stay after school so I could watch it. During the course of each day the electrical clocks in the various classrooms might be either a few minutes ahead or behind. They would be out of sync. At exactly four o'clock the central clock system would "magically" reset every clock in the school. But this central system could only move the hands on the clock forward, so sometimes, if a clock was two minutes ahead, the hands on the clock would swing wildly round and round in an attempt to catch up. I was fascinated by the fact that in that moment every clock in the school would show exactly the same time and it was like the whole system became one clock.

In quantum physics there is something similar to the school clocks. When energy is pumped into a system of vibrating, electrically charged molecules, the vibrating molecules in the cell walls of living tissue emit electromagnetic vibrations (photons). Beyond a certain threshold, any additional energy pumped into the system causes its molecules to vibrate in unison, just like the various clocks on the classroom walls. They do so increasingly until they pull themselves into an ordered condensed phase. Zohar applies this principle of condensation to the working of the brain and to human consciousness.

> The crucial distinguishing feature of the Bose-Einstein condensate[16] is that the many parts that go to make up an ordered system not only *behave* as a whole, they *become* whole; their identities merge or overlap in such a way that they lose their individuality entirely. A good analogy would be the many voices in a choir, which merge to become "one voice" at certain levels of harmony, or the plucking of the many strings of several violins to become "the sound of the violins." This merging of identities is crucial to giving any physical accounting of the way consciousness draws together various "subunities" within experience.[17]

The unity of the conscious self can be accounted for only if all the separate but interrelated brain activities can somehow become unified like the classroom clocks, and, beyond that, become a whole, a quantum self, like a condensation when the many parts of a system not only behave as a whole,

---

[16]The technical term for this condensed phase is Bose-Einstein condensate. For the sake of simplicity I will use the word condensation in its place.

[17]Zohar, *The Quantum Self*, p. 83.

but become a whole. To use the language of holons, the conscious self is a holon whose parts are the many interrelated brain activities, but the whole, the self, is greater than the parts. The new holon is the conscious self that emerges from a quantum physical basis, but it transcends the sum of its parts and becomes a human person.

The physical basis of the conscious self is the condensation among neuron constituents in the brain. This simple statement carries with it some profound implications for the relationship between brain and mind, between matter and spirit, and between body and soul. We now can trace the development of human consciousness right back to its roots in quantum physics. Human consciousness and mental activity are rooted in a quantum reality common to the whole universe. The basic idea found in the biblical creation story and in the new creation story, namely, that *the human is the earth become conscious,* now takes on new meaning.

> We are, in our essential makeup, composed of the same stuff and held together by the same dynamics as those which account for everything else in the universe. And equally—which brings out the enormity of this realization—the universe is made of the same stuff and held together by the same dynamics as those which account for us.[18]

If human consciousness emerges from the potentiality of the universe, then there must be a way in which consciousness is latent in the whole evolutionary process. We are closer to the earth than we have ever before imagined. Even though the human emerges from the earth and is dependent on quantum physical processes, the human transcends its parts and is a new holon, just as water emerges from hydrogen and oxygen and transcends its parts and becomes a new holon.

In discussing holons in Chapter 3, we described the capacities of holons as self-preservation, self-adaptation, self-transcendence, and self-dissolution, and we can use these capacities to understand human emergence as well. As a deeper awareness gradually emerges within living creatures, there is a tendency toward self-preservation founded in the particle dimension of reality as well as a tendency to self-adaptation founded in the wave dimension of reality that tends toward interrelationships. At a particular point this tension between preservation and adaptation gives rise to self-transcendence and the emergence of a new holon, human consciousness and the human person.

Thus it is essential to maintain a balance in our perception of the human in which we can affirm both our rootedness in the quantum physical processes and our emergence into a new holon, a new way of life. This dependence on a quantum physical process is not a limiting factor in the evolution of the human but an empowering factor giving evidence of the inner

---

[18] Zohar, *The Quantum Self,* p. 101.

presence of the Creator Spirit as the ultimate source of our selfhood. As Chet Raymo says, "To admit that the mind is electrochemical does not diminish our concept of self; rather, it suggests that the cosmos was charged with the possibility of being conscious from the first instant of creation."[19] This development of our human consciousness opens up for us the ability to reflect on ourselves, to make free choices, to love deeply, and to search for meaning, something no other member of the community of species on this earth has been able to do.

Thus the unfolding of the entire universe from within is the internal creative presence of the Creator Spirit in all of creation; and the emergence of the entire human person is the result of the internal creative presence and extravagant love of God that brings forth a creature who is able to return that love in a freely chosen way. This way of understanding creation gives us a deeper personal awareness of the intimate presence of God within our life and of the internal unity of the human person.

As we ponder the meaning of our lives and the mystery of God, a practical question arises. Is there a relationship between the quantum view of consciousness and the various ways of prayer and contemplation as practiced by many different religions and cultures? Zohar tells us that the coherence of the brain's quantum system helps to focus our energy and to find a deeper unity of consciousness.

> The condensation that gives us the physical basis of consciousness arises from the correlated jiggling of molecules in the neuron cell walls. [Like the clocks on the schoolroom walls.] The extent to which these molecules are correlated, and hence the extent to which the condensation is coherent, depends upon the amount of energy pumped into the brain's quantum system at any given moment. If there is less energy available to the system, then the unity of consciousness will be less marked; if there is more energy, there will be greater unity. The range of unity possible in both directions is enormous.[20]

This need to focus our energy and our attention in order to achieve deeper consciousness is found in almost every culture, every spiritual tradition, and every religion. It is found in Zen Buddhism, tai chi chuan, vision quests, the desert monks, the medieval mystics, transcendental meditation, centering prayer, contemplation, and retreat times. Deeper consciousness requires a sense of peace and integration, and over the millennia people have developed practices and postures that contribute to that deeper experience of unity and centering. As we reach a certain level of calm, the energies of the system can be focused in the brain leading to a more coherent personality based on a more coherent quantum system in the brain.

---

[19] Raymo, *Skeptics and True Believers,* p. 194.

[20] Zohar, *The Quantum Self,* p. 115.

It should come as no surprise that this more coherent system in the brain, often brought about through various meditative and religious practices, would open people to a deeper consciousness of the meaning of human life, of our interconnectedness with the universe, and of the presence of God as the fundamental mystery embracing the whole. Our treatment of self-awareness and wholeness leads us to a deeper consciousness and to an awareness of the God within us. Zohar's study of human consciousness and the quantum self leads us to a realization of the deeper mystery within the universe, which can be called God. This deeper awareness and deeper mystery calls us to reflect on the spirituality found within our human lives as well as within the earth and the whole cosmos.

SPIRITUALITY

Spirituality is written into the weaving and unweaving tapestry of evolution and creation. Our prehistoric ancestors behaved spiritually because they remained connected to the cosmic womb of life, which itself is innately spiritual. And it is only by reconnecting with that primordial source . . . that we can hope to regain our spiritual, planetary and cosmic dignity as a human species. The divine meaning of creation is not derived from us, humans; creation itself is the source and wellspring; we, humans, are the derivative species![21]

Human spirituality can be variously described as a discovery of the sacred in all dimensions of life, or as a life-long process of growth and development under the guidance of the Spirit, or as the discovery of the divine presence and the Self within the self. We often tend to begin our history of spirituality with the appearance of Christianity, but spirituality has permeated the evolution of the human race from the first glimmer of consciousness approximately three million years ago. For this reason this section will be divided into four parts: the spirituality of our ancestors, the spirituality of Jesus, the spirituality of the creation story, and the relationship between spirituality and religion.

In discussing these various dimensions of spirituality I am not placing them over against one another, or seeing one as more mature than another. There is a spiral movement in spirituality based on the people's various creation stories, their cultural settings, and their experiences of God. People's in-depth contact with God in these stories, cultural settings, and experiences circle around one another and throw light on the constant search of the human race for the mystery of God within us, among us, and beyond us.

THE SPIRITUALITY OF OUR ANCESTORS

Spiritual consciousness is not the sudden appearance of a new reality, but the gradual unfolding of something already present in the earth and in the

---

[21] O'Murchu, Diarmuid, *Reclaiming Spirituality,* New York, Crossroad, 1998, pp. 60–61.

universe. Spirituality is an intimate dimension of the cosmos from the first flashing forth of the universe fifteen billion years ago because its source is the Creator Spirit whether that source is called God or Gaia or Jahweh or Wisdom/ Sophia or the Omega Point or the Holomovement. The evolutionary and cocreative process of cosmic growth and development was guided from within by the Creator Spirit. This divine Wisdom, so evident in the self-organizing capacity of the universe, manifests itself in the galaxies and the stars, in our solar system, and in the overwhelming beauty of planet earth with its rich diversity of mountains and plains and deserts, and finally in life, awareness, and human consciousness. With the advent of self-consciousness, the human now becomes a mirror of divine wisdom able to know, love, and worship the deepest mystery who is God.

There is little archaeological evidence for the dawning of human consciousness, and there is no way of knowing exactly where or how humans first discovered the sacred and reflected on the deeper mysteries of life. The first several million years of our history are shrouded, and we can only speculate how our ancestors became aware of a spiritual presence within the earth and within themselves.

The first humans apparently lived in intimacy with all of the creatures of the earth on which they depended for food and shelter. Their first web of relationships was that of the community of species that surrounded them and the innate and mysterious powers of the earth. They began to use simple wooden and stone implements, and they discovered the controlled use of fire for warmth and light and cooking. "With the fire in the hearth a communing with mythic powers takes place, social unity is experienced, a context for reflection on the awesome aspects of existence is established."[22] We can imagine the awe and reverence our ancestors had for the order of the cosmos as well as for the power of the wind and rain. They developed a rapport with the spiritual powers of nature and a reverence for death leading to ceremonial practices relating to their belief in the meaning of life. The mysterious power of human sexuality and reproduction became part of their rituals and their art forms.

We should not, however, romanticize the Paleolithic culture as we tend to romanticize Native American culture. Life was difficult and many conflicts were present. The search for food and shelter was perpetual, often requiring a nomadic way of life and the necessity of defending grazing lands and food supplies. Violence and chaos were present and at times disrupted the settled life of the people. But these early cultures did have a deep sense of the sacred in their lives, along with their dependence on the community of species, and their need for worship and ritual.

There is growing archaeological evidence that by 40,000 B.C.E. artistic skills, music, and dance, and some competence in simple technological proc-

---

[22]Swimme, Brian, and Thomas Berry, *The Universe Story,* San Francisco, HarperSanFrancisco, 1992, p. 149.

esses were widespread. Humans also began to use spoken language. This increased ability to communicate resulted in a significant transformation of human consciousness and a higher level of human culture and spirituality. As Swimme and Berry point out:

> The earlier paleolithic period when humans survived by hunting and gathering culminated, in Europe, in the grandeur of its Magdalenian phase, with its implements shaped in wood, stone, horn, and bone; its necklaces and pendants for personal adornments; its shamanic capacity for communing with the spirit powers beyond the world of appearances; its esthetic sensitivities and artistic skills as manifested in its cave paintings. All this was associated with a deep indwelling of the human within the natural rhythms of the cosmological order.[23]

The spirituality of our ancestors flowed from their intimacy with the earth, their experience of interacting spirit forces, their need for protection from evil powers, and their development of a more personal God. Our ancestors, at the beginning of the Neolithic period, 10,000 years ago, saw the universe in its inexhaustible fecundity in a feminine image that led to a sense of awe and worship for Mother Earth. This was a relatively peaceful period based on community life and shared decision making. The spirituality of this period was discovered in the presence of the sacred in the maternal dimension of the universe and in the seasonal cycles so intimately bound up with the feminine.

With the coming of the agricultural revolution and the domestication of animals there was a gradual change in the web of relationships among the humans and the rest of the community of species and within the human community itself. In terms of spirituality, the rise of a patriarchal society had a deep impact on the perception of God and the understanding of the divine presence in the universe. Two significant changes took place: (1) a transition from female to predominantly male deities; (2) the development of institutionalized religions about 5,000 years ago. The Jewish tradition was influenced by both of these factors. The Israelite nation from its beginning was surrounded by other patriarchal cultures, and this left an imprint not only on its concept of a transcendent, patriarchal God, but also on its internal social structure from the great patriarchs—Abraham, Isaac, and Jacob—to the Davidic kingly dynasty. The Jewish tradition also became an institutionalized religion based on the Mosaic law and the Levitical priesthood.

But enfolded within this idea of a patriarchal God and an institutional religion flows a stream of deep spirituality. As Richard Woods says, "Whether among the patriarchs, the prophets or sages, the dominant characteristic of Jewish spirituality has centered implicitly or explicitly, as it does

---

[23]Swimme and Berry, *The Universe Story,* p. 163.

today, on the presence of God."[24] This special presence of God is found in the call of Abram (Gen. 12:1–3), in the powerful story of Jacob wrestling with God (Gen. 28:10–19), and especially in the theophany to Moses in the burning bush and the revealing of the divine name (Ex. 3:1–14). This divine name, stressing the intimate presence as well as the transcendence of God, might be paraphrased to say, "I shall be there as who I am shall I be there."[25] In other words, God is always intimately present to the people, but in a way that is uniquely transcendent. All these formative experiences show both the intimacy of God with the patriarchs and the people, and the powerful guiding presence of that God.

A second stream of spirituality in Israel is that of the Spirit of Yahweh. The word *spirit* in Hebrew is *ruah*, and it means both "breath" and "wind." "Spirit" is often used to explain the overpowering and life-giving presence of God, and it is something dwelling not only in Moses as the leader and lawgiver but something shared by all the elders. "The Lord then came down in the cloud and spoke to Moses. Taking some of the spirit that was on Moses, he bestowed it on the seventy elders; and as the spirit came to rest on them, they prophesied" (Num. 11:25). During the time of Samuel there are references to ecstatic bands of prophets who are overwhelmed by the breath of God. Samuel speaks to Saul, "As you enter that city, you will meet a band of prophets, in a prophetic state, coming down from the high place. . . . The spirit of the Lord will rush upon you, and you will join them in their prophetic state and will be changed into another man" (1 Sam. 10:5–6; also see 1 Sam. 19:18–24).

The spirit plays a major role in the later prophetic literature, and we can look at examples from three prophetic sources: Isaiah, Ezekiel, and Jeremiah. Isaiah sees the spirit as a source of the wonderful gifts that are poured out upon the people in the person of the messianic king. "The spirit of the Lord shall rest upon him: a spirit of wisdom and of understanding, a spirit of counsel and of strength, a spirit of knowledge and of fear of the Lord, and his delight shall be the fear of the Lord" (Isa. 11:2).

In the story of the dry bones in Ezekiel the spirit is graphically described as the source of new life for the Israelites.

> Then the Lord said to me: Prophesy to the spirit, prophesy, son of man, and say to the spirit: Thus says the Lord God: From the four winds come, O spirit, and breathe into these slain that they may come to life. I prophesied as he told me, and the spirit came into them; they came alive and stood upright, a vast army. (Ezek. 37:9–10)

---

[24] Woods, Richard, *Mysterion: An Approach to Mystical Spirituality,* Chicago, The Thomas More Press, 1981, p. 239.

[25] Murray, John Courtney, *The Problem of God,* New Haven, CT, Yale University Press, 1964, p. 10.

Finally, Jeremiah looks to the future and sees the spirit as a source of a renewed covenant between God and the people—a covenant based not on an external law or temple sacrifices, but on a law written on the heart.

> But this is the covenant which I will make with the house of Israel after those days, says the Lord. I will place my law within them, and write it upon their hearts; I will be their God, and they shall be my people. No longer will they have need to teach their friends and kinsfolk how to know the Lord. All, from the least to the greatest shall know me, says the Lord.   (Jer. 31:33–34)

Another stream of this spirituality is found in the wisdom tradition that reached its full flowering in the figure of Sophia/Wisdom treated in Chapter 3. Sophia/Wisdom is a feminine figure imaged as the source of all creation and the mediator of revelation and salvation, and her power and presence is reminiscent of the earth mother of our early ancestors. This Jewish spirituality, based on the Israelite's experience of the abiding presence of God and their prophetic and wisdom traditions, became a major source of the spirituality of Jesus.

THE SPIRITUALITY OF JESUS

In the Christian tradition, as reflected in the Gospel stories, we see Jesus as a person of a deep spirituality grounded in and going beyond the Jewish spiritual tradition. Perhaps we can get a better understanding of the deeper consciousness of Jesus and his growth in the spirit by using the more modern language of heteronomy, autonomy, and theonomy as described earlier in this chapter.

Heteronomy, remember, is that dimension of life in which someone primarily lives up to the expectations of others, such as family and friends, social and religious traditions. The parents of Jesus are presented in the Gospels as observant Jews who followed the law of Moses. They brought the child Jesus to the temple for circumcision, and later they took him up to Jerusalem to present him to the Lord (Lk. 2:21–24). When Jesus was twelve years old he was taken to Jerusalem for the feast of Passover, and he worried his parents by staying behind sitting in the midst of the teachers listening to them and asking questions. Jesus and his parents lived up to the expectations of the law, and they participated in the life of the community as Jesus advanced in wisdom, age, and favor before God and the people (Lk. 2:52).

An autonomous person is one who not only lives according to the expectations of others, but begins to discover and live out of a deeper consciousness of self. This movement toward autonomy is portrayed in the baptism of Jesus and his temptation in the desert. It is clear from the Gospel stories that the baptism of Jesus was a deep spiritual experience expressed symbolically in the Holy Spirit descending upon Jesus in the form of a dove and the voice from heaven saying, "You are my beloved Son; with you I am well pleased" (Lk. 3:22). This is most likely the symbolic culmination of the spiritual journey of Jesus as a young man as he struggled with the presence of God within him and discovered his profound personal and filial relationship with God. This was the beginning of Jesus' awareness of God as an intimate parent, a Father, Abba/Daddy, an awareness that continued to mature throughout his life.

Autonomy is an essential part of the dynamic of human and spiritual growth, but there are also hidden dangers in autonomy such as a false sense of self, an exaggerated assertion of self-importance, a tendency to seek power and control, and a temptation to be like God. After his baptism by John, "The Spirit drove Jesus out into the desert, and he remained in the desert for forty days, tempted by Satan. He was among wild beasts, and the angels ministered to him" (Mk. 1:12–13). The autonomy of Jesus was purified in the Spirit by facing the challenges of self-discovery, by symbolically embracing the harshness of the desert and its wild animals, and by overcoming the temptations to a false sense of self. The chaos of the desert gives way to a deeper consciousness of self before God as symbolized in the presence of the angels serving him.

After his baptism and desert experience, both of which took place outside of institutional Judaism, Jesus returned to Galilee and to Jewish society in the power of the Spirit, and news of him spread throughout the whole region. Jesus began to move beyond himself into theonomy, a reaching out to others and to God. In the beginning of the Gospel of Mark, the temptation in the desert is immediately followed by the proclamation of the good news of the reign of God and the need for a change of heart. "Jesus came to Galilee proclaiming the gospel of God: 'This is the time of fulfillment. And the kingdom of God is at hand. Repent, and believe in the gospel'" (Mk. 1:14–15).

Jesus began to teach in their synagogues and was praised by all. On one occasion he unrolled the scroll and found the passage in Isaiah where it is written: "The Spirit of the Lord is upon me, because the Spirit has anointed me to bring glad tidings to the poor, has sent me to proclaim liberty to captives and recovery of sight to the blind, to let the oppressed go free, and to proclaim a year acceptable to the Lord" (Lk. 4:18–19).

Then Jesus said to the people, "Today this scripture passage is fulfilled in your hearing" (Lk. 4:21). The Spirit, who led Jesus to autonomy through his baptism and drove him into the desert to overcome temptation, is now calling him to theonomy and leading him to reach out to those in need—the poor, the captives, the blind, and the oppressed. His consciousness of himself leads Jesus to a compassion for and a willingness to serve others. As a result of this challenge to the people in the synagogue, Jesus was driven out of Nazareth and threatened with death, a preview of his ultimate suffering and death on a cross.

The spirituality of Jesus flowed from his Jewish roots, but the Spirit also brought him to a deeper consciousness of his own self and his intimate relationship to God that became the foundation of his call to minister to those in need and to preach the coming reign of God. This coming of the rule of God in the lives of individuals and within Jewish society demanded a change of heart and a conversion that would turn the religious system upside down. It would free the oppressed; it would bring prostitutes and tax collectors into the kingdom before the Scribes and Pharisees; it would teach that the poor woman who put a couple pennies in the temple treasury gave more than the wealthy patrons. The religious leaders were angered by the message and miracles of Jesus, and this led to his suffering and death and his vindication in the Resurrection.

The early Christian community saw the spirituality of Jesus in terms of images from the Jewish scriptures. Jesus is the new Adam (earthling) who was created in the likeness of God but did not cling to the desire to be equal to God as did the first Adam (earthling). Rather he emptied himself, becoming obedient to death, even death on a cross, and God exalted him in the Resurrection (Phil. 2:6–8). Jesus is the suffering servant portrayed in Isaiah as one who was beaten and insulted, oppressed and condemned, spurned and avoided as a victim of suffering. Yet it was *our* infirmities he carried, and he was crushed by our sins. By his suffering we are healed, and by his chastisements we are made whole (Isa. 52:13–53:12). For the early Christians, the spirituality of Jesus embraced the reality of human suffering and the reality of new life arising from the power of God.

The death and resurrection of Jesus became the defining moment and event in early Christian spirituality. The author of the Acts of the Apostles describes an address of Peter to the people of Israel in which is traced briefly the mighty works of Jesus.

> This man [Jesus], delivered up by the set plan and foreknowledge of God, you killed, using lawless men to crucify him. But God raised him up releasing him from the throes of death, because it was impossible for him to be held by it. . . . Therefore let the whole house of Israel know for certain that God has made both Lord and Messiah, this Jesus whom you crucified.   (Acts 2:23, 24, 36)

The theme of death and resurrection, so obvious in the dynamics of creation and in the cycles of the seasons and in the order rising out of chaos, is now played out in the life of Jesus and in the faith of the early Christians. By entering into the waters of baptism, his followers entered into his death, and by rising up out of the waters they shared in his resurrection.

The spirituality of our ancestors was based on a deeply woven web of relationships with creation as they experienced it and with the whole community of species. Within the Jewish community, this web was articulated in terms of intimate presence of God, the prophetic power of the Spirit, and the role of Sophia/Wisdom. The spirituality of Jesus was based on a more intimate and personal relationship to God and on the call of God to transform the social and religious web of relationships through self-sacrificing love. What does the new creation story contribute to our spiritual journey?

SPIRITUALITY OF THE NEW CREATION STORY

The spirituality of the new creation story embraces three dimensions: (1) the sacredness of the cosmos and the earth that surrounds us with the presence of Mystery; (2) the intimate presence of God within all things as a spiritual field flowing from internal causality and cocreativity; and (3) the theme of death and resurrection that permeates all aspects of life. The new creation story with its new mentality and new way of thinking will inevitably bring out new dimensions to our personal and collective spirituality. It will incorporate much of the spirituality of our ancestors and the spirituality of Jesus, but the new creation story shines a new light on the traditions and opens up new depths and new horizons for the people of the next century.

Sacredness of the Cosmos and the Earth. I am reminded of an incident that occurred shortly after a new baptismal font large enough for baptism by immersion was installed in the church where I was working. One Sunday morning I was standing near the font and an elderly woman came in and looked with wonder on the font with water flowing in and out of it. She said to me, "Is this water blessed?" My response was, "Yes, it is blessed by God." There was a pause as she looked at the large font, and she said questioningly, "You mean, *all* of it?"

This incident illustrates a new dimension to spirituality in the new creation story. The water in the font is not blessed because we bless it, but we are blessed because the water by its very existence is blessed by God. We do not make creation holy, but it is creation that makes us holy. Our ritual of blessing simply recognizes the sacredness of creation as it is used in our rituals.

A deeper awareness of the sacredness of all creation leads to a change in our attitude toward the earth. Our relationship to the earth should not be one of control but of conscious attunement; our awareness and our spirituality must be attuned to the sacred presence in all of creation. Our spirituality flows from deep within us as we touch the mysterious power dwelling at the depth of our being. It is as if we had a well within us and as we go down into that well we discover the common sacred stream that feeds our well and the wells of all people and even of all creation. Patricia Mische describes this *inward journey* into the sacred as a journey through our deep *past,* but in a real sense it is a description of the *present* because, in quantum terms, the past is always present to us. Her words describe the powerful web of relationships that embraces all that we are in the present and all that we have been in the past and all the potential within us for the future.

> The inward journey is a journey through our deep past—all that has formed us. It cuts through the many layers of tradition, belief, culture, history, symbols that are part of our personal and collective experience. We travel inward through all the individual and collective sufferings, joys, struggles, discoveries, changes that have brought us to this present time; through all the history and all the choices that have separated us and divided us and broken us, and

all the choices that have bound us together, healed us, made us one. We journey back to a common source, back through the ages of history; back through the birth of human consciousness and the birth of the human; back through the birth of life and the birth of the planet; back to the origins of the universe to the startling moment when the universe was charged to Become; back to the eye of God; back into divine love.[26]

Relationships are central to the quantum makeup of all of creation and are a distinctive feature of the human experience. Among humans there are four general types of relationships: (1) to family and friends; (2) to institutions and societies; (3) to the natural world; (4) to ourselves. Each of these kinds of relationship needs to be fostered in our human growth and development. But where does God fit into these relationships? Is God a fifth kind of relationship?

The new creation story sees God, not as a new or fifth kind of relationship, but rather the depth dimension of all relationships. God is not separate from us, our families and friends, our institutions and societies, the natural world, but, as we have seen, is intimately present within us and the source of being for all relationships. Thus the more we love and care for our spouse, our families, and our friends, the more we will love and care for God. Our service to institutions and societies is simply a service to the God who lives within all human relations. The deeper our consciousness and love of ourselves the deeper will be our consciousness and love of God. As we nurture and protect our Mother Earth, we are nurturing and protecting our God. God as the depth dimension of all things is the source of all, but our loving and personal God is also beyond all.

There is a story about three men in India: Two men were standing in the marketplace, when another man riding on his donkey came rushing through the market. One of the men said to the other, "Where is Josef going in such a hurry?" The other answered, "He is looking for his donkey." We often dash around looking for God, when God is right here present at the depths of all relationships and all that exists. The spirituality of the new creation story begins with the sacredness of the cosmos and of the earth and takes us into the depths of the inner presence of God in all relationships.

The Presence of God as a Spiritual Field.   The new creation story enables us to have a *spirituality of internal causality.* As described previously in this chapter, when Newtonian billiard balls are bouncing around on a table they do have a kind of relationship to each other, but it is an *external* relation. When electrons are bouncing around in a box they relate in an entirely different way. Their wave aspects interfere with each other and overlap, and they have an *internal* relation. Thus the spirituality of the new creation story includes both internal relations and internal causality.

---

[26] Mische, "Towards a Global Spirituality," p. 7.

Internal relationships help us to experience spirituality as a universal field that is a powerful and yet invisible force in our lives. In Chapter 3 we quoted Jaworski's description of the characteristics of fields, and it is worth citing again.

> Fields are nonmaterial regions of influence—invisible forces that structure space or behavior. The earth's gravitational field, for example, is all around us. We cannot see it, it's not a material object, but it's nevertheless real. It gives things weight and makes things full. There are also magnetic fields that underlie the functioning of our brains and bodies. . . . There are also fundamental quantum matter fields recognized by physicists—electron fields, neutron fields, and others. They are "invisible, intangible, inaudible, tasteless, and odorless," and yet in quantum theory, they are the substance of the universe.[27]

Thus spirituality is a field that is within us and surrounds us like the water around a fish. It impacts our lives at every moment and in every relationship, and this impact is from the inside out. We experience the Creator Spirit in nature when we feel the warm sun as we walk on the lake shore at sunrise and in the harvest moon rising in the fall sky. We experience God in the loving presence of our families and in the feelings of belonging to a neighborhood or a faith community. We experience inner presence of Mystery in the quiet of prayer, in the exultation of life in a newborn, and in the deep peace that comes from the sense of the infinite within us. We can also discover some sense of God's presence in the negative experiences of life such as the power of a tornado ripping through a city, or the struggle to rebuild a broken family, or the grief over the death of a loved one. God is present in such tragic events, not as one who is the direct cause of these tragedies, but as one who suffers with us, supports us, and gives us new courage and new life in the face of adversity. Spirituality is a field that is "invisible, intangible, inaudible, tasteless, and odorless," and yet it is the most powerful force in our lives whether we are aware of it or not.

The spirituality of *internal causality* can be described as cocreativity. Typically the Jewish-Christian tradition imagines God as the external cause of creation and as one who impacts the lives of individuals and communities from without. This is the image of a transcendent God or what John Shea calls the interventionist God.[28] As noted earlier in this chapter, seeing through the prism of the new paradigm, we can use the image of an internal unfolding of God's power and presence (God's causality) within the whole of creation. This is the image of an immanent God, or what Shea calls the

---

[27] Jaworski, Joseph, *Synchronicity: The Inner Path of Leadership*, San Francisco, Berrett-Koehler Publishers, 1996, pp. 149–150.

[28] For a more extensive treatment of the interventionist God and the intentional God, see John Shea, *Stories of God*, Chicago, Thomas More Press, 1978, pp. 89–116.

intentional God. God impacts the evolutionary process not so much by intervening in creation as an external cause, but as an internal cause through which God's intention and purpose for creation is fulfilled.

This internal causality of God does not deny the dynamic and collaborative role of all creation in the evolutionary process, but it calls us to a deeper awareness of the cocreative dimension of this process. In the words of O'Murchu, "One of the major shifts in consciousness required for our time is that we belong to the evolutionary cocreative process, and it is in rediscovering our mutual interdependence with the cosmos, and particularly with planet Earth, that we will begin to reclaim our spiritual identity."[29] Thus the unfolding of the entire universe from within is the internal cocreative presence of the Creator Spirit in all of creation, and the emergence of the human spirit is the result of the internal cocreative presence and extravagant love of God. This way of understanding creation gives us a deeper personal awareness of the intimate presence of God within creation and within the whole of our life. Elizabeth Johnson describes this internal causality in a beautifully poetic way.

> The One who blows the wild wind of life, who fires the blaze of being, who gives birth to the world, or who midwifes it into existence does not stand over against it or rule it hierarchically from afar but dwells in intimate, quickening relationship with humanity and the life of the earth. . . . Enfolding and unfolding the universe, the Spirit is holy mystery "over all and through all and in all" (Eph. 4:6).[30]

The spirituality of internal causality and cocreativity is expressed in the following prayer, my paraphrase of Psalm 16, that has become my constant refrain.

> I am sure God is here, right inside me.
> I cannot be shaken.
> So my heart rejoices,
> My body thrills with life,
> My whole being rests secure.
> O God, show me the road to life;
> Boundless joy at your side forever.

Spirituality of Death and Resurrection.   As we have seen above the defining moment in the story of Jesus is his death and resurrection. Likewise, death and resurrection is the defining reality in the story of the cosmos, the story of our earth, the story of human society and the church, and our individual stories. In the cosmos the massive explosion of a supernova leads to the formation of the heavy metals, an essential element in the development

---

[29] O'Murchu, *Reclaiming Spirituality*, p. 41.

[30] Johnson, Elizabeth, *Women, Earth, and Creator Spirit*, New York, Paulist Press, 1993, p. 57.

of life. In the story of the earth, mass extinctions of species and the ice ages left the earth and its populations devastated, but later this "death" of the earth's inhabitants brought about a flourishing of new species and creative new communities of species. In our own days the destruction following the volcanic eruption of Mount St. Helens and the fire damage in Yellowstone Park brought about a rejuvenation of plant and animal life. Each year we experience the seeming death of trees and plant life during the winter and the inevitable rebirth of the earth's beauty in the springtime.

Human societies and the church often share in the same death and resurrection experience. The fall of Jerusalem in 587 B.C.E. and the subsequent exile became a creative source of new life and new messianic hope as found in Second Isaiah, Chapters 40–66. Even the terrible violence of war will, at times, bring out the new powers of renewal within a society. The neighborhood violence found in many cities will force us to reexamine the broader violence in our political and economic systems, and it will call us to transform the very systems that are the roots of the violence. Even in the lives of individuals the experience of the "dark night of the soul" becomes the source of new light and a deeper spirituality. Often in my own ministry, when people share their stories of struggling with addiction or domestic abuse, with divorce and ruptured relationships, with doubt and confusion about their faith, I can rejoice with them because the very recognition of these "deaths" and a willingness to deal with them are the first signs of resurrection.

I am not suggesting that we should become passive in the presence of the many faces of death in nature and in human society. It is easy to say, "Why bother about these tragedies? Why not just let evil make its way, eventually it will come full circle and God will take care of it?" (There were some Christians in the early centuries of the church who asked others to club them to death so they could go to heaven!) I am suggesting that we must accept the inevitability of natural disasters and human evil. I am suggesting that we use all of our abilities to avoid natural disasters by living in tune with the earth, and to prevent the conditions leading to human violence and destruction. But I am also suggesting that even in the worst of circumstances *new life will win out.*

The spirituality of death and resurrection has already been discussed in terms of the chaos theory and the theory of dissipative structures in Chapter 1, and in Chapter 2 in the section on chaos, darkness, and the shadow side. The spirituality of death and resurrection can also be found in Chapter 3 in the section on the earth as tomb or womb, in which the tomb was seen as patriarchy and the womb was seen as ecofeminism. The spirituality of death and resurrection informs not only our personal spirituality but also the future of our society and our church.

We cannot address the future in a serious or comprehensive way without embracing the dark and perilous threat that hangs over us as a human and planetary species. And in quantum terms, we are compelled to assert what seems initially to be an outrageous claim: a radically new future demands the destruction and death of the old reality. It is from the dying seeds that new life sprouts forth. Destruction becomes a precondition for reconstruction; disintegration undergirds reintegration; Calvary is a prerequisite for resurrection.[31]

The entire cosmos from its beginning fifteen billion years ago has a spiritual dimension because of the presence of the Creator Spirit, and human spirituality emerged about three million years ago with the gradual development of human consciousness. But what about institutional religion that seems to have begun only about five thousand years ago? What is the relationship between spirituality and religion? It appears that religion cannot be the originating source of spirituality, because spirituality is the more basic and fundamental reality. Does that mean that spirituality is the origin of religion? Or is religion simply the result of a particular social and cultural setting?

SPIRITUALITY AND RELIGION

The word "religion" has many different meanings for different people in different contexts. For example, in an article in *Atlantic Monthly* entitled "The Biological Basis of Morality," Edward Wilson uses the word *religion* in a very broad sense that includes not only contemporary organized religions but ancient tribal religions. "The tribalistic roots of religion are similar to those of moral reasoning and may be identical. Religious rites, such as burial ceremonies, are very old."[32] He sees religion as an essential dimension of any culture and as an instinctual behavior pattern much as we saw spirituality emerging from the beginnings of consciousness.[33] This would seem to *equate religion and spirituality.*

Religion in current Western society, as part of a general tendency toward privatization, has moved from being an organized community toward becoming a personal choice of the individual. *Religion becomes not a community but a personal belief system.* Danah Zohar in her book *The Quantum Society* describes this reality.

> Religion itself has not escaped this privatization. It, too, has been marginalized, its once overarching values now a matter of private belief, even of private choice. . . . Flooded with choice and aware that all these choices are available to us, we can move from one religious belief system to another, sometimes in an ephemeral or shallow way. Among the potpourri of religions now available to which

---

[31] O'Murchu, *Quantum Theology,* p. 181.

[32] Wilson, Edward O., "The Biological Basis of Morality," in *Atlantic Monthly,* April 1998, p. 65.

[33] See Wilson, "The Biological Basis of Morality," p. 64.

any one of us might give our (limited) adherence, there is none that all of us can share as the underlying basis for our common social reality.[34]

None of these authors distinguishes clearly between religion and spirituality, but they see religion either as an instinctual part of the human species or as the private choice of a belief system. Diarmuid O'Murchu, however, does make a clear distinction between spirituality and religion and proposes that formal religion began about 4,500 years ago during the period of the Agricultural Revolution.

Our spiritual story as a human species is at least 70,000 years old; by comparison, the formal religions have existed for a mere 4,500 years. At the outset, therefore, I wish to establish the centrally important distinction between spirituality and religion. The latter refers to those formally institutionalized structures, rituals and beliefs which belong to one or other of the official religious systems, which include Hinduism, Buddhism, Judaism, Christianity, Islam, Sikhism, etc. Spirituality concerns an ancient and primal search for meaning that is as old as humanity itself and . . . belongs—as an inherent energy—to the evolutionary unfolding of creation itself.[35]

O'Murchu's view is that spirituality is inherent to the human condition whereas religion serves a temporary and social purpose. Religion arose as part of the ethos of the Agricultural Revolution, a time when humans attempted to exercise control over the forces of nature and a time when patriarchal structures began to emerge. Beyond that, according to O'Murchu, "We humans tried to conquer and control the Godhead itself, that divine, mysterious force, that fascinates, puzzles, and frightens us. And how did we decide to do it? *By inventing religion!*"[36]

Formal institutionalized religion is something that arises out of a particular cultural setting, but, according to O'Murchu, it is only a temporary stage of human evolution.

That religion should have arisen as part of the ethos of the Agricultural Revolution is understandable. One could even argue that it was appropriate and necessary for that phase of our evolution as a human species. What we cannot escape is that we as a species have outlived that phase of our evolutionary development.[37]

---

[34] Zohar, Danah, and Ian Marshall, *The Quantum Society: Mind, Physics, and a New Social Vision,* New York, Quill/William Morrow, 1994, pp. 271–272.

[35] O'Murchu, *Reclaiming Spirituality,* p. vii.

[36] O'Murchu, *Quantum Theology,* p. 11 (emphasis original).

[37] O'Murchu, *Quantum Theology,* pp. 11–12.

O'Murchu's view of society is overly negative because it focuses on only the destructive aspects of patriarchy, and it is an overly negative view of religion because it sees religion as a contingent and short-lived aspect of spirituality. Moreover, he does not deal adequately with the community dimension of spirituality. True spirituality, as found throughout the evolution of the human species, always involves a community within which it grows and develops. It is not something privatized and individual, and it is not merely an internal reality. Human spirituality, like human consciousness, is a web of relationships that nourishes and guides and inspires us as we walk the journey of life hand in hand as a people of God, a community of the Spirit, and, for us as Christians, the Body of Christ.

My own view of the future of religion and spirituality is more in line with that of Thomas Berry.

> Any effective response to these issues [raised by the new cosmology] requires a religious context, but . . . the existing religious traditions are too distant from our new sense of the universe to be adequate to the task that is before us. We cannot do without the traditional religions, but they cannot presently do what needs to be done. We need a new type of religious orientation. This must, in my view, emerge from our new story of the universe. This constitutes, it seems, a new revelatory experience that can be understood as soon as we recognize that the evolutionary process is from the beginning a spiritual as well as a physical process.[38]

A healthy sense of religion will unfold from the deepest spiritual dimension of the universe. It will involve the discovery of a new paradigm, and a new way of thinking, that integrates the spirituality of our ancestors, the spirituality of Jesus, and the spirituality of the new creation story. A healthy sense of religion will maintain its usefulness if it takes as its purpose the development of the spirituality of the community by providing rituals that express its inner life and foster its continual growth in the Spirit. A healthy sense of religion will involve a sacramental community that helps people find images, rituals, and symbols, both new and old, to express their self-awareness, their awareness of God within, and their awareness of Jesus who embodies the reality of "God with us." A healthy sense of religion will contribute to the fullness of life for all people by becoming a servant community built on love, justice, and service.

RITUALS, SYMBOLS, AND SACRAMENTS

All over the world people perform rituals; and, from the archaeological evidence, it looks as if they always have. I find this an amazing fact. Most people in our society are not educated to think that the performance of rituals is

---

[38] Berry, Thomas, *The Dream of the Earth,* San Francisco, Sierra Club Books, 1988, p. 87.

as characteristic of human beings as is speaking language and living in social groups; yet this is what the record seems to show.[39]

Rituals, symbols, and sacraments are essential dimensions of deeper consciousness, so much so that only with a vibrant and life-giving liturgical life will the church be able to foster, develop, and live out its spirituality and carry out its servant role in society. Central to the life of any religion are the rituals that express symbolically the mystery of the presence of God within the community. The depth of this mystery and of our relationship to God is so powerful that words alone are inadequate. As we have already discussed, communities have an inner life involving a communal memory and a particular energy field. It is only in symbolic rituals that the community can adequately articulate this inner life with its memory and energy field.

In order to rediscover meaningful rituals, symbols, and sacraments we must first of all examine the foundations of ritual in the creation story and begin to understand the crucial role in human life of ritual and performance. Then we will discuss three different but interrelated modes of performance: (1) the ritual dimension of performance; (2) the confessional or faith dimension of performance; (3) the ethical or social justice dimension of performance. Finally, we will look at the Christian sacraments in terms of ritual performance.

FOUNDATIONS OF RITUAL

Human rituals are rooted deeply in nature, as is evident from the fact that many animals seem to have an ability to communicate by actions that are very similar to rituals among humans. Often domestic animals will have a ritualistic routine in greeting a stranger in the house or in approaching their food. We are all familiar with the stylized mating rituals of many species. Animals of many different species engage in highly patterned behaviors that are akin to the rituals of human behavior.

In fact, as we look into the history of the human race, it is clear that the earliest modes of communication were not in the form of speech but in the form of rituals. This use of ritual as communication lasted for hundreds of thousands of years and changed only because the evolution of the humanoid line had the potential for turning ritualized behavior into spoken words that other species apparently did not. Nonverbal behaviors preceded speech and provided the basis for spoken language that developed only about 40,000 years ago. According to Driver, "If we did not ritualize, we would not speak. Ritualizing is our first language, not our 'mother' but our 'grandmother' tongue, and as such it is something we do not outgrow."[40]

Over the millennia this ability to ritualize, that is, to combine nonverbal gestures with the spoken word, became the basis of the social life of hu-

---

[39] Driver, Tom, *The Magic of Ritual*, San Francisco, HarperSanFrancisco, 1991, p. 12.

[40] Driver, *The Magic of Ritual*, p. 13.

mans, giving them the capacity to express the deeper dimensions of self-consciousness, a capacity that goes beyond that of other living things. To ritualize is to make a new *pathway* through uncharted trails, in the way Johnny Murphy and I, as young boys, with fear and trembling blazed a trail through the rough woods behind our homes. Our ancestors used rituals as a way of finding a path through their rough cultural woods to discover a growing sense of themselves as a species. They ritualized their experience of the mysterious powers of the earth that surrounded them. Ritualization has played a powerful role in the evolution of our species and the development of all its cultures.

A pathway first blazed through the woods by two young boys can later become a *shelter* in which they can escape the intrusions of their families. They repeat the rituals they developed to overcome their fears, and later they find comfort in these now familiar surroundings. Ritualization is a pathway, but, as ritual becomes more and more familiar and is often repeated, it can also become a shelter within which to hide.

> These two elements provide a way of distinguishing the words "ritualization" and "ritual" in reference to human activity. The former (ritualization) emphasizes the making of new forms through which expressive behavior can flow, while the latter (ritual) connotes an already known, richly symbolic pattern of behavior, the emphasis falling less upon the making and more upon the valued pattern and its panoply of associations.[41]

Both of these tendencies are present in contemporary Christianity. On the one hand there are those who sense the inadequacy of Christian rituals and liturgy, as rich as they are, to express the contemporary life experiences of space travel, the quantum view of consciousness, and nuclear war. They feel the need to improvise and find new ways to ritualize their sense of a new spirituality and a new way of life. On the other hand there are those who fear the destruction and/or loss of the traditional rituals and liturgy that have nourished the faith of countless believers. They feel the need to rediscover and strengthen the rituals that shelter them.

In the life of the Christian community, these two viewpoints must engage in open conversation in which participants will discover that at times ritualization and experimentation are called for, and at other times traditional rituals meet the needs of the community. Such dialogue will calm the fears of those who feel the tradition might be destroyed, and it will help remove the barriers to new cultural expressions. Both traditional worship practices and new liturgical expressions are necessary for a vibrant community. If ritualization (the pathway) and ritual (the shelter) can be allowed to evolve in open conversation, the tensions between these two viewpoints can become creative and not divisive.

---

[41] Driver, *The Magic of Ritual*, p. 30.

THE RITUAL DIMENSION OF PERFORMANCE

In many ways ritual is the cousin of other cultural realities such as theater, drama, and music. Their common ancestor is *performance*. One of my Dominican colleagues commented that liturgy is drama and it is a performance. He went on to say that in the Easter Vigil each year Mother Church kicks up her pagan heels in rituals of fire, light and darkness, and water. Liturgy can be dramatic and theatrical, but the theater and drama are not, strictly speaking, rituals or liturgies. What makes true ritual different from other forms of performance?

Before answering that question, it is important to be clear about what ritual and performance have in common. Theater, drama, and ritual are all performances that involve symbolic and expressive actions and words; they all involve doing and showing. Moreover, they all involve *creativity*. It is clear that the theater involves creativity, but creativity in ritual may sound strange to those whose experience of ritual is identified with repetitive patterns based on external rules and regulations. But ritual and liturgy, although they flow from tradition, are influenced by cultural creativity and ethnic differences. These differences are experienced in the worship practices in Native American, African American, and Hispanic communities. The Asian Synod of Roman Catholic Bishops held in Rome in the spring of 1998 stressed the necessity of developing rituals flowing from the Asians' own cultural experience. Ritualization as a pathway is by its very nature creative and brings a life-giving dimension to ritual action. Creativity is as important to ritual as to the performing arts.

In all manner of performances the symbolic and expressive actions and words are characterized by deliberate, disciplined *use of the body*. The stylized performance of a Japanese tea ceremony and the exuberant display of African dancers both require a strong bodily commitment to the performance. No less does true ritual necessitate the disciplined use of the body. In many parishes it is often difficult to encourage people to this bodily commitment through practice and rehearsal, yet without discipline rituals become sloppy and distracting rather than vibrant and engaging.

Every good performance is also *infused with a spirit*, whether it be the spirit of Beethoven or Shakespeare, the spirit of the ancestors, or the Holy Spirit. Without this spirit there can be no life-giving performance. There is no good ritual without the spirit of the people and the spirit of the gods, and this requires full and active participation of the gathered assembly.

The common elements of performance are creativity, bodily commitment, and spirit, but what is it that makes true ritual different from other forms of performance? Driver answers this question in terms of the ability of rituals to bring about personal and social transformation.

> Rituals are not merely another form of art or play, although they are surely artful and playful. Rituals are perhaps the oldest, they are in many ways the oddest, members of the performance family.

Their business in society is to effect transformation that cannot otherwise be brought about.[42]

Attending a performance of Shakespeare's *Much Ado about Nothing* can be an entertaining and thought-provoking experience, but participating in a religious ritual, although it may be entertaining and thought provoking, also has as its fundamental purpose a change of heart and a new way of living in the participants. The marriage ritual brings about a change in the spouses themselves as well as a change in their relationship to families and to society at large. The large crowds attending a professional football game are enthusiastically involved in the action and are often entertained by the game, but the large crowds of people attending a Billy Graham crusade are asked to change their lives and become active participators in the action.

The purpose of rituals is to effect a transformation, and this transformation is effective at many levels. The baptismal ritual is a rite of passage in which the child, by being ritually plunged into the waters of death and rising to new life, shares in the death and resurrection of Jesus and the cosmic dying and rising within the whole of creation. In a symbolic way the child is clothed with Christ, that is, becomes a new member of the Body of Christ. Within the Roman Catholic tradition the eucharistic ritual involves the transformation of bread and wine into the Body and Blood of Christ, and at a deeper level it calls for a transformation of both individuals and the assembly as they become what they are—the Body of Christ and a community of the Spirit. Christian rituals are efficacious performances that symbolize and make present the transforming power of God in building up a believing community within a deeper web of relationships within the universe.

There is, however, ambiguity embedded within rituals in the very fact that they are efficacious performances.

Rituals are indeed necessary sources of limit, steering human behavior in socially desirable ways; but they are also inciters of extreme behavior, including murder. Prophetic voices, from the time of ancient Israel if not before, have warned that both religion and ritual are morally ambiguous. As they bring grace and provide protection from evil, so they may also bring falsity and the destruction of all that is humane.[43]

This ambiguity is found in the biblical story of Cain and Abel in which the outcome of the offering of the first fruits of the soil by Cain and firstlings of the flock by Abel eventually ended in the murder of one brother by the other (Gen. 4:1–8). Later, in the story of Abraham, there is the ambiguity of God's apparent command to Abraham to sacrifice his son Isaac, a command that, at the last moment, was rescinded (Gen. 22:1–14). In our

---

[42] Driver, *The Magic of Ritual*, p. 91.
[43] Driver, *The Magic of Ritual*, pp. 105–106.

own recent history there is at least one example of ritual gone awry—the mass suicide in Jonestown.

Is there any way of determining whether certain rituals are bringing grace and providing protection from evil or are bringing falsity and destruction? According to Driver, it is the confessional dimension of performance that can help to set the moral direction of rituals insofar as it verbally and publicly manifests the deeper consciousness of the participants in the rituals.

> Hence there comes a time when people need, for the sake of moral development, to assume responsibility for their rituals, and it is this which brings them to the confessional mode of performance. The confessional mode transcends the ritual mode inasmuch as the performers recognize and speak out (confess) their moral responsibility for the rituals they perform.[44]

In the ritual dimension of performance the focus is on ritual as an external manifestation of the efficacious power and presence of God's Spirit. It is now important to turn to the confessional or faith dimension of performance and discuss how ritual can affect the identity of the participant.

THE CONFESSIONAL OR FAITH DIMENSION OF PERFORMANCE

Perhaps the most commonly recognized example of the confessional mode of ritual is found in the Billy Graham crusades when, as part of the ritual, people are invited come forward and profess their faith and claim Jesus as their Lord and Savior. Many other religious traditions include a clear call for personal professions of faith as an integral part of their rituals, and in particular those rituals that have to do with rites of passage. In the Christian tradition many of the creeds grew out of the confession of faith integral to the baptismal ritual. To confess is to reveal oneself, to expose the heart.

Performances in the confessional mode are primarily concerned with identity and self-disclosure. Confession is not only taking a stand subjectively but demonstrating it publicly. Sometimes coming out publicly is the best or only way to make the subjective stand possible. For example, in the Alcoholics Anonymous program, an essential step in the recovery process is the public announcement that "I am an alcoholic." It is important not only to profess this fact in a meeting but also to share it with other people. In a similar way the coming out of people who are gay or lesbian discloses a part of their identity that previously had been hidden or unknown. It enables them to live out more authentically their own self-awareness.

The confessional mode of ritual makes something that already exists "really real." For example, a couple may love each other deeply and have formed a profound mutual relationship prior to the marriage ritual. In the marriage ritual, however, they publicly profess their mutual love and their mutual consent to a life-long partnership, and this profession is publicly af-

---

[44] Driver, *The Magic of Ritual*, pp. 112–113.

firmed by the official witnesses. The mutual love and relationship becomes "really real" in its ritualization. This profession becomes a public affirmation that calls the couple to a sense of responsibility to the religious community and calls the religious community and society at large to provide support for the couple. Driver explains this in terms of confessional truth.

> The performance of confessional truth is not only its disclosure but also its formation. Confessional truth is not simply a known truth performed but also the transformation of a partial truth into a truth more fully formed. Prior to its confession, such a truth is not entirely true, only potentially true. It becomes "true" in the act of disclosure.[45]

The selfhood that is realized in the confessional dimension of ritual is both personal and communal. It involves the transformation of the individual and the community within which the ritual is performed. In my parish experience I have seen the baptism of a child not only transform the identity of the child as he or she becomes a member of a faith community, but it transforms the family by bringing the family to a deeper participation in the community, and it transforms the community by helping it renew its own identity. The baptismal as well as the marriage ritual calls both the individuals and the community to responsibility for the living out of the reality of their faith.

The public and communal character of the confessional dimension of rituals helps to determine whether they are the source of life or the source of death. There is always a certain amount of risk in any ritual performance because of the awesome power and ambiguity contained within the symbolic actions. When the gay and lesbian community is oppressed and forced to live "in the closet," it is not only possible but probable that destructive rituals and lifestyles will be developed. When people who are gay or lesbian can openly and publicly claim their identity, their rituals and lifestyles call them to responsibility not only to themselves but to the larger religious and social communities. Religious cults that remain hidden and secret are those that can become destructive to their members; remember the Jonestown suicide.

Nevertheless religious communities, which seem to be open and public, can have rituals or teachings that are harmful to other individuals. For example, certain evangelical Christians believe that if you do not accept their interpretation of the Bible you cannot be a "Christian," and this can lead to elitism and divisiveness. In the Roman Catholic Church the exclusion of women from full participation in liturgical life as well as the use of ritual language that excludes certain people is also harmful and destructive for those excluded and for the community at large. But the fact that these rituals and teachings are public means that these communities are subject to

---

[45] Driver, *The Magic of Ritual*, p. 119.

scrutiny and negative criticism, and this can, and sometimes does, bring about discussion and eventually a change.

This personal and communal transformation and a deeper sense of identity does not exhaust the potential of ritual. Arising from the ritual mode, the confessional mode drives on to the ethical. It raises the question of what is the larger ethical impact of this transformation in the social and political sphere.

THE ETHICAL OR SOCIAL JUSTICE DIMENSION OF PERFORMANCE

The confessional mode, if it is authentic, always changes the relation between the self and God and between the self and the world, and confession of self-identity leads to ethical action in the social and political arena. This was evident in the civil rights struggles in the 1960s. It is no accident that these struggles took place in the context of a deeply committed faith community with prophetic religious leaders.

In the same way various women's groups emphasized the need for women to speak their identity in their own "voice." As women regained their "voice," they could ritualize their lives in a new way. They needed new images and a new language to speak their experience of God. These rituals led them to a deeper consciousness of their own dignity and self-worth that expanded into a desire to be free of social, political, economic, and religious oppression. External rituals beget a deeper sense of autonomy that bursts forth into social action and the call for justice.

Another example of the relationship between ritual performance, the profession of faith, and social justice is found in those who *demonstrate publicly* in civil disobedience. On May 17, 1998, the Gods of Metal Plowshares ritually enacted the biblical prophecy of Isaiah to beat swords into plowshares at a Pentagon air show outside of Washington, D.C. This was clearly a ritual performance as the five activists symbolically hammered and poured their blood on a B-52 bomber. One of the demonstrators joyfully announced to supporters, "The action was good liturgy." This action also flowed from a profession of faith as one of the demonstrators, a parish priest, explained to his congregation, "Put simply, the bottom-line reasoning behind my nonviolent resistance to war and nuclear weapons is my faith in Jesus Christ." It was a faith-based ritual calling for peace and the end to nuclear violence; it was calling for both a personal and social conversion of heart and of action.

In a similar way, as people absorb the new creation story, they celebrate that story in rituals and symbols, such as the national celebration of Earth Day, the various solstice rituals around the country, the dances and nature rituals of the Native Americans, and the powerful revised ceremonies of the Easter Vigil with their use of such earth symbols as fire, water, light, and darkness. These rituals embody our closeness to the earth, our unity in the earth, and our dependence on the earth. We are absorbed into a whole web of relationships with and in all of creation. These rituals call us to confess our new and deeper sense of identity, not as a Lion King ruling over creation, but as a member of the community of species sharing in the bounty of the earth. We are the earth become conscious. We are cocreators in the search for a new adult phase of human life that stresses collaboration and mutuality, justice and equal rights, wholeness and world peace. The full flowering of this self-awareness will guide us into social and political action for the welfare of our Earth Mother and the equitable distribution of the earth's sustainable resources among all creatures.

The three dimensions of performance (the ritual, confessional, and ethical) recall the faith journey of the priest named Peter described above as well as the spirituality of Jesus in terms of the three stages of human development from heteronomy to autonomy to theonomy. Peter moved from an overemphasis on the external expectations of others (heteronomy) to a new sense of self (autonomy) to an experience of God within and a desire to reach out to others (theonomy). Jesus moved from the external rituals of his Jewish traditions into a deep sense of self, symbolized in his baptism by John and the temptations in the desert, to a new experience of God and a passionate caring for the outcasts and the oppressed. Heteronomy and the ritual mode of performance deal with the externals which, if authentic, will lead to autonomy and the confessional mode of self-identity that will blossom into the ethical mode and action for justice. There is a close connection between communal rituals and personal development, and this mutuality can be found explicitly in the sacraments of the church.

THE SACRAMENTS AS RITUALS

> Ritual and sacraments are not merely inventions of formal religion. We humans are essentially creatures of symbol and ritual. We use symbolic behavior to express and communicate some of our deepest relational intentions.
> . . . A rediscovery of meaningful ritual and inspirational sacrament is one of the more urgent needs of our time, a prerequisite for rediscovering an authentic sense of human, planetary, and global community.[46]

Among the various rituals of the Christian tradition, the sacraments hold a primary place. The sacraments of baptism and the Eucharist (or Communion) are basic to most Christian communities, and within the Roman Catholic tradition there are seven sacraments that help ritualize the major turning points and events in human life. Baptism has always been the first sacrament of initiation symbolizing a rebirth in Christ and the incorporation of the candidate into the community. Confirmation ritualizes the power and presence of the Holy Spirit and the call for an adult participation in the life of the community. The Eucharist celebrates God's liberating power found in the death and resurrection of Jesus, builds up the inclusive community of faith, and provides nourishment for the journey. The sacraments of recon-

---

[46] O'Murchu, *Quantum Theology,* pp. 88–89.

ciliation and anointing are symbols calling forth the reconciling and healing power of God in the community. The sacrament of matrimony is the ritual celebration of the mystery of human and divine love embodied in the mutual love and commitment of two people, and in the multiple creative dimensions of that love for the couple, the religious community, and society. The sacrament of ordination is the ritual recognition that the power of the Spirit within the community is calling forth individuals for sacramental leadership within the sacramental community.

These sacraments are ways in which the Church of Deeper Consciousness expresses in symbolic actions its experience of God and its call to community. And these rituals should incorporate the three dimensions of performance—the ritual, the confessional, and the ethical. Each sacrament as a prophetic symbol should transform the individual and the community, should lead to a deeper confessional sense of identity, and should include the prophetic call to social action in the world. Michael Lawler points out the dynamic power of the sacraments, "A prophetic symbol, unlike a simple sign, is not just a bearer of information but it is also a provocation of personal action and reaction that affects the participant's total being."[47]

Unfortunately, in our times many sacramental rituals have lost much of their power and have often become ritual shelters in which people can hide behind the customs and practices of the past. Ritual rigor and regulations are in the forefront, and many of our symbols have lost their ability to provoke personal responses that affect the participants' total being. At a deeper level many of our current liturgical symbols and rituals emerged within the context of a patriarchal society and a patriarchal church, and, as a result, they are celebrated in ways that tend to alienate many people.

What can be done to turn our sacramental celebrations into powerful, transforming rituals? There are two directions in which we can move: (1) to modify our current liturgical celebrations in order to express more truthfully the reality of our experience of mystery; and (2) to reform our liturgical celebrations more radically by discovering new pathways into the wilderness of God's presence among us.

The Modification of Current Liturgical Celebrations. Many Christian communities are attempting to modify their rituals and to bring forth a greater level of participation within the assembly. The following is my description of a Sunday liturgy in one parish. As you follow the story be aware of the various dimensions of ritual (transformation, self-identity, and social action) as they are woven into the fabric of the liturgy.

> On a particular Sunday morning as the folks came into the back of church, there was a growing sense of anticipation. Dipping their finger into the water in the baptismal font, the early arrivals realized that the water was warm, a sure sign that this morning there

---

[47] Lawler, Michael G., *Symbol and Sacrament: A Contemporary Sacramental Theology,* New York, Paulist Press, 1987, p. 25.

was to be a baptism during the Eucharist. Then the level of excitement rose as the young couple arrived along with their baby, their family, and their friends. The family was greeted by other parishioners, and the family, with the exception of the parents and the child, found their way to the front pews.

The celebration began with the presider blessing the baptismal water and recalling the many ways in which water is a symbol of life. The blessing describes the saving presence of God in Jewish history, retells the story of the baptism of Jesus, and reminds the assembly of the role of baptism in the Christian community. Then the parents and the child along with the presider entered the assembly as it was singing the gathering song.

The members of the assembly and especially any guests were welcomed by the presider, and the readers came forward to share the Word of God with the assembly. Then the homilist, the staff member who had prepared the family for Baptism, came forward into the pulpit and preached about the themes from the readings and their relationship to baptism and to the newly baptized child.

After the homily the parents and the child, the sponsors and the families and friends are invited to gather around the baptismal font. The parishioners either join the family at the font or turn in their seats so that everyone can participate in the sacramental ritual. The parents remove all of the clothes from the baby and come to the font. The child is naked before the community. The parents, the sponsors, and the whole community join in confessing the faith of the community into which the child will be baptized. Then, as a sign of dying and rising with Christ, the parents immerse the baby into the water, and the presider pours water over the baby and repeats the ancient formula, "I baptize you in the name of the Father and of the Son and of the Holy Spirit." The assembly breaks into an acclamation of great joy, and the baby is anointed with chrism as a sign of its entrance into the priestly people and its sharing in the priesthood of Christ. The parents clothe the child in a white baptismal robe and, as they carry the child into the body of the church, the entire assembly rises and welcomes the newly baptized into the community with clapping and songs of praise.

On this day the Eucharistic prayer of the community was a communal prayer sung by the assembly with the choir and led by the music director and the presider. The focus of the singing went from the assembly to the choir to the leaders and back to the assembly. As the ritual reached its central point and the presider raised the bread and wine and sang, "This is my Body" and "This is my Blood," there were tears of joy among the assembly. The Eucharistic prayer ended with a doxology, the Lord's prayer, and a loving and exuberant exchange of peace and blessings among all the people.

Eucharistic ministers approached from various parts of the assembly for the communion ritual of sharing in the Body and Blood of Christ. The family of the newly baptized came first and then the members of the community, young and old, male and female, gay and straight, married and single, and people of all colors, approached the table of Jesus as a sign of our communal faith as a Christian community.

At the end of the communion ritual the parents and the child along with the sponsors came forward and stood on the altar platform facing the assembly. The members of the assembly extended their hands in blessing as the presider recited a prayer of blessing for the mother and father of the newly baptized. The presider then prayed that the child, who was clothed with a white garment, will put on Christ and keep that garment unspotted. The sponsors lighted a baptismal candle from the Pascal candle, the symbol of the presence of Christ in the assembly, and they were exhorted to keep the light of Christ burning brightly for all to see. The entire service ended with a blessing and a call to go forth to bring that light of justice and peace to all peoples.

Notice the focus on the assembly and its integral participation in each ritual moment from the opening song to the final blessing. Various people carried out different roles such as readers, choir, music director, presider, homilist, and eucharistic minister. The confessional dimension of the ritual was expressed in the blessing of the baptismal water, in the confession of faith just prior to the actual baptism, in the communal singing of the eucharistic prayer, and in the sharing of communion. The transformative dimension of the ritual was found in the white garment as a symbol of new life in Christ, in the deeper faith of the assembly, and in the call for all the participants to bring the light of justice to all peoples. The external rituals led to a deeper self-awareness and moved the assembly beyond itself to become a servant community to the world.

The More Radical Reformation of Our Liturgical Celebrations. It is important to modify our current liturgical celebrations, but we must go beyond this to a more radical transformation of both our liturgical celebrations and our sacramental system. Some of the reasons for this deeper need for change are found in Chapter 1 above, "The Winds of Change." There are three realities that call immediately for re-formation of the sacraments: (1) the new creation story; (2) the experience of women; and (3) the diversity of cultures in the church.

As we have seen the major theme of the creation story is the web of relationships. As the creation story enters more deeply in the consciousness of people, there will be a desire to express in symbols and rituals this web of relationships rather than the more hierarchical and patriarchal symbols in current sacramental rites. It will be important to ritualize our closeness to

the earth, our awareness of our role as a member of the community of species, and the value of inclusiveness in our language and our ritual. We can
learn much from other world religions and especially from the native peoples whose lives remain rooted in the earth and the mystery within the earth
family.

Many women's groups have tried to find new ritual pathways to celebrate their experience of God and of their Christian faith. Some have turned
to Mother Earth, Gaia, for inspiration, others have found a deep sense of
faith in Sophia and the concept of Wisdom, and others have struggled in
small and large groups to search out a pathway in the wilderness. A recent
Reimagining Conference brought together women and men from across the
various Christian traditions to experience ways of imaging and celebrating
God's presence. They took time to talk about the re-formation of Christian
rituals in the light of their faith. Ecofeminism will be a fertile source of liturgical renewal in the church.

As Christianity comes into contact with other cultures, both locally and
worldwide, it becomes clear how cultural diversity impacts our use of rituals. People now have the opportunity to participate in the rituals and prayer
forms of various world religions, such as Buddhists and Muslims, and Asian
and African religions. Even within the Christian communities there are significant differences, such as Roman Catholic churches with large, ornate
tabernacles and a Native American church with a tabernacle set within the
earth and covered by something resembling an awning made out of buffalo
skin.

The marvelous richness of ritual possibilities available to Christian
communities can be almost overwhelming. A question arises, particularly
among those for whom rituals are a shelter: How is it permissible for us to
bring into our liturgies these new images and symbols that were unknown in
the time of Jesus and throughout the history of the church? There are several answers to this question. First, there have always been innovations in
Christian liturgies from the time of the Gospels to the present day. There has
been a variety of rites in both the Eastern and Western churches. Rituals
have been constantly reformed as cultural changes appeared in various parts
of the world. An acquaintance with history shows the great creativity in the
ritual history of the Christian churches, and our culture with its massive social and religious upheavals will also eventuate in radical liturgical changes.

Second, we are becoming more and more aware of the surplus meaning
of symbols and rituals. In our awareness of a quantum world lived out in an
all-encompassing holy web of relationships, there are realities that escape
our ability to rationalize and to comprehend. It is just such realities that are
symbolized in our sacraments.

> A symbol is charged with many meanings, and once it has caused
> an interpreter to take account of its many meanings, its work still
> continues. For there is always more depth of meaning to be uncov-
> ered in it, more questions to be asked of it, because the abundance

and richness of its meanings are inexhaustible. The human mind can never get to the bottom of a symbol and be done with it.[48]

Symbols are necessary to grasp something of our deeper consciousness of reality, but our minds can never embrace the fullness of meaning in symbols.

This is a time for ritualizing. Ritualizing makes demands upon us. We must have a strong and vibrant spirituality that will guide us through the darkness and help us overcome our fear of the unknown. We must be willing to free the community for creativity and for the freedom to use the richness of diversity in our human family. We must constantly monitor our ritual experiences to make sure they express the living faith of the community and its memories of the living traditions. This will be a scary journey, but perhaps no more scary than the journey of our ancestors as they awakened to consciousness, or the journey of the Hebrew people out of Egypt, or the journey of Paul to the Gentiles, or our Christian forbearers as they set out to evangelize the world.

The Church of Deeper Consciousness has in its hands the richness of two thousand years of tradition, but it also has at hand a creation story and a new cosmology unknown and unheard of in the whole history of the world. It has a new vision of a fifteen-billion-year history of the universe and a sense of the total interconnectedness of the earth and its creatures. It has a growing sense of who we are as humans and what our role is in bringing ourselves and creation to maturity. The Church of Deeper Consciousness as a community of disciples has the responsibility to enter into this cosmic journey, to bring the good news of God's extravagant love and powerful presence to all people, and to celebrate that love and presence in life-giving rituals.

---

[48] Lawler, *Symbol and Sacrament*, pp. 21–22.

5

HOLARCHICAL CHURCH

All visible organizations arise out of invisible fields. Everything
and everybody is the subject and beneficiary of field influence.
All of us belong to a web of interrelations, empowered by an
intricate and mysterious life force. And it is the ability to self-
organize, more than anything else, which promotes and en-
hances life in our universe.[1]

This chapter recapitulates the theme of the web of relationships, but now
applies it to the organization of the church. It begins with a discussion of
three ways of describing church structures: hierarchy, heterarchy, and holarchy. The chapter then deals with the Creator Spirit and unravels the inner
sources of the universe in terms of the psyche and the self-organizing principle. The church as a self-organizing system is based on an analogy to bioregions with a vision of the reign of God as its guiding principle. The holarchical structure of the church and its leadership raises three major concerns: (1)
the viability of the traditional distinction between clergy and laity; (2) the
meaning of ministry; and (3) the role of leadership in a Holarchical Church.

HIERARCHY, HETERARCHY, AND HOLARCHY

If the Church of the Earth and the Church of Deeper Consciousness are to
fulfill their role in the human community, some organizational structure is
necessary. Over the church's two-thousand-year history its structure has
continually changed and developed, frequently in response to the cultural
situation in which it existed. When I first studied ecclesiology in the 1950s,
a major portion of the course and the textbook was given over to the hierarchical structure of the church focusing on the role of the pope, the bishops,
and priests. The first draft of the proposed Dogmatic Constitution on the
Church of the Second Vatican Council placed heavy emphasis on the hierarchical and juridical aspects of the church, including the supremacy of the
pope. The final draft of the constitution (1964), instead of beginning with a
discussion of the structures and government of the church, starts with a
chapter on "The Mystery of the Church" and a second chapter on the "Peo-

---

[1] O'Murchu, Diarmuid, *Quantum Theology,* Crossroad, 1997, p. 96.

ple of God." It is hard to overemphasize the importance of that change, which was a premonition of further changes to come. However, the final draft of the constitution, in the third chapter on "The Hierarchical Structure of the Church," still presents the church structures as a hierarchy.

The word *hierarchy* means sacred (*hieros*) structure or order (*arche*). It refers to what was seen as the God-given vision of a hierarchy of being, involving various levels with the angels holding the highest position followed by humans, the animals, plants, and nonliving things. This hierarchy of being was paralleled by a social hierarchy that placed the human over the earth and its other creatures, men over women, masters over slaves, the rich over the poor, the rulers over the people, and the clergy over the laity. This was thought to be the "sacred order."

In more recent times this sacred order has been challenged in many ways. Such a social hierarchy and a hierarchy of being seems to be the result of the development of patriarchy dating from about 8000 B.C.E. As we will see in more depth as this chapter proceeds, it does not fit well into the political and social developments of the last two hundred years or the vision of the new creation story that has emerged in the last fifty years. Ken Wilber points out:

> Now, the opponents of hierarchy—their names are legion—basically maintain that all hierarchies involve a *ranking* or dominating judgment that oppresses other values and the individuals who hold them . . . and that a linking or *nonranking* model of reality is not only more accurate but, we might say, kinder and gentler and more just.[2]

This dissatisfaction with hierarchy led many authors in organizational theory and in future studies to begin using two new words: networking and heterarchy. When first working with these ideas of networking I, so I thought, coined the term heterarchy and applied it to the structures of the church. Later I attended a lecture by a futurist in which he described the coming of a new society based on mutual relationships called heterarchy. After the lecture I asked him where he discovered the word *heterarchy*, and he said that he had coined the word himself! Another example of this development can be found in a work by John Naisbitt in which he writes, "It has to do with the deployment of power and that is shifting from the state to the individual. From vertical to horizontal. From hierarchy to networking."[3] Naisbitt also quotes an article from the *Harvard Business Review*:

> Brooktree is not a hierarchy but an information heterarchy, with multiple centers of power and hundreds of on-line work stations around the globe. The company has no one factory of its own but

---

[2] Wilber, Ken, *Sex, Ecology, Spirituality: The Spirit of Evolution,* Boston, Shambhala, 1995, p. 15.

[3] Naisbitt, John, *Global Paradox,* New York, William Morrow and Co., 1994, p. 45.

links its process technology with any number of chip fabs [fabricators] around the world.[4]

Thus the word *heterarchy*, meaning other (*hetero*) ordered (*arche*), entered into the organizational lexicon. It carries the meaning of complex relationships, networking, horizontal rather than vertical lines, all based on information technology. "In a heterarchy, rule or governance is established by a pluralistic and egalitarian interplay of all parties."[5] At the time I thought this would be the precise word to describe the structural dimension of a new paradigm of the church because it did away with the hierarchy of being and the social hierarchy that seemed to afflict the church.

Gradually, however, the concept of heterarchy began to lose its value. It tended to flatten out all of reality and to leave social structures without any organization. With heterarchy how can we deal with the reality of wholes that are made up of parts, wholes that are greater than their parts while still being dependent on their parts? How can there be a web of relationships, if there is no organizing principle within the web? "Heterarchy, in and by itself, is merely differentiation without integration, disjointed parts recognizing no common and deeper purpose or organization: heaps not wholes."[6] Social structures are not flat, and they are not heaps. There are some people who have a deeper sense of the sacred than others, some who have a power of healing, and some who have leadership qualities. Heterarchy is not the answer because it fails to deal with the complexity of nature and the diversity of gifts.

Where can we turn? I began to realize that there is a hierarchy, a sacred order, rooted deeply within the new creation story. It is not the hierarchy of patriarchy, which is seriously flawed if not pathological. This new sacred order is written deeply into the fabric of the unfolding of the universe. It is found in the theory of holons, which is a way of describing the holy web within the entire universe.[7] A holon is not a kind of matter or a particle or a wave or a process; a holon is a whole/part. Whatever exists in the universe is a whole/part; every whole is also a part, and every part is also a whole. This is true in the realms of matter, of life, and of mind. "It is for these reasons that Koestler, after noting that all hierarchies are composed of holons, or increasing orders of wholeness, pointed out that the correct word for 'hierarchy' is actually *holarchy*."[8] Holarchy is an ordering (*arche*) of holons (*whole/parts*).

In many of the social and religious organizations that we experience, we often find a pathological hierarchy, but it is essential to realize that there is

---

[4] Naisbitt, *Global Paradox*, p. 16, quote from George Gilder in the *Harvard Business Review*.

[5] Wilber, *Sex, Ecology, Spirituality*, p. 16.

[6] Wilber, *Sex, Ecology, Spirituality*, p. 21.

[7] This theory has been discussed in Chapter 3.

[8] Wilber, *Sex, Ecology, Spirituality*, p. 21.

nothing intrinsically wrong with finding a sacred order in the universe. The unfolding presence of God is found in every dimension of the universe. It is the burden of this chapter to describe the sacred order, or the hierarchy, of the inner depths of the church in terms of holarchy based on the theory of holons. In order to do so, we will go on a journey back to the earliest foundations of the church. Prior to the development of the traditional hierarchical structure of the church, there already existed evidence of an inner depth in the experience of the early Christians. Their experience underpins any past or future structures of the church, and it is described by the early church in the story of the coming of the Holy Spirit.

THE CREATOR SPIRIT

When the time for Pentecost was fulfilled, they were all in one place together. And suddenly there came from the sky a noise like a strong driving wind, and it filled the entire house in which they were. Then there appeared to them tongues as of fire, which parted and came to rest on each one of them. And they were all filled with the Holy Spirit and began to speak in different tongues, as the Spirit enabled them to proclaim.   (Acts 2:1–4)

PENTECOST

The Jewish feast of Pentecost was a time to recall and relive the experience of the ancient covenant of God with the Israelites, and in choosing this time as the context for the coming of the Spirit, the author of Acts describes the coming of a new covenant of God within the Christian community. The image of the driving wind heralded a new action of God's Spirit within the community, and it appeared "suddenly" and "from the sky" and it "filled the entire house." These words describe the overpowering presence of the Spirit and are reminiscent of the divine power that overshadowed Mary at the Annunciation and the descent of the Holy Spirit at the baptism of Jesus. The tongues of fire recall the great theophany on Mount Sinai: "Mount Sinai was all wrapped in smoke, for the Lord came down upon it in fire" (Ex. 19:18). All the people were filled with the Holy Spirit who enabled them to speak in different tongues. All the people were empowered by the Spirit to speak, and as the crowd representing all the nations gathered, "each one heard them speaking in his own language" (Acts 2:6).

The history of the apostolic church is the story of a Spirit-guided community and a Spirit-guided spread of the Word of God. This history is summarized in the story of the Pentecost experience told in symbolic language taken from the Jewish tradition and expressing the faith of the early church.

It is important to notice the universality of this story. All the people were gathered, and the tongues of fire rested on each one, and all were filled with the Holy Spirit, and all were enabled to proclaim the message, and they were heard by all the people in their native languages. The Holy Spirit empowered all with a message heard by all. This is reaffirmed in the speech of

Peter immediately following the Pentecost story. Peter uses the words of the prophet Joel to explain the meaning of this event:

> "It will come to pass in the last days," God says, "that I will pour out a portion of my spirit upon all flesh. Your sons and daughters shall prophesy, your young men shall see visions, your old men shall dream dreams. Indeed, upon my servants and handmaids I will pour out a portion of my spirit in those days, and they will prophesy."
>
> (Acts 2:17–18)

The Holy Spirit is the *biblical* way of explaining the power and presence of God within the life of the community, within the lives of individuals, and within the whole of creation. The Spirit is the inner source of energy, movement, and life. It is unpredictable and sometimes overwhelming. The Spirit gives knowledge, light, inspiration, and guidance; the Spirit is internal and relational, compassionate and loving. The Holy Spirit is eternal and unlimited, overpowering and life-giving, and it is the source of both diversity and freedom, as well as of unity and order.

The Spirit is *ruah,* a wind and a breath, present in creation, revelation, and salvation. *Ruah* is the wind hovering over the chaos at creation and the breath of life given to Adam (the earthling) (Gen. 1:1 and 2:7). According to Eduard Schweizer, "everything within this universe is permeated by the spirit of God, which fills everything like a kind of electric current."[9] The Holy Spirit is the driving force within the prophet, and it is the advocate, the spirit of truth who teaches, guides, and defends us. In the Spirit, God lives in the hearts of all people, inspiring them and calling them to action. The Holy Spirit is also the promise for the future and the source of new birth and a new creation. The psalmist says to God, "You send forth your Spirit, . . . and you renew the face of the earth" (Ps. 104:30). Schweizer tells us that "God gave his church the Holy Spirit as a foretaste and promise for all that was yet to come. . . . The Spirit acts as a liberating, reforming, and healing power in individual, social, and political life."[10]

In describing the Holy Spirit in the Jewish-Christian tradition, I am reminded of an important experience of synchronicity that took place while I was teaching in the mid-1980s. One semester I was simultaneously teaching one course entitled "The Holy Spirit, God and Gift," and a second course entitled "Religion and Adult Development." One of the focal points of the course on adult development was the concept from depth psychology called the *psyche*, which has already been briefly discussed in Chapter 4. As I prepared for and taught these two courses, I became excited by the realization that the biblical description of the Holy Spirit and the psychological description of the psyche were almost identical. Is it possible that these two concepts are in fact describing one underlying reality?

---

[9] Schweizer, Eduard, *The Holy Spirit,* Philadelphia, Fortress Press, 1980, p. 29.
[10] Schweizer, *The Holy Spirit,* p. 110.

THE PSYCHE

At various times in life there is a tendency to reflect on our past and to search for meaning in our lives. This typically happens as we reach a significant turning point such as our fiftieth birthday or the age of retirement. Often we discover a definite pattern in our life, and it seems as if there is some inner reality providing direction and meaning within the disparate events of our personal history. This has happened to me as I have discovered the central place of nature and the natural sciences in my life.

When I was a high school student, I had a deep interest in the natural sciences, and I helped to found a science club, called the Tri-Sci Club, for students studying biology, chemistry, and physics. Later I went to college in order to become a chemist and worked as a lab assistant in the chemistry department. In some ways I apparently turned away from this focus by entering the Dominican Order studying for the priesthood. Not so! During the years that I studied philosophy there was a strong emphasis on the relationship of philosophy and science, and my master's thesis in philosophy was entitled *The Nature of the Science of Nature Is Naturally Nature*. After studying theology for three years I was asked to pursue graduate work, and my interest in nature and the sciences continued to flourish. My doctoral dissertation was on the maternity of Mary, the Mother of Jesus, and a significant portion of it was concerned with the biology of human conception.

During my first year of seminary teaching I was asked to teach a major course on the theology of creation that once again called me to do more research on both the biblical and scientific dimensions of the creation story. I became concerned about environmental issues and was led to an interest in camping and hiking. For about eight summers I taught in an institute for human growth and development that brought me into contact with the issues of depth psychology. The science of nature became integral to my teaching and my life.

Later, when I became a parish pastor, these interests were broadened as I tried to integrate my awareness of nature and the new story of creation into my pastoral work and into the structure of a parish community. I began to bring some of these ideas into the rituals of the parish, and we integrated the new creation story into the Easter Vigil ceremonies. The creation story became the foundation for the program for the confirmation candidates, and, for one year, it was the central focus of the parish adult education program. And now I am in the midst of writing this book on *The Holy Web: Church and the New Universe Story*.

There is a definite pattern that emerges in my story, a pattern that I did not consciously choose or plan. Although it involved personal choices and a constant interplay with outside forces, there seems to be a deeper source of this pattern in my life. Ira Progoff, who has written extensively on the *psyche*, compares such an unfolding pattern with the growth of an acorn into an oak tree.

The human organism unfolds in the course of its growth toward maturity as an acorn becomes a tree. It moves unknowingly, and yet with a significant development of consciousness along the way, toward a purpose that is inherent in its nature, a purpose contained in the seed of what its nature is to become. What guides the unfoldment of the whole person is the unconscious psychic processes.[11]

The unconscious is often perceived as the home of the repressed and of the negative dimensions of the human person that are hidden deep within us and are the source of our mental and emotional problems. Although not denying the reality of a repressed unconscious, Progoff focuses more on the unconscious as a dynamic source of growth.

The primary quality of the unconscious would have to be seen as a growth or unfoldment of patterns of potentiality. Its tone would express not the backward movement of repression but the forward movement of a development by which the nature of the individual fulfills itself. . . . The question to be asked of it [the psyche] is not: what is it hiding? But: what is it trying to unfold?[12]

The psyche, which is "the directive principle in the human being which guides its growth from the moment of conception forward,"[13] is the driving force within us that teaches and guides us. "The *psyche* refers to the totality of the personality. It is a spaceless space, an inner cosmos that incorporates all psychic processes, conscious as well as unconscious."[14] It can be compared to the genetic coding found imprinted in every cell of the human body, which, unless it is impeded by an accident or illness, will develop in accord with that coding. The psyche is the inner source of unity directing both the conscious and unconscious, the inward and outward dimensions of the human person.

The psyche is also a connective principle. We begin to realize that the pattern of development unfolding in our personal existence is not only the unfolding of our individual life but also in some ways connected to a larger purpose unfolding transpersonally in the universe.

By its very nature, therefore, the functioning of the psyche tends to have a connective effect. As it brings about an experience of meaning within the person, it awakens in the finite being a sensitivity to the infinite. It leads to the realization that since this sensitivity is

---

[11] Progoff, Ira, *Depth Psychology and Modern Man,* New York, McGraw-Hill, 1959, p. 13.

[12] Progoff, Ira, *The Symbolic and the Real,* New York, McGraw-Hill, 1973, p. 71.

[13] Progoff, *The Symbolic and the Real,* p. 73.

[14] Welch, John, *Spiritual Pilgrims,* New York, Paulist Press, 1982, p. 66.

possible it must be that somewhere in the depths of the finite person there lies a capacity to perceive some of the meanings implicit in the infinite.[15]

We are opened to an experience of the infinite within us!

The psyche is the inner source of a web of relationship within the human person bringing a deep sense of unity both within and without. Just as the Holy Spirit is like a breath hovering over all creation, Progoff also sees the psyche as a principle operating in the whole of creation and supporting the web of relationships in the entire universe.

> The essence of the psyche is that it is the directive principle by means of which meaning unfolds in the individual's existence. It is a principle that operates not only in human beings but in sub-human species as well. The tendency is observed throughout the natural world that individual beings are drawn in a direction that fulfills the potentialities of their nature. The psyche is the faculty by means of which this occurs. When the principle of meaning, which the psyche embodies, is experienced intensely by an individual, it has the effect of opening in him a sensitivity to meaningfulness not only in his personal life but in the universe around him. He feels connected to a purpose that expresses itself through him in his personal existence and that also encompasses him in a way that he can feel but can define only with difficulty.[16]

The psyche, as well as the Spirit, is the inner source of energy, movement and life; it is unpredictable and sometimes overwhelming. The psyche, as well as the Spirit, gives knowledge, light, inspiration, and guidance and is internal and relational, compassionate and loving. If the Holy Spirit is the *biblical* way of explaining the power and presence of God within the life of the community, the lives of individuals, and the whole of creation, then the psyche in its deepest dimension is the *psychological* way of explaining the power and presence of God within the life of the community, the lives of individuals, and the whole of creation.

This way of perceiving the Spirit and the psyche is reminiscent of the way Thomas Aquinas describes the law of the Gospel or the "New Law." In his *Summa* he asks "Whether the New Law is a written law?" He responds:

> Now that which is most powerful in the law of the New Testament, and upon which all its efficacy is based, is the grace of the Holy

---

[15] Progoff, *The Symbolic and the Real,* p. 81.

[16] Progoff, *The Symbolic and the Real,* p. 80. Also Progoff, *Depth Psychology and Modern Man,* p. 32: "Human life has aspects in which it reaches beyond itself, . . . there are illimitable dimensions in man by which man is connected to the cosmos in more ways that he knows; and the central means of this connection is his psyche. The illimitable magnitude of the human personality in all the forms in which it is experienced by the individual expresses the ontological, the metaphysical core of life in which the human and the cosmic are essentially one."

Spirit, which is given through faith in Christ. Consequently that which is primary in the New Law is the grace of the Holy Spirit which is given to those who believe in Christ. . . . Consequently, we must say that the New Law is primarily a law that is written on our hearts, but secondarily it is a written law.[17]

Aquinas describes the New Law in terms of belief in Christ because he is speaking only in the context of the Christian community. In the light of our growing sense of the universal presence of the Spirit of God, it is possible to apply his words to all believers. In a similar way, when Jeremiah describes the "new covenant" with Israel, he is speaking within the context of the Jewish nation. In our times our experience of the reality of God's inner presence with all people enables us to see the inclusivity of this law and covenant.

But this is the covenant which I will make with the house of Israel after those days, says the Lord. I will place my law within them, and write it upon their hearts; I will be their God, and they shall be my people. No longer will they have need to teach their friends and kinsfolk how to know the Lord. All, from least to greatest, shall know me, says the Lord, for I will forgive their evildoing and remember their sins no more.

(Jer. 31:33–34)

The Holy Spirit, the psyche, the new law, and the new covenant are all ways of articulating God's inner presence in the human and the power of God unfolding in the story of the universe. According to Progoff, "The particular hypothesis with which holistic depth psychology does its work is that the seed of growth, the seed of creativity, the seed of divinity in man are one and the same. They are not separate from one another."[18] The deeper we probe the psyche the more we become experientially aware that the power within us is also the power of the universe around us. We become experientially aware of a power within us and yet beyond us that embraces the whole of life and the entire universe. Divinity is found in the transcendent depths of our humanity—a humbling yet transforming experience of cosmic awareness.

Now a new question arises. Does this transforming experience of cosmic awareness have anything to say about the way we structure organizations? Is there a sacred order, something akin to a psyche, that guides the growth and development of organizations and institutions?

---

[17] Thomas Aquinas, *Summa Theologiae*, I–II, q. 106, a. 1. "*Id autem quod est potissimum in lege novi testamenti, et in quo tota virtus eius consistit, est gratia Spiritus Sancti, quae datur per fidem Christi. Et ideo principaliter lex nova est ipsa gratia Spiritus Sancti, quae datur Christi fidelibus.*"

[18] Progoff, *Depth Psychology and Modern Man*, p. 15.

The Self-Organizing Principle

> The Earth is a self-organizing process of astounding complexity and achievement. It's a matter of intimacy: The closer we get to an understanding of the dynamism of the integral Earth, the more obvious it becomes that the four and a half billion years of terrestrial evolution resembles one vast embryogenesis. Something is developing, hatching, unfolding, and we are the self-reflexive mind and heart of the whole numinous process.[19]

In Chapter 1 we discussed the meaning of dissipative structures. You may recall the story of the configuration of a lecture hall that brought about disequilibrium as the speaker began his lecture. As the audience became more and more disturbed, they spontaneously reconfigured the whole space. Disequilibrium is necessary for any system's growth, but it also is a threat to the future of the system. When the turbulence in a system reaches a certain level, it tends to dissipate its energy in maintaining its current structure. "Faced with amplifying levels of disturbance, these systems possess innate properties to reconfigure themselves so that they can deal with the new information. For this reason, they are frequently call self-organizing or self-renewing systems."[20]

Thus, according to the self-organizing principle, systems seem to have an inner sense of direction and guidance that enables them to change and restructure themselves from within, and this dynamic is found in all aspects of the universe. A galaxy is a self-organizing system as it takes its spiral form while adapting to the tremendous forces of it neighbors and its inner dynamics. The water flowing out of a drain is a self-organizing system as it forms a spiral based on the movement of the earth and the force of gravity. A flock of geese is a self-organizing system as it makes its way north to its feeding grounds. The brain is a self-organizing system as it processes millions of pieces of information to form holistic dimensions of reality. And we are beginning to discover that organizations, whether large or small, are (or could be) self-organizing systems if they become systems with "shifting patterns of dynamic energy in constant creative dialogue with their surrounding environments."[21] Although it is important to realize that the self-organizing principle is fundamental to the whole of creation, our primary interest here is to consider this principle as it applies to human organizations and to the church.

One of the characteristics of such a self-organizing system is its flexibility and its ability to interact with the environment. According to Margaret Wheatley such a system "possesses the capacity for spontaneously emerging

---

[19] Swimme, Brian, *The Universe Is a Green Dragon*, Sante Fe, NM, Bear & Company, 1985, p. 133.

[20] Wheatley, Margaret J., *Leadership and the New Science*, San Francisco, Berrett-Koehler Publishers, 1994, p. 88.

[21] Zohar, Dana, and Ian Marshal, *The Quantum Society: Mind, Physics, and a New Social Vision*, New York, Quill/William Morrow, 1994, p. 190.

structures, depending on what is required. It is not locked into any one form but instead is capable of organizing information in the structure that best suits the present need."[22] But does not the system's very flexibility and openness to new forms make it too fluid, spineless, and hard to define? Does not a self-organizing system leave itself open to every wind of change and new fad?

Research seems to indicate that one of the basic principles of these systems is that of *self-reference*. Self-reference in an organization is similar to the psyche in the human person. It is an inner directive principle guiding the organization in its dynamic relationship with its environment. Margaret Wheatley describes self-reference in this way:

> In response to environmental disturbances that signal the need for change, the system changes in a way that remains consistent with itself in that environment. . . . Changes do not occur randomly, in any direction. They always are consistent with what has gone on before, with the history and identity of the system. . . . Self-reference is what facilitates orderly change in turbulent environments.[23]

Because of the principle of self-reference, openness to environmental information in self-organizing systems leads to a firmer sense of identity and to a development of clear and useful boundaries. Not only that but it becomes apparent that the openness and creativity of a system also affects the environment of the system. Self-organizing systems do not simply take in information; they change their environment as well. This is important because the church is called not only to adapt to its environment but to minister within its environment in terms of its own identity.

> In the world of self-organizing structures, everything is open and susceptible to change. But change is not random and incoherent. Instead, we get a glimpse of systems that evolve to greater independence and resiliency because they are free to adapt, and because they maintain a coherent identity throughout their history.[24]

Another way of describing this paradox of flexibility and coherence is to look once again at the theory of holons. Among the four capacities of holons there are two that are applicable here: self-preservation and self-adaptation. Self-preservation is the capacity of all holons to preserve their individuality and their own particular wholeness or autonomy. Because every holon functions not only as a whole but also as a part, it must have the capacity to accommodate itself to its environment. These capacities are found in an individual holon, such as the human person, that seeks to maintain its personal identity while it is adapting to its multiple external relation-

---

[22]Wheatley, *Leadership and the New Science,* p. 91.

[23]Wheatley, *Leadership and the New Science,* p. 94.

[24]Wheatley, *Leadership and the New Science,* p. 98.

ships, and in social holons, such as a corporation, that seeks to maintain its corporate identity while adapting to its external business climate.

Zohar and Marshall explain this same paradox of flexibility and coherence in the quantum terms of particles and waves. Speaking of individual holons, they explain that "at our core (our particle aspect) we are a recognizable but ever-changing pattern. At our 'periphery' (our wave aspect) we are a teeming web of relationships. Each of us is *both* self *and* other."[25] They see this same dynamic among social holons. "Communities, too, can be perceived as dual-aspect quantum systems. Like the individuals of which they are composed, each community has a 'core' and a 'periphery,' a particle aspect and a wave aspect. Each is to some extent both self and other, the other or others with which it shares a public space."[26]

Perhaps the most powerful dimension of self-organizing systems is seen when the stress between self-preservation (the particle aspect) and self-adaptation (the wave aspect) of any holon reaches a critical point, and it actualizes its capacity for self-transcendence. A poignant human example of this dynamic is found at times of personal crisis or loss, such as a divorce or the death of a child or spouse. This creates such a radically different external environment that the person's very identity is at stake. This is also a moment of self-transcendence when a new dimension of the person's identity emerges. In self-transcendence something novel emerges that results in a new and different holon. Self-organizing systems are also self-renewing systems, and this internal power to renew and transcend itself is found in all holons in all dimensions of the universe, whether in the physiosphere, the biosphere, or the noosphere.

What is the source of this power for renewal? As we have discussed throughout this book, the unfolding of the entire universe from within over the fifteen-billion-year story of creation is derived from the internal presence of the Creator Spirit. God is the ultimate source of the whole evolutionary process, and God does not create as an external cause but as an internal cause. And this internal causality is found not only in physical evolution of living and nonliving things but also in the development of human consciousness and human society.

As we have said above, the Holy Spirit is the *biblical* way of explaining the power and presence of God within the life of the community, the lives of individuals, and the whole of creation. The psyche in its deepest dimension is the *psychological* way of explaining the power and presence of God within the life of the community, the lives of individuals, and the whole of creation. And now we can add that the self-organizing system is the *organizational* way of explaining the power and presence of God within the life of the community, the lives of individuals, and the whole of creation.

------

[25] Zohar and Marshall, *The Quantum Society,* p. 190.

[26] Zohar and Marshall, *The Quantum Society,* p. 191.

This means that there is, in fact, a sacred order (a hierarchy) that can be found embedded deeply within creation. We see this sacred order in the holy web within and among all holons, in the subatomic structure of waves and particles, in the quantum view of consciousness, in the psyche, in the self-organizing principle, and most of all in the all-pervading power and presence of the Creator Spirit. It is now our task to discover how to use that sacred order as a means of articulating the structures of a new paradigm of the church. Can we discover a new model of structure and leadership in the church in terms of the Creator Spirit, the psyche, and the self-organizing principle?

THE HOLARCHICAL MODEL

> I will maintain that holarchy, as universal in nature, reflects a divinely intended principle of order in creation, which is applicable to society and the Church.[27]

We have already discussed two of the four characteristics of a new paradigm of the church: The Church of the Earth and the Church of Deeper Consciousness. The Church of the Earth is built upon the web of relationships as found in the theory of holons, the field theory, and the implicate order. This web manifests itself as a community of disciples with the greatest possible diversity with each person being a subject within the communion in the one body of Christ. The Church of Deeper Consciousness is a web of relationships built on a quantum sense of consciousness and flowing from a spirituality based on our ancestors, on the life and message of Jesus the Christ, and on the new creation story. This consciousness and spirituality is expressed in rituals, symbols, and sacraments. With this as a background we will explore a model of church structure and leadership based on holarchy and the self-organizing principle.

THE ANALOGY: BIOREGIONS

> On the contrary, the whole community is the temple of the spirit, the body of Christ. Unless the whole community is unfaithful to the Lord in word or deed, *what arises spontaneously from the community of Jesus is at the same time experienced as a gift of the Spirit.*[28]

Certainly Christians during apostolic times were not explicitly aware of the idea of self-organizing systems, but in Edward Schillebeeckx's description of the early church there is a sense of a spontaneous development of church structures as an internal gift of the Spirit: "What arises spontaneously from

---

[27] Nichols, Terence, *That All May Be One: Hierarchy and Participation in the Church,* Collegeville, MN, The Liturgical Press, 1997, p. 17.

[28] Schillebeeckx, Edward, *Ministry: Leadership in the Community of Jesus Christ,* New York, Crossroad, 1981, pp. 5–6 (emphasis added).

the community of Jesus is at the same time experienced as a gift of the Spirit." There is a self-organizing principle at the heart of Christianity prior to any model of structure and leadership in the church, whether it be sacramental, ontological, or legal. It is this principle that I want to explore using a new model based on the creation story and the reality of *bioregions*.

In recent decades environmentalists and ecologists have begun to think about the earth in terms of bioregions, and the following is Thomas Berry's description of the planet earth and its differentiated regions. We can see mirrored in this description the global church (the planet) and the local or regional churches (the bioregions).

> The planet presents itself to us, not as a uniform global reality, but as a complex of highly differentiated regions caught up in the comprehensive unity of the planet itself. There are arctic and tropical, coastal and inland regions, mountains and plains, river valleys and deserts. Each of these regions has its distinctive geological formation, climatic conditions, and living forms. Together these constitute the wide variety of life communities that may be referred to as bioregions. Each is coherent within itself and intimately related to the others. Together they express the wonder and splendor of this garden planet of the universe.[29]

This description is a useful analogy that points out the great variety of local and regional Christian churches, differing in culture, language, ritual, and theological expressions. Each church is coherent within itself and yet intimately related to the others. In the totality of these various churches, in the global church, is found the wonder and splendor of the Christian faith and way of life. How can we describe in more detail the way these bioregions (local churches) function as self-organizing systems? Berry provides an apt description.

> A bioregion is an identifiable geographic area of interacting life systems that is relatively self-sustaining in the ever-renewing processes of nature. The full diversity of life functions is carried out, not as individuals or as species, or even as organic beings, but as a community that includes the physical as well as the organic components of the region. Such a bioregion is a self-propagating, self-nourishing, self-educating, self-governing, self-healing, and self-fulfilling community. Each of the component life systems must integrate its own functioning within this community to survive in an effective manner.[30]

---

[29] Berry, Thomas, *The Dream of the Earth*, San Francisco, Sierra Club Books, 1988, pp. 163–164.

[30] Berry, *The Dream of the Earth*, p. 166.

This is a valuable analogy because the local church, most commonly the diocese, is a life system that is self-sustaining and self-renewing and that possesses within itself as a community the full diversity of life-giving functions. The six functions of a bioregion can also apply to the church.

The first function, *self-propagation*, requires that we recognize the rights of each species to its habitat, to its migratory routes, to its place in the community. Likewise the church must recognize the rights of various individuals and groups to express their gifts, charism, and cultures with one another. The church also propagates itself as a community by welcoming and integrating new members into its life. *Self-nourishment* requires that the members of the community, whether the earth community or the faith community, sustain one another through mutual love and care and through rituals and celebrations.

Just as *self-education* in the bioregion is accomplished by the remarkable feat of billions of experiments throughout the entire evolutionary process, so the church is a self-educating community by continually experimenting with different ways to live out the Christian faith and to be of service to all peoples. *Self-governance* is an integral functional order within every regional life community. There is a similar order in the church, and this order is not an extrinsic imposition, but an interior bonding within the community that enables each of its members to participate in its governance and to achieve that fullness of life expression that is proper to each.

The church community, as well as the earth community, carries within itself not only the nourishing energies that are needed by each member of the community, but also the special powers of *self-healing*. Within the church there are the sacraments of healing and reconciliation, and there are many individuals and groups who exercise in the name of the community ministries of healing and reconciliation among the poor, the sick, and the dying.

The final function of both the bioregional community and the church is found in its *self-fulfilling* activities. The earth community is fulfilled when each of its component parts, whether individuals or species, is able to fulfill its potential to the fullest. The church community is fulfilled in each of its component parts when individuals and groups are able to live out their faith to the fullest, and when various cultures and ethnic groups flourish within the community with all their differences and richness. The church community fulfills its potential when the subjectivity of every individual is respected and the contribution of everyone is received and valued, and when this self-fulfillment is celebrated in rituals, drama, art, and festivals.

"Each of these bioregions is . . . *relatively* self-sustaining. None is fully self-sustaining since air and water flow across the entire planet, across all its regions. . . . Eventually all bioregions are interdependent."[31] This interde-

---

[31] Berry, *The Dream of the Earth*, p. 169.

pendence as found in the communion among local churches will be discussed in Chapter 6.

A bioregion is an excellent example of a self-organizing system, but it differs in many ways from a human organization such as a business corporation or the church. All human organizations are made up of members who have consciousness and who make conscious decisions that affect the entire organization. Human communities can choose their own organizational structures and leadership styles, and these structures may differ radically from one another as, for example, in monarchy, oligarchy, and democracy. However, a new understanding of organizational structure and leadership is emerging from our understanding of self-organizing systems and the kind of leadership that promotes these systems.

The study of self-organizing systems in nature reveals a deep tension between disequilibrium and chaos on the one hand and equilibrium and order on the other. We have already seen this phenomenon in the description of dissipative structures in which the tension between self-preservation and self-adaptation leads to either self-transcendence or self-dissolution. This tension is described graphically by Alvin Toffler.

> At times, a single fluctuation or a combination of them may become so powerful, as a result of positive feedback, that it shatters the preexisting organization. At this revolutionary moment . . . it is inherently impossible to determine in advance which direction change will take: whether the system will disintegrate into "chaos" or leap to a new, more differentiated, higher level or "order" of organization which they call a "dissipative structure."[32]

As we approach the turn of the century, many observers of the ecclesial scene would see Toffler's description as a reflection of the current situation in the Christian church. With all the divisions within the church, the turmoil over doctrines and lifestyles, the dissent of theologians, it may seem that the church will either disintegrate into chaos or remain stuck in a stultifying rigidity. I am more optimistic. I believe all these signs are leading to a quantum leap into a new level of organization and a more powerful grasp of the Christian faith and tradition. The inner presence of the Creator Spirit, as seen in self-organizing systems, can and will, as Jesus promised, lead us to a deeper knowledge of the truth (Jn. 16:13). I share Marilyn Ferguson's more positive assessment.

> The continuous movement of energy through the system results in fluctuations; if they are minor, the system damps them and they do not alter its structural integrity. But if the fluctuations reach a critical size, they "perturb" the system. They increase the number of

---

[32] Toffler, Alvin, "Forward: Science and Change," in Prigogine, Ilya, and Isabelle Stengers, *Order Out of Chaos,* New York, Bantam Books, 1984, p. xv.

novel interactions within it. They shake it up. The elements of the old pattern come into contact with each other in new ways and make new connections. *The parts reorganize into a new whole. The system escapes into a higher order.*[33]

Based on the study of self-organizing systems, there are a number of ways in which we can help the current conflict and chaos to move in the direction of self-transcendence. First, we have to realize that in any system *power is energy*, and this energy needs to flow from and through the entire organization. There have been positive results of this flowing organizational energy in experiences with participative management and self-managed teams, and it is clear that what gives power its charge, positive or negative, is the quality of relationships.

> Those who relate through coercion, or from a disregard for the other person, create negative energy. Those who are open to others and who see others in their fullness create positive energy. Love in organizations, then, is the most potent source of power we have available. And all because we inhabit a quantum universe that knows nothing of itself, independent of its relationships.[34]

Thus the first requirement within the church is to foster the positive energy flowing through the system by restoring the primacy of love among us, by deepening the interactions and relationships within the church, and by increasing our active exchange with the world around us. In order to accomplish this, we need *to maximize the information available within the system.* In theories of evolution and in the development of human organizations, information is a dynamic element that must take center stage. Information gives order, prompts growth, and defines what is alive. At every level of the universal web of relationships there is a constant exchange of information within the various fields that keep the universe pulsing with energy and with life. The sharing of information is the underlying dynamic process that ensures the life of any organization.

Often within the church the open sharing of information is seen as harmful to the order of the church and as a way of misleading the faithful. Many times decisions are made without consultation, or people are censured without clear information about their accusers or the charges against them, or people are denied the opportunity for open discussion of controversial issues. Such secrecy leads to negative energy in the church, and it results in a climate of fear within the community. On the other hand an open system and an open sharing of information leads to positive energy and the building up of the community.

---

[33] Ferguson, Marilyn, *The Aquarian Conspiracy*, New York, St. Martin's Press, 1980, pp. 164–165 (emphasis original).

[34] Wheatley, *Leadership and the New Science*, p. 39.

The fuel of life is new information—novelty—ordered into new structures. We need to have information coursing through our systems, disturbing the peace, imbuing everything it touches with new life. We need, therefore, to develop new approaches to information—not management but encouragement, not control but genesis. . . . If information is to function as a self-generating source of organizational vitality, we must abandon our dark cloaks of control and trust in the principles of self-organization, even in our own organizations.[35]

Perhaps a comparison of the church with an amoeba is helpful. An amoeba, when seen under a microscope, has evident boundaries, but it does not have a stable shape—sometimes circular, sometimes oblong, and sometimes variegated. At various times and in various cultures the church, as well, has evident boundaries but not always the same shape. An amoeba, when it finds a foreign object in its path, will surround it. If the object is edible, it will be absorbed; if the object is not edible, the amoeba will reject it. The church, when faced by new ideas or new cultures or new theories, should not run or hide from them but should surround them and look at them from every direction. If the new reality is in accord with the church's deep faith, the church will absorb it; if the new reality is not in accord with this faith, the church will reject it.

The free flow of information can often disturb a system and open it to the challenges of the environment and social milieu in which it exists. In this situation how can the church maintain its identity? We often think that the best way to solidify someone's identity is to isolate the person from outside influences. A good example was the situation that I experienced in my early days of formation as a Dominican. In the novitiate and the house of studies we were seldom outside of the building and grounds in which we lived, and we had minimal contact with families and friends. Our only source of information was that provided by the Order. This same separation is often found in the context of seminary education. It has become clear to me that this regime only builds an *external* sense of identity. An *internal* sense of identity comes only through interaction with the larger environment and through the open flow of information. This openness can be and frequently is a challenge, and it can bring chaos and conflict. The outcome, however, is a more solid self-identity and identification with the organization. Wheatley gives a good explanation of this dynamic.

Openness to environmental information over time spawns a firmer sense of identity, one that is less permeable to externally induced change. Some fluctuations will always break through, but what comes to dominate the system over time is not environmental influences, but the self-organizing dynamics of the system itself. High

---

[35] Wheatley, *Leadership and the New Science*, p. 105.

levels of autonomy and identity result from staying open to information from the outside.[36]

The tension between identity and environment perhaps can be better understood in quantum terms of the wave/particle duality. Quantum stuff is both wavelike and particlelike simultaneously, and the nature of things has to be understood from both its wavelike and particlelike aspects. The organizational identity is the particle dimension that seeks self-preservation, and the openness to the environment is the wave dimension that seeks self-adaptation. A healthy church is one that is simultaneously both building its identity in response to its environment and affecting its environment in terms of its identity. This demands a continuous flow of information within the church and with its environment.

From this analogy to a bioregion, the church can be seen as a self-sustaining and self-renewing life system that possesses within itself as a community the full diversity of life-giving functions. It is a system capable of dealing with chaos and environmental change out of a sense of its internal identity and by maximizing the free flow of information available in the system. In the church, as well as in all holons, the source of its ability to maintain identity is self-reference that can also be called its inner vision. In the early church that vision is often described as the apostolic faith of the community that has the reality of the reign of God as its origin, inspiration, and orientation.

THE VISION: THE REIGN OF GOD

> The goal [of the new People of God] is the kingdom of God, which has been begun by God Himself on earth, and which is to be further extended until it is brought to perfection by Him at the end of time. (*Lumen Gentium*, #9)

How can we discover the role of *vision* in a self-organizing system? Sometimes we perceive of vision as a destination that draws us into the future. We develop objectives and strategies that will enable us to reach our vision according to definite time lines. Such a concept of vision can be helpful to an organization, but what if we looked at *vision* as a field[37] that needs to permeate organizational space, rather than as a linear destination.

> If vision *is* a field, think about what we could do differently to create one. We would do our best to get it permeating through the entire organization so that we could take advantage of its formative properties. All employees, in any part of the company, who bumped up against that field would be influenced by it.[38]

---

[36]Wheatley, *Leadership and the New Science*, p. 92.

[37]See Chapter 3.

[38]Wheatley, *Leadership and the New Science*, p. 54.

Thus vision as a field can be something in the present that influences the nature and the development of the whole organization, and it requires the active involvement of each person in the organization. A senior member of a large nonprofit foundation said that she always saw to it that the vision statement was in the office and on the desk of every employee, and she encouraged all employees to assimilate this vision and actively use it as a source of guidance and inspiration. In order to create a field, the vision must reach all corners of the organization, involve everyone, and be available everywhere because it is the vision that maintains the identity of the organization.

> We need all of us out there, stating, clarifying, discussing, modeling, filling all of space with the messages we care about. If we do that, fields develop—and with them their wondrous capacity to bring energy into form. Field creation is not just a task for senior managers. Every employee has energy to contribute; in a field-filled space, there are no unimportant players.[39]

What is the apostolic vision of the Christian church? Typically within the Roman Catholic tradition when we say that the church is "apostolic," we are referring to the apostolic succession of leadership in the church. Although this is true in the sense that the succession of leaders is a dimension of apostolicity, there is a deeper vision that underpins and guards the apostolic nature of the community. Patrick Granfield makes the "Christ event" the vision that is the directing idea of the church and that determines the purpose and identity of the church.

> The Christ event is the directing idea of the Church; it determines its purpose and shapes its identity. The Church, remaining permanently dependent on God's saving acts in Jesus Christ, preserves its character and authenticity insofar as it is faithful to its mission. The unity and continuity of the Church are maintained as long as Jesus Christ is the center of its memory and meaning. Believers, by actively participating in the faith, form a stable communion. They share ideas and operations for the development and integration of values that are intimately linked to their deep, personal, and subjective appropriation of the Christ event.[40]

The Christ event is central to the sense of identity in the church, but there is an even deeper and more operative vision in the preaching of Jesus, namely, the reign of God that is the overarching purpose, the big dream, the visionary concept, and the ultimate consummation of the life and preaching of Jesus. This is clear from the preaching and parables of Jesus, which he

---

[39] Wheatley, *Leadership and the New Science*, p. 56.

[40] Granfield, Patrick, *The Limits of the Papacy*, New York, Crossroad, 1987, p. 58.

used to describe his mission. According to Jon Sobrino, "The most certain historical datum about Jesus' life is that the concept which dominated his preaching, the reality which gave meaningfulness to all his activity was 'the kingdom of God.'"[41] The fundamental importance of this concept is also found in the way that Mark sets out the theme of Jesus' preaching at the very beginning of his public ministry. "This is the time of fulfillment. The kingdom of God is at hand. Repent and believe in the gospel" (Mk. 1:15).

When the early Christians talked about the apostolic vision of the Christian community, I believe they had in mind this powerful vision of the reign of God, and maintaining this vision is the underlying foundation of apostolicity.

If the apostolic vision of the Christian community and the field in which it develops is the reign of God, how can we clarify the meaning of this fundamental concept? There are many ways of explaining the kingdom of God. Every book on either christology or ecclesiology attempts to describe it, and there is a whole range of opinions expressed about how it should be understood. Clearly we cannot give here an extended treatment of the meaning of the reign of God, but we can describe it in broad strokes and show how it can become a living vision for a self-organizing, Holarchical Church structure.

One dimension of the reign of God is that, whenever and wherever God rules, there is both an inner change of heart and a change in the order of things. Albert Nolan in his work *Jesus before Christianity* stresses the fact that the reign of God takes place not in heaven but on earth. "The good news of the 'kingdom' of God was news about a future state of affairs *on earth* when the poor would no longer be poor, the hungry would be satisfied and the oppressed would no longer be miserable." Nolan also describes the reign of God in political terms by saying, "The fact that his [Jesus] way of speaking about a 'kingdom' is based on a pictorial image of a house, a city or a community leaves no doubt about what he had in mind: a politically structured society of people here on earth."[42] When God rules in the lives of people and of societies, there will be a visible and tangible restructuring of relationships, a restructuring that will be good news for the poor, the hungry, the sad, the sick, the lame, the outcasts, and the unclean.

Donald Goergen brings out a second significant dimension of the reign of God in the preaching of Jesus.

> The reign of God was primarily a way of speaking, one of Jesus' ways of speaking about God, about God in relationship to humankind, a circumlocutional, periphrastic way of speaking. In the end, the reign of God *is* God, God as near, or as coming in strength, or as ruling, but still God. Talk about the reign of heaven or reign of

---

[41] Sobrino, Jon, *Christology at the Crossroads,* Maryknoll, NY, Orbis Books, 1978, p. 41.

[42] Nolan, Albert, *Jesus before Christianity,* Maryknoll, NY, Orbis Books, 1992, pp. 58–59.

God was simply Jesus' way of talking about God, but God in relationship to us, God under the aspect of his power, God as active in
our history, God as reigning on earth as in heaven.[43]

Without minimizing the social and political aspects of the kingdom of
God, it is very important to see that the *reign of God is the presence of God
within us*. It is God's inner presence in the unfolding of human history and,
in a deeper sense, the unfolding of the whole of creation. The flashing forth
of the universe, the formation of our galaxy, and the birth of our earth with
all of its glory are the result of the reign of God and God's presence within
the universe. Thus the reign of God is a universal reality that is found in
every nook and cranny of the whole of creation. In a profound sense *the
reign of God unfolds as the holy web that binds us all to each other and to
all of creation.*

That same God is Emmanuel, God with us, guiding and ruling human
history. The difference is that the human has become conscious of itself and
has the freedom to make choices. The human has often rejected the rule of
God. Jesus was very aware of the personal and social evils of his time, and
he described those evils as the rule of Satan. Nolan comments on this in language that could easily be transposed to our own day.

> As Jesus understood it, Satan ruled the world. It was a perverse and
> sinful generation, a world in which evil reigned supreme. This was
> evident not only in the sufferings of the poor and oppressed and in
> the power which evil spirits had over them; it was also evident in
> the hypocrisy, heartlessness and blindness of the religious leaders
> (the scribes and Pharisees) and in the merciless avarice and oppres-
> sion of the ruling classes.[44]

The reign of God is present and active within all creation. The reign of
God overcomes the evil within and around us, and it results in a new creation and a new social and political structure that will be good news to the
poor and oppressed. How can we know where and how this reign of God is
manifested in our lives and in the institutional structures of our society? If
the reign of God is the guiding vision of the self-organizing church, what are
the signs of God's presence and reign? Are there any manifestations of the
reign of God that will clarify this fundamental apostolic vision and help
keep that vision alive in the church? I suggest that, in order to find those
signs, we look to the *fundamental needs* within our contemporary society in
relationship to the *biblical awareness* of the early Christian community. In
doing so we discover three basic manifestations of the reign of God: (1) reconciliation; (2) healing; and (3) liberation.

---

[43] Goergen, Donald J., *The Mission and Ministry of Jesus*, Wilmington, DE, Michael Glazier,
1985, pp. 229–230.

[44] Nolan, *Jesus before Christianity*, p. 60.

Reconciliation.   At the heart of contemporary society there is division, alienation, and loneliness. We have known the awful horror of war and the divisions that result from war. There are tribal, ethnic, and religious divisions that seem almost unsolvable. We know of racial divisions and violence in our streets. We are a nation of strangers who have lost our roots and become alienated from one another. The fragmentation and alienation we experience within ourselves is manifested in emotional distress, personal breakdowns, and the record sales of Valium. We have experienced an alienation from God, even the "death of God" in our times. The church, itself, is racked with divisions, oppression, and alienation evident in the number of people rejecting and/or leaving the church. There is a deep need for reconciliation within ourselves, within our institutions, and with our God.

The theme of reconciliation is found in the biblical witness of the early church. It can be seen in the way in which Jesus brought people together by eating and drinking with "sinners" and "prostitutes" and "tax collectors" who were the outcasts of society. It is evident in the stories of banquets to which all the alienated were invited. Reconciliation is also central to the teaching of Paul:

> So whoever is in Christ is a new creation: the old things have passed away; behold, new things have come. And all this is from God, who has reconciled us to himself through Christ and given us the ministry of reconciliation, namely, God was reconciling the world to himself through Christ, not counting their trespasses against them and entrusting to us the message of reconciliation.   (2 Cor. 5:17–19)

We do find God's reconciling power present in our society. Many people are being reconciled to the earth in their pursuit of sustainable agriculture and a simpler way of life. The experience of the Reconciliation Commission in South Africa is moving that nation toward a healing of the wounds of apartheid. Ecumenical relations among many Christian churches are breaking down many barriers that have long divided communities. Wherever reconciliation is found, there is the reign of God.

Healing.   The theme of healing is constant throughout the Gospels, with Jesus being portrayed as one with a power of healing so great that even to touch the tassel of his cloak could bring relief. The Gospel of Matthew summarizes this healing ministry.

> Jesus went around all of Galilee, teaching in their synagogues, proclaiming the gospel of the kingdom, and curing every disease and illness among the people. His fame spread to all Syria and they brought to him all who were sick with various diseases and racked with pain, those who were possessed, lunatics, and paralytics, and he cured them.
> (Matt. 4:23–24)

The healing ministry of Jesus was seen as the manifestation of the reign of God and the overcoming of the power of Satan. This healing power was often interrelated with a change of heart and a new faith on the part of the one being healed. At times, such as the case of the lepers, it reintegrated the person into the religious society.

The need for healing is very broad and deep in our society. There is good evidence for this need. The number of new medicines and drugs coming on the market along with their constant commercials on television indicate our "addiction" to drugs and our need for healing. The spiraling cost of health care and health insurance bears witness to the demand for healing. In some parts of our society seeing a psychiatrist is almost as normal as seeing a dentist. The physical and emotional illnesses of so many people indicate the need for healing in society, in our neighborhoods, and in our planet. The church itself needs healing from the wounds of power politics, clergy sexual abuse, and the oppression of women.

We do find God's healing power present in our society. Many people are discovering the effectiveness of alternative health care such as diet, massage, imaging, emotional counseling, prayer, and hypnosis. Neighborhoods are being healed through block clubs, affordable housing, and antidrug programs. Our churches are becoming a source of healing through small groups for those grieving death in a family, for those suffering from family breakdowns, and for survivors of domestic or clergy abuse. There is an overwhelming need for healing in our institutions, and where there is healing, whether physical, personal, social, or environmental, there is the reign of God.

Liberation.   Liberation movements are found throughout our global society from ethnic groups seeking freedom from oppression to the tribal struggles in the former Soviet Union, from the call for black power among African Americans to the liberation theology in Latin America to the American Indian Movement. The feminist movement is calling for a recognition of the social and religious oppression of women and the need to bring the feminine viewpoint into our culture and our churches. There is a growing climate of fear in the Catholic Church as the pope and Vatican officials are attempting to silence dissent, a climate that is oppressive and places unnecessary limits on freedom of expression and exchange of information. Those with power, whether political, military, or religious, tend to use fear of guilt and physical harm, economic sanctions and social oppression, as ways of maintaining control. In the process they take away the freedom of the people.[45]

Liberation from oppression is a central theme of the biblical tradition of the early Christians. Jesus came to set us free. "Jesus said to those Jews who believed in him, 'If you remain in my word, you will truly be my disciples, and you will know the truth, and the truth will set you free'" (Jn. 8:31–32). The celebration of Easter is surrounded by the liberation themes in the retelling of the story of the freeing of the Israelites from oppression and slav-

---

[45] See Wessels, Cletus, "Coping with Conspiracy of Silence, Climate of Fear," in *National Catholic Reporter,* January 29, 1988.

ery in Egypt. Jesus, as the Pascal lamb, sets us free from sin and death through his own death and resurrection. In the Letter to the Romans, Paul says, "Now there is no condemnation for those who are in Christ Jesus. For the law of the spirit of life in Christ Jesus has freed you from the law of sin and death" (Rom. 8:1–2). Later, in the Letter to the Galatians, he repeats the call to freedom. "For freedom Christ set us free; so stand firm and do not submit again to the yoke of slavery" (Gal. 5:1).

We do find God's liberating power present in our society. Many women in the church and in secular society are living out their rightful freedom from oppression and for the free use of their gifts and abilities. Ethnic groups and legal immigrants are reaching out for the freedom to live and work without the fear of arrest and deportation. Many people are claiming their freedom from unjust and oppressive laws. Wherever the spirit of freedom and liberation appears, there is the reign of God.

It is very important to recall that liberation, just as reconciliation and healing, must come from within. The oppressor never sets the oppressed free, and freedom given by another is easily taken away. The only true freedom is the freedom that comes from within when the oppressed overcome their fear and choose to be free. Reconciliation, healing, and liberation all involve a deep personal transformation, and they ultimately lead to a transformation of society. "This is the time of fulfillment. The Kingdom of God is at hand. Repent, and believe in the gospel" (Mk. 1:15). Reconciliation, healing, and liberation are manifestations of the presence of the reign of God.

The Holarchical Church is a self-organizing system guided by a vision of the reign of God manifested in reconciliation, healing, and liberation. There is deeply embedded in the life of the church, especially in its sacramental system, a source of reconciliation, healing, and liberation. In the church, as well as in all human organizations, a clear sense of identity and vision enables the church to interact creatively with any culture and any environment. The task of leadership in the Holarchical Church, as in any self-organizing system, is to communicate the guiding vision and strong values of the church, to keep them ever present and clear, and then allow the system to function with its own dynamics flowing from the abiding presence of the Spirit of God.

> If we allow autonomy at the local level, letting individuals or units be directed in their decisions by guideposts for organizational self-reference, we can achieve coherence and continuity. Self-organization succeeds when the system supports the independent activity of its members by giving them, quite literally, a strong frame of reference. When it does this, the global system achieves even greater levels of autonomy and integrity.[46]

---

[46]Wheatley, *Leadership and the New Science*, p. 95.

The coming of the Holarchical Church requires a new way of thinking because it is a new paradigm. It has solid roots in Christian tradition, but it is based in a radical new creation story and a new science that calls for concepts, images, and structures unknown to previous generations. This will demand a letting go of certain ways of thinking and acting, but it will also provide deeper insights into the meaning of apostolicity based on the powerful reign of God within the church and within the whole universe. It will require moving from a pattern based on a highly structured social system with a strong central leadership to a self-organizing system that emerges from within based on an apostolic vision with maximum local autonomy and integrity. This move calls for a new mentality and a deep trust in the presence of God in all creation. It calls for a church that is a dynamic web of relationships held together by the faith of the community.

Before we move on to specific concerns in the church, I want to conclude this section with a quote from Margaret Wheatley, a woman of deep faith, which identifies the fear that can result from a new paradigm, the risk that is involved, and the need of faith to sustain us. She tells us that we should not base our hope on visible, external structures but rather on the invisible, immaterial fields that support the entire structure of the universe.

> Those who try to convince us to manage from values or vision, rather than from traditional authority, usually scare us. Their organizations seem devoid of the management controls that ensure order. Values, vision, ethics—these are too soft, many feel, too translucent to serve as management tools. How can they create the kind of order we crave in the face of chaos?
>
> What if we slip out quietly along the curvature of space, out into its far reaches? What if, once there, we adjust our eyes magically to the invisible world? There we will see a plenitude of structure—potential structure, emerging structure—and we will stop doubting. We once were made to feel secure by things visible, by structures we could see. Now it is time to embrace the invisible. In a world where matter can be immaterial, where the substance of everything is something we can't see, why not ally ourselves with fields? For such a little act of faith, space awaits, filled with possibilities.[47]

THE CONCERNS

Shortly after beginning my term as a parish pastor I invited parishioners to join me after the Sunday Mass for a discussion of any and all of the issues that concerned them. At one point someone asked me, "What would you do if someone donated one million dollars to the parish?" I immediately made several suggestions, such as, renovating the church, improving the salaries of the staff and teachers, and paying off the debt. Then I turned to one of

---

[47]Wheatley, *Leadership and the New Science*, p. 57.

the staff members and asked her what she would do. She responded, "I would ask the people what *they* wanted to do!" That simple phrase, *ask the people,* is the underlying theme of all the concerns discussed in this section.

As we look to the future unfolding of a new paradigm of the church, there are three specific concerns that need to be discussed and integrated into the concept of the Holarchical Church: (1) the viability of the traditional distinction between clergy and laity in a self-organizing system; (2) the meaning of ministry; and (3) the role of leadership. It is beyond the scope of this book to treat of these concerns in depth, but we can lay out the context of these concerns and suggest some guidelines for further study and dialogue.

CLERGY AND LAITY

Any attempt to portray the structure of the church in the early centuries of its life is complicated by the variety and diversity of the written sources and by the difficulty of interpreting these sources out of each person's own experiences and biases. We can, however, discover a general consensus on the broad outline of the way in which the distinction between clergy and laity developed in the first six centuries.[48]

In the New Testament and during the early apostolic times, there is no mention of "clergy" or "laity." The whole believing community was seen as a royal priesthood, a holy nation, a people set apart (1 Pet. 2:9), and each member offered true spiritual worship to God. According to the Letter to the Hebrews, Jesus is the one and only high priest.

> The priestly function—the true priesthood—is peculiar to Christ, who has enabled all Christians to share in it. In the Christian communities of the first century, there was no independent priestly function that was exercised by a special caste or minister. The laity as such was not recognized in the New Testament, which speaks only of people, a holy people, a chosen people, a people set apart, a *kleros* entirely responsible for carrying out a royal priesthood and calling on each one of its members to give to God true worship in spirit.[49]

Schillebeeckx describes the situation as the church moved into the second century. "At the beginning of this transitional period the church's ministry was in no way detached from the community or so to speak set above it; ministry is clearly incorporated into the totality of all kinds of services which are necessary for the community."[50] In the ongoing life of the church

---

[48] See Faivre, Alexandre, *The Emergence of the Laity in the Early Church,* New York, Paulist Press, 1990; and Schillebeeckx, Edward, *The Church with a Human Face,* New York, Crossroad, 1990.

[49] Faivre, *The Emergence of the Laity in the Early Church,* p. 7.

[50] Schillebeeckx, *Ministry,* p. 13.

during the biblical and early apostolic times, there is no evidence for a distinction between clergy and laity either linguistically or practically.

According to Faivre, the turning point in the history of the community came at the beginning of the third century. "The term 'lay'—a word that we have barely encountered in the first century in the epistle of Clement of Rome—suddenly came into use again. At the same time, the idea of 'clergy' was formed and became used more extensively."[51] With Cyprian, an influential African bishop of the third century, the new position of the clergy precisely as clergy, a closed group within, and in some sense above, the community was solidified.

What has happened? How and why, over a period of two centuries, did the clear distinction between clergy and laity become an integral part of the life of the Christian community? The reasons are many and complex, but we can point out briefly some of the factors that were involved. As the number of Christians increased and spread out over much of the known world, and as Christians came into contact with the Roman empire—first as victims of persecution and later, in the time of Constantine, as a recognized religion—profound changes took place in the life of the community.

- Among the earliest Christians there were multiple charisms and ministries, but by the third century the eucharistic celebration became the central focus of community life. This gave the presider at the Eucharist, ordinarily the bishop, a leadership role of greater importance and visibility within the community.

- The bishop also became something of a father figure and an economic manager because he was the recipient of the financial contributions from the community and the one who dispersed the funds to the presbyters and deacons as well as to the poor and needy. A primary function of the layperson was to contribute to the community and the bishop became the steward of the wealth of the community.

- Although the traditional Jewish typology of priesthood with its high priest and a Levitical priestly family was not generally used by Christians in the first two centuries, in the third century it became widely used as a model for the church and for the distinction between the clergy and laity.

- The challenges to unity in the church from without (pagans) and from within (heretics) further strengthened the leadership role of the bishop as a source of intellectual and doctrinal unity.

- During this period monarchy was seen as the ideal system both for civil society and for the church. This is clearly stated in a quote from the *Pseudo-Clementine Writings* of the third century: "The great number of believers must obey one leader if they are to live in harmony together. For the means of government which, based on the model of the monar-

---

[51]Faivre, *The Emergence of the Laity in the Early Church*, p. 44.

chy, results in one leader being in command enables all that leader's subjects, through good order, to enjoy peace."[52]

Whatever the historical reasons, an important transformation took place in the church over the first six centuries. As Faivre illustrates this development, in the second century, "It is impossible to find a dependence in the early church of lay people on a clergy. There were only Christians and disciples claiming Christ as their master,"[53] but "During the period beginning at the dawn of the third century and ending with the death of Gregory the Great (604), a frontier that was increasingly difficult to cross was established in the church's structures between the clergy and the laity."[54]

The clear distinction between clergy and laity continued almost undisturbed as a part of the structure of the church. It became a more important dimension of the life of the community as well when, over the centuries, the church's institutional character became more clearly articulated. At the beginning of the twentieth century the relationship between clergy and laity was clearly articulated by Pius X, and it was seen by the pope as part of the essence of the church.

> It follows that the church is by essence an *unequal* society, that is, a society comprising two categories of persons, the Pastors and the flock, those who occupy a rank in the different degrees of the hierarchy and the multitude of the faithful. So distinct are these categories that with the pastoral body only rests the necessary right and authority for promoting the end of the society and directing all its members toward that end; the one duty of the multitude is to allow themselves to be led, and, like a docile flock, to follow the Pastors.[55]

In what way can the relationship between the clergy and laity be essential to the structure of the church? It cannot be essential to the very life of the church in such a way that the church cannot exist without it because the church in fact existed for two centuries without such a structure. Perhaps it was essential to the life of the church as the church found itself surrounded by a patriarchal and monarchical society. Without the rise of a strong clerical leadership the church could probably not have survived in such a society. But in a radically different social and cultural setting the distinction between clergy and laity may no longer be a viable structure of the church.

The first hints of this possible change in the structure of the church appeared in the discussions during the Second Vatican Council and in the documents that were subsequently promulgated. The Dogmatic Constitu-

---

[52] Found in Faivre, *The Emergence of the Laity in the Early Church*, pp. 85–86.

[53] Faivre, *The Emergence of the Laity in the Early Church*, p. 40.

[54] Faivre, *The Emergence of the Laity in the Early Church*, p. 150.

[55] Pius X, "*Vehementer Nos*," No. 8, February 11, 1906, in *The Papal Encyclicals 1903–1939*, McGrath Publishing Company, 1981, pp. 47–48.

tion on the Church (*Lumen Gentium*), with its focus on the Mystery of the Church and the People of God, hinted at the fact that the basic reality of the church is the mystery of God's presence within the entire community of the people of God. The hierarchical structure of the church was treated later in the third chapter, and it was seen as "a variety of offices which aim at the good of the whole body" (*Lumen Gentium*, #18). The code word in Vatican II was "collegiality," and in the postconciliar times there were great hopes for an international synod of bishops, episcopal conferences, and pastoral councils as a means of embodying the people of God as the basic structure of the church. According to Richard Gaillardetz, Vatican II presented us with a new vision.

> The vision of the Church developed at Vatican II represented a decisive move away from an excessively institutional view of the Church and toward an ecclesiology grounded in the concept of communion, which . . . has its roots in the biblical notion of *koinonia*. . . . It suggests that the Church is constituted by a set of relationships that possess a particular character. . . . This means that, as with the Trinitarian relations, all ecclesial relations will be 1) egalitarian yet differentiated and 2) mutual and reciprocal. This has significant implications, needless to say, for the exercise of power and authority in the Church.[56]

This future vision of ecclesial relations as egalitarian yet differentiated, mutual and reciprocal, has not been realized despite the honest efforts of many people in every sector of the church's life. Gaillardetz, himself, reaches the conclusion that the vision, after more than thirty years, has not yet been embraced by the leadership of the church.

> While Paul VI established the world synod of bishops, the synod was not granted deliberative power, as many bishops at the council had hoped. The authority of episcopal conferences has been challenged by the Roman curia. Pastoral councils, eagerly established in the 1960s and 1970s, have too often been marginalized in the 1980s and 1990s. Symbolic gestures suggesting a renewed vision of ecclesial authority have frequently been undermined by undue curial interventions in matters pertaining to local Churches, questionable litmus tests for the appointment of Church officeholders, and an intolerance for responsible theological dissent. It is difficult to avoid the conclusion that, in spite of important developments, the ecclesiological renewal brought about by the council has been only partially realized in the area of Church authority.[57]

---

[56] Gaillardetz, Richard, *Teaching with Authority*, Collegeville, MN, The Liturgical Press, 1997, p. xii.

[57] Gaillardetz, *Teaching with Authority*, p. x.

Given that there is a deeply felt need within the church for a change in the overall structure of the church resulting in ecclesial relations that are egalitarian yet differentiated, mutual and reciprocal, what is the impediment to addressing it? The solution to this problem is not found in simply improving clergy/laity relations or calling for more collegiality among the clergy and more docility among the laity. Something more radical is needed, something that goes to the very roots of the problem.

Perhaps the root of the problem is that relationships in a society comprising two categories of person in which one group has all the rights and authority and the other group allows itself to be led simply cannot be egalitarian yet differentiated, mutual and reciprocal. The relationship between clergy and laity is like a Gordian knot which, in Greek legend, could be undone only by the future master of Asia. Alexander the Great, failing to untie it, cut the knot with his sword. Vatican II tried but could not untie the knot because it did not deal directly with the clergy/laity relationship. I agree with Remi Parent that the only way to cut the Gordian knot is to do away entirely with the distinction between clergy and laity as it is now understood in the church. "To put it crudely, I think that the future of the clergy and of the laity requires that the clerics cease being clerics and that lay people cease being lay people."[58]

This is not only a very difficult task, as has become clear with the more modest attempts of Vatican II to modify the ecclesial relationships within the church, but it is a task that can be accomplished only by seeing current clergy/laity relationship as part of a complex authoritative hierarchy of relations that constitute our religious mentality. "If people think of God as a commanding autocrat, they will likely create an ecclesial autocracy, and justify it by reference to God's authority." [59] This network of relations can be seen graphically in the diagram on the next page. Each element is a passive object in relationship to what is above it and an active subject in relationship to what is below it.[60]

It is clear that in this religious universe the movement indicated by the arrows only goes from top to bottom, and the clergy/laity relationship is deeply embedded in this larger religious mentality. The image of God portrayed in this schema is a transcendent God who, in *his* transcendence, is the external cause of all that exists. God in relationship to all other things is the only active subject and all other creatures are passive objects. Jesus Christ can be an active subject only insofar as he is seen in his divinity as God, whereas in his humanity Jesus is seen as the passive object. Clergy are passive in relationship to Christ and are active only as they participate in a spe-

---

[58] Parent, Remi, *A Church of the Baptized: Overcoming the Tension between the Clergy and the Laity,* New York, Paulist Press, 1989, p. 6.

[59] Nichols, *That All May Be One,* pp. 10–11.

[60] See Parent, *A Church of the Baptized,* p. 28.

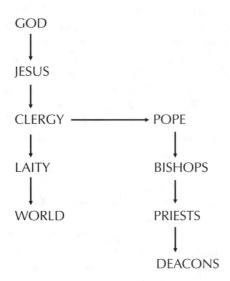

cial way in the divine power of Christ, and the downward flow of this power goes from the pope to bishops to priests to deacons. The laity are passive in the internal workings of the church, but the laity, empowered by the clergy, can be active in the world. The world is entirely a passive object waiting to be sanctified by the presence and preaching of the church.

Thus the Gordian knot is a much larger and a much broader religious universe than it seemed at first, and this knot cannot be untied within the current paradigm of the church. In my opinion the only way to cut the almost universal Gordian knot is by using the sword of a new paradigm, which is found in the Holarchical Church.

The basis of a new paradigm is a radically new creation story and a new science calling for concepts, images, and structures unknown to previous generations. It is a vision of God as the internal cause of creation who is immediately present within the world and unfolding in the fifteen-billion-year story of the universe. This is a vision that does not see God's presence as mediated from top to bottom through Jesus Christ to the clergy to the laity to the world. Rather the presence of God is the center of a web of relationships, with the power and presence of God expanding in all directions from within. The new paradigm is a vision of the church as a community of disciples with the greatest possible diversity in which all are treated as subjects filled with a deep sense of communion in the one body of Christ, a church that is not a pyramid but a web of relationships. As Parent says, "The church must pass today *from the uniformity of a clerico-pyramidal church to a church of communion.*"[61]

---

[61]Parent, *A Church of the Baptized*, p. 133 (emphasis original).

It is not possible to describe in any detail a Holarchical Church in which clerics cease being clerics and lay people cease being lay people because in the new paradigm the church as a self-organizing system unfolds and emerges out of the presence of God within it. We also know that, as we see in the universe, God emerges in many strange and unanticipated ways. Moreover, it is important to recall that, in terms of liberation, the only true freedom is the freedom that comes from within when the oppressed choose to be free. Thus, wherever there is oppression in the church, freedom will come when the laity themselves choose to cease being laity and the clergy, who can also be the object of oppression, choose to cease being clergy. To live out such a new paradigm will require a deep and strong faith in the presence and power of God. It requires the kind of trust described by Margaret Wheatley.

> I want to move into a universe I trust so much that I give up playing God. I want to stop holding things together. I want to experience such safety that the concept of "allowing"—trusting that the appropriate forms can emerge—ceases to be scary. I want to surrender my care of the universe and become a participating member, with everyone I work with, in an organization that moves gracefully with its environment, trusting in the unfolding dance of order.[62]

It is possible, however, to discover some signs of the new directions by looking at the meaning of ministry and the role of leadership in a Holarchical Church. If the church is truly apostolic, it will be guided by the vision of the reign of God as manifested in reconciliation, healing, and liberation. If the church is truly the Body of Christ, it will be open to all and will foster relationships that are egalitarian yet differentiated, mutual, and reciprocal. Within these parameters, ministry and leadership will emerge within the self-organizing system by the power and presence of the Holy Spirit.

THE MEANING OF MINISTRY

Several years ago I guided a retreat for the leadership and administrative team of a congregation of Sisters. At the opening session I informed them of an imaginary rescript from Rome indicating that we could create and celebrate the closing Eucharist for the retreat in any way we wanted. There was only one restriction—whatever we did had to express the shared faith of the group. They were excited and immediately started thinking about how to organize this liturgy. For example, one suggestion was that we use beer and pizza in place of bread and wine. This would be so much more in tune with the culture of the time. Over the next few days they mulled over this suggestion in the light of their faith. They began to realize that the Eucharist was not just a meal but a ritual memorial of an historic event, the Last Supper. It

---

[62] Wheatley, *Leadership and the New Science,* p. 23.

was a celebration, not just of this small group, but also of the worldwide community of believers for whom bread and wine is a more common and more basic food. In light of these two insights the Sisters decided to have bread and wine as the elements of the Eucharist. Many other suggestions were made and discussed in terms of their faith. The outcome was a Eucharist that, although in many ways very traditional, was a ritual that deeply expressed the faith of this group in its relationship to Christian history and the larger global community.

As we search for the meaning of ministry within a new paradigm of the church we need to be open and creative but always in terms of the vision of the reign of God that guides our Christian experience and our Christian faith. The search will involve an honest sharing of faith in an environment of freedom. The underlying assumption is that openness, honesty, and freedom will allow the presence of God to emerge within the local community and to energize the community from within. The ministry that flows from such a community will be validated or challenged by the extent to which it embodies the reality of reconciliation, healing, and liberation, and by its web of relationships with the larger faith community. Our concern here is similar to that proposed to the Sisters on retreat. In terms of the vision of the reign of God and our response in faith to that vision, how can the emerging forms of ministry within a Holarchical Church without clergy and laity be identified and implemented?

The first requirement in ministry is an awareness that we do not bring God to individuals or to our society. God is already present in the world. The task of ministry is *to discover the presence of God* within a believing community, whether within the local Christian community, within other religious communities, or within the civic communities that form the environment for ministry. Second, we are called *to foster and develop an awareness of the presence of God* in every possible way by helping to bring it into full growth and maturity for the welfare of all the people. Third, we are called *to challenge those aspects of our society and culture that obscure or conceal the presence of God* and are destructive to human community, the community of species, or the planet earth.

Over the centuries, multiple offices and ministries have developed to carry out these functions. As would be expected in a self-organizing church, the structure of ministry will be different in various cultures and in varying circumstances, just as different plant and animal life emerges in varying bioregions. However, in light of past experiences as well as current developments in Christian life, it is possible to discover certain common elements of ministry. Yet even these common elements will emerge quite differently in the variety of local churches. For the sake of our current discussion I will describe these ministries and the role of leadership from the experience of the North American church.

For any ministry within the Christian community there are three prerequisites: (1) the inner *call* by which the individual and the community become aware of their gifts and charisms; (2) the necessary *competence* to carry out particular ministries; and (3) the *consent or acceptance* of the community by which the ministry of the individual is affirmed within the community. This affirmation can be given in a variety of ways, from an implicit acceptance of the ministry within the church to a public installation of the minister to a sacramental ritual of affirmation, but some manifestation of consent is necessary for the authenticity of ministry.

The most fundamental ministries are those that embody God's presence in the church as a faith community, a servant community, and a sacramental community. Preaching, teaching, and evangelizing are ways in which *the faith community* is built up and the good news is brought to the world, and these theological and educational dimensions of the church's mission are essential to the building up of the community. How this ministry is carried out will be determined by the particular circumstances of each local church. Within *a servant community* pastoral outreach to the poor, the oppressed, the outcasts, and the grieving is essential to the life of the Christian church, and social justice concerns are an integral part of ministry in the church. Evangelization and pastoral outreach both deal directly with the reconciling, healing, and liberating dimensions of the reign of God. The church is also *a sacramental community*, and it lives out this sacramentality in the many rituals, symbols, and sacraments that have emerged in the long history of Christianity. From the earliest times the Eucharist has been the central ritual for the Christian community. The community gathered together to remember the Paschal meal that Jesus celebrated with the disciples the night before he died. This ritual meal was a celebration of the presence of the Risen Christ, a means of building up the community, and an expression of the deep unity of the church. The Eucharist also became a memorial of the death and resurrection of Jesus and the beginning of a new covenant with God.

Throughout this work the major theme of the creation story is the web of relationships. It is my hope that, as the creation story enters more deeply into the consciousness of people, there will be a desire to express in symbols and rituals this web of relationships in place of the more hierarchical and patriarchal symbols often found in current sacramental rites. We can learn much from other world religions and especially from the native peoples whose lives remain rooted in the earth. It is important for the Christian community as the church of the earth to ritualize its closeness to the earth, its awareness of its role as a member of the community of species and the intimate relationship of these realities to the death and resurrection theme found in the Christian churches.

The Christian community, guided by the Holy Spirit, has an inner self-organizing principle out of which all these ministries will develop and diversify in response to the environment in which the community exists. Membership in that ministering community is ritualized in the sacrament of baptism through which the believer is incorporated into the community and comes to share in the priesthood of Christ. There are many priestly roles for the members of the church. Whenever someone helps to build up and strengthen the community or reaches out to share the good news with others, that is a priestly role emerging from the priesthood of Christ. Whenever someone gives bread to the hungry, clothes the naked, or welcomes the homeless, that is a priestly role emerging from the priesthood of Christ. Whenever someone participates actively in the Eucharist celebrating the presence of the Risen Christ in the community, that is a priestly role emerging from the priesthood of Christ. All the members of the community share in the common ministry of the community in accordance with their gifts, their competency, and the affirmation of the community.

If this vision fails to recognize that the church is a *human* self-organizing system, there is a danger of romanticism and idealism. As we have previously seen in Chapter 2, the new creation story tells us not only about the beauty of the earth but also what appears to be the ugliness, the chaos, the darkness, and the shadow side of creation. Every human self-organizing system is limited and subject to inner conflicts and divisions. The church as well has had in the past, and will continue to have in the future, a diversity of opinions on doctrinal and pastoral issues leading to conflicts and divisions within itself. Tensions will arise as we live through these turbulent times in which there is a changing sense of ministry and a search for new ways to be of service to the church and our society. Like the apostle Paul we will find it necessary to live with these tensions and to trust the powerful presence of Christ within this self-organizing web of relationships called the Christian church.

> Living the truth in love, we should grow in every way into him who is the head, Christ, from whom the whole body, joined and held together by every supporting ligament, with the proper functioning of each part, brings about the body's growth and builds itself up in love.
>
> (Eph. 4:15–16)

THE ROLE OF LEADERSHIP

> The conventional view of leadership emphasizes positional power and conspicuous accomplishment. But true leadership is about creating a domain in which we continually learn and become more capable of participating in our unfolding future. A true leader thus sets the stage on which predictable miracles, synchronistic in nature, can—and do—occur.[63]

One of the most important dimensions of any human self-organizing system is the role of leadership. In our culture the very words *leader* and *leadership* are sometimes seen to be negative insofar as they express a relationship in which one party is dominant and sometimes oppressive. As we saw above in

---

[63] Jaworski, Joseph, *Synchronicity: The Inner Path of Leadership*, San Francisco, Berrett-Koehler Publishers, 1996, p. 182.

the discussion on clergy and laity, an active leader seems to demand a passive follower. As a result in recent years people have experimented with new language to describe the leadership function, such as enabler, facilitator, one who empowers, and so forth. Some have looked for a model in communities, such as the Quakers, who function almost entirely as leaderless groups. Others have developed models of small Christian communities as the basic parish structure.

These efforts at the reform of leadership in the church help to make us aware of new ways of looking at leadership in the church, and they are useful in certain situations. Yet none of these words or models seem to capture the reality of leadership as it is developing in the dialogue with the new science.[64] Like many other organizations the church, even a church without clergy and laity, needs a leadership function as part of its structure. The church, however, needs to reexamine its vision of how leadership actually functions because its traditional leadership roles are grounded in a structure that is often obsolete and counterproductive. We need to develop a deeper and more accurate vision of how that role of leadership might develop within a Holarchical Church.

Robert Greenleaf, in his book *Servant Leadership*, describes two organizational traditions.

> The first . . . is the hierarchical principle that places one person in charge as the lone chief atop a pyramidal structure. Nearly all institutions we know about—businesses, governments, armies, churches, universities—have been organized this way so long that it is rare for anyone to question the assumptions that underlie them. We see no other course than to hold one person responsible. And so the natural reaction to a call for stronger leadership is to try to strengthen the control of the person at the top. This reaction, in most cases, exacerbates rather than alleviates the problem.
>
> The second tradition . . . is the form where the principal leader is *primus inter pares*—first among equals. There is still a "first," a leader, but that leader is not the chief. The difference may appear to be subtle, but it is important that the primus constantly test and prove that leadership among the group of able peers. This principle is more difficult to find in practice, but it does exist in important places—with conspicuous success.[65]

This second tradition is very familiar to me because the government of the Dominican Order is based on this concept. The leader of the local or provincial community is called the Prior, meaning the *prior inter pares*, and, in terms of decision making, it is the local community that ultimately makes any major decisions. In the parish in which I worked, the staff also used this

---

[64] See Wheatley, *Leadership and the New Science.*

[65] Greenleaf, Robert K., *Servant Leadership*, New York, Paulist Press, 1977, p. 61.

second tradition as the model on which its leadership was based. This form of collective leadership brings about more informed decisions and provides the opportunity for a more creative organizational structure. Often in staff meetings someone would ask for a discussion of an issue in her area of responsibility. With the input of many different points of view and a free and open discussion, a solution would emerge that was more effective and more creative than that of any one person. According to Greenleaf:

> The major conclusion I have reached after much searching is that we have at long last come to grips with the liabilities in the obsolete idea of the single chief atop a pyramidal structure, and that henceforth the ultimate authority should be placed in a balanced team of equals under the leadership of a true servant who serves as *primus inter pares,* first among equals.[66]

At a deeper level, if we see the church as a self-organizing system unfolding from within, leadership in the church is called to create a climate in which the people as well as the leaders continually learn and become more capable of participating in the unfolding future of the church. Leadership involves collectively listening to the people and to what is wanting to emerge in the world, and then having the courage to do what is required.

Leadership in a self-organizing church is not about controlling the organization with negative energy but about freeing it through positive energy to discover the internal movement and guidance of the Creator Spirit. The leaders are those who are open to the inspiration of the Spirit present in the community and within the individuals. The leader assists the members of the community to discover the law written on their hearts, and the psyche that is the inner directive principle in each person. The leader invites the community to discover and articulate its guiding visions, strong values, and organizational beliefs and "to communicate them, to keep them ever-present and clear, and then allow individuals in the system their random, sometimes chaotic-looking meanderings."[67]

Servant leadership at every level in the church involves:

- *Creating a climate* in which the community and its leaders continually learn and become more capable of participating in the unfolding future of the church.
- *Freeing the community* through positive energy to discover the internal movement and guidance of the Creator Spirit.
- *Collectively listening* to what is wanting to emerge in the world, and then having the courage to do what is required.
- *Enabling the community* to discover and articulate its guiding visions, strong values, and organizational beliefs.

---

[66] Greenleaf, *Servant Leadership,* p. 241.

[67] Wheatley, *Leadership and the New Science,* p. 133.

What is the source of the authority of leadership within the church? Throughout much of its history, as we saw in the section on clergy and laity, there has been a tendency within the church to see authority as flowing down from above—from God to the pope, the bishops, the priests, and the laity. Often the contemporary church functions as if all enlightenment and decision making comes from above, and there is no need for horizontal or collective interaction in decision making. One example would be the English translation of the catechism of the Catholic Church. After extensive discussion among English-speaking scholars and theologians over a long period of time, a translation of the document was completed using the *inclusive* language that has become common in English usage. The translation was sent to Rome, and the Vatican officials made radical changes in the English version and used language that is *exclusive* in its meaning. Apparently they felt that they knew better how to express the contents of the document than the local scholars.[68] Another example is the continual reminder from church officials that parish councils and boards are only advisory to the pastor, as if parishioners were unable to study, discuss, and make decisions in a collaborative fashion.

As we have seen, this view that all actions and decisions within the church always move downward from above is contrary to the unfolding flow of all of creation, and the evolutionary process that produced the great beauty of our earth emerging from the inner presence of God within creation. It is contrary to the idea of the psyche as the inner directive power within human development, and it opposes the self-organizing principle in nature and in organizations. The view that all power comes from above denies the presence of the new law written on the heart and the presence of the Holy Spirit within all people as exemplified in the experience of Pentecost. It reverses the incarnational principle that the divine is found in the transcendent depths of the human; and if God is not found in the depths of the human, how could the Word become flesh? The Word becomes flesh from within not from without. Here we can see clearly the need for a new way of thinking in the church and a new vision of leadership within the church.

In practice it has become clear that real authority must come from within and will work effectively only when the leader's authority is granted and/or accepted by the members of the organization. This is stated by Greenleaf.

A new moral principle is emerging which holds that the only authority deserving one's allegiance is that which is freely and knowingly granted by the led to the leader in response to, and in

---

[68] A bishop from Indonesia echoes this sentiment: "Since the Second Vatican Council the role of episcopal conferences in guiding the movement for renewal and mission has been crucial. Episcopal conferences have overseen liturgical translation and adaptation. At present all this vital work has to go to Rome for approval—to people who just do not speak or understand our language!" Hadisumarta, Bishop Francis, "Enhanced Role for Bishops' Conferences," in *Origins,* May 7, 1998, p. 774.

proportion to, the clearly evident servant stature of the leader. Those who choose to follow this principle will not casually accept the authority of existing institutions. *Rather, they will freely respond only to individuals who are chosen as leaders because they are proven and trusted as servants.* To the extent that this principle prevails in the future, the only truly viable institutions will be those that are predominantly servant-led.[69]

Karl Rahner also views the practical necessity of authority being conceded by believers to officeholders, and he recognizes this as part of the dynamic of the faith community.

In practice, in the future, the office-holders will have as much effective authority—not merely a theoretical claim to authority—as is conceded to them freely by believers through their faith. The assumption of an authority in the Church will always have to consist in an appeal to the free act of faith of each individual and must be authorized in the light of this act in order to be effective at all; in the concrete the office-holder's appeal to his authority will be a proclamation of *faith*.[70]

Edward Schillebeeckx, in his book *Ministry: Leadership in the Community of Jesus Christ,* presents a more deeply rooted and theologically nuanced challenge to the hierarchical model of leadership in the church. In the following text Schillebeeckx describes some of the dimensions of ministry and leadership as found in the early history of the church. His description in many ways shows that the self-organizing model was present early on in the dynamics of the church.

Ministry is a necessary function of the community and therefore the community has the right to ministers. Furthermore, the local church tests the apostolic faith of the candidate and bears witness to it. This is an expression of the ancient conviction that primarily the community itself is apostolic; but because in turn the bishop takes on a specific responsibility for the community and thus for its apostolicity, the community which receives him first examines the apostolic foundation of his faith.[71]

There was a definite concern in the early church for what will be later called *apostolic succession.* J. M. R. Tillard also places the primary basis for apostolicity within the community. "The local church itself in its communion of clergy and laity comes first and is as a whole the guardian of apos-

---

[69] Greenleaf, *Servant Leadership,* p. 10 (emphasis original).

[70] Rahner, Karl, *Shape of the Church to Come,* New York, Seabury Press, 1974, p. 58.

[71] Schillebeeckx, *Ministry,* p. 42.

tolicity. The bishops follow each other on the *sedes*."[72] Both of these authors conclude that the foundation for apostolic succession is the community of faith as manifested by a succession of leaders, a conclusion that is consistent with the self-organizing principle. The primary qualification for leadership is the apostolic faith of the candidate, and the determination of this qualification is part of the role of the community because the community itself is apostolic.

Although the community is the inner source of ministry, without some pastoral institutionalization of its ministry, it "runs the risk of losing for good the apostolicity and thus ultimately the Christian character of its origin, inspiration and orientation—and in the last resort its own identity. Ministry is connected with a special concern for the preservation of the Christian identity of the community in constantly changing circumstances."[73] This calls for an organizational structure in which there is constant interaction between the community and its leaders. "Therefore the minister is not merely a mouthpiece of the community, but occasionally can also reprimand it, just as on the other hand the community can also call its ministers to order."[74]

Within the Christian community, there are diverse kinds of servant leadership that will differ in a variety of social and ethnic situations. It is possible to describe in general the various leadership functions that might emerge in the American church. First, there are what can be called ad hoc leaders, those people who come forward at times for specific functions, such as coordinating the parish festival, being the head sacristan for Holy Week, or preparing a parish breakfast. They have a specific competence for a specific task. Other people take on leadership positions for a period of time, such as serving as parish councilors and/or board members, or chairing the school committee or a fund drive. Some people choose to use their talents for a specific responsibility within the parish structure. Second, there are servant leaders who minister on a full-time basis and provide leadership in a particular area of the life of the community, such as liturgy, social justice, Christian formation, pastoral outreach, or administration. These people usually have some formal training, certification, or experience in their fields and may pursue such ministry as their personal career. In all cases leadership, as any other ministry, requires a call, competence, and the implicit or explicit affirmation of the people.

The Christian community is a community of disciples, and in this it differs from business corporations and political organizations. The church functions within the context of an explicit belief in God with a specific vision that we have defined as the reign of God. This community celebrates its life and the mystery of God's presence in rituals, symbols, and sacraments.

---

[72] Tillard, J. M. R., *The Bishop of Rome*, Wilmington, DE, Michael Glazier, Inc., 1983, p. 69.

[73] Schillebeeckx, *Ministry*, p. 24.

[74] Schillebeeckx, *Ministry*, p. 31.

Does this require another leadership role of presiding at the central Christian celebration of the Eucharist? If so, who should preside at these celebrations and what are the necessary qualities and competencies of the one who presides?

History shows that in human societies there have been men and women who were spirit people with an in-depth experience of the mystery of God, and who exercised spiritual leadership in their community. During the Neolithic period, 10,000 years ago, the primary focus of worship was the Earth Mother Goddess and women provided leadership in cultural, religious, and social affairs.[75] The so-called primitive people in the Americas had women and men who were medicine people and spirit people. Jesus, himself, was a spirit person as evidenced by the appearance of the Holy Spirit at his baptism, the voice from the cloud at his transfiguration, and his intimacy with God found in the name, Abba. In the Christian community from the beginning there have been spirit people and spiritual leaders who have built up local communities and who, because of their leadership gifts, have served as the presider at the community celebrations.

It is my opinion that the one who presides at the Eucharist does have a special function as a sacramental leader because the church is a sacramental community. This leader is not sacramental in the narrow sense of one who does sacraments, but as a person who helps build up and animate the community, one who then becomes the natural leader of the eucharistic ritual. Sacramental leadership within a sacramental church is essential because, as was noted above, ritual is so crucial in making visible the presence of God within the community, for the building up of the community, and for the celebration of the death and resurrection of Christ Jesus.

This kind of leadership requires a spiritual person with an intimate experience of the inner power and presence of God and whose transparency allows the presence of God to shine through in word and action. The sacramental leader is one who is a member of the community, and one who lives at the heart of the community sharing its hopes, fears, and dreams. This leader must know well the apostolic vision of the community and must be competent in building up the community through rituals, symbols, and sacraments. The leader is also one who is led because others may be more knowledgeable and competent in liturgical celebration, in pastoral practice, in faith formation, or in administrative affairs. The spiritual leader, however, helps the community to discover the vision of the reign of God in every dimension of the community and draws the community together in the celebration of the Eucharist. Sacramental leaders are storytellers and servants of the story. They are chosen, not because of their gender or their marital status, but because they are proven and trusted servants of the apostolic vision and of the community that professes that vision.

---

[75] See Swimme, Brian, and Thomas Berry, *The Universe Story*, San Francisco, HarperSanFrancisco, 1992, p. 175.

This concept of a spiritual and sacramental leader will demand radical changes in our current seminary system. There are many who believe that priestly formation is best secured when professors are mainly priests and when the students are predominantly seminarians. It is my belief that the isolation of the seminarians from others during their formation years often produces merely an external conformity to the demands of the role because there are no other roles or role models with which to interact. Young men or women who are formed and educated separately from the majority of the church membership will find it difficult to share the lives of the faithful in the deeply pastoral and collaborative way described above. A mature sense of personal and role identity is developed and internalized primarily by interaction and dialogue with others, some of whom share the role and some of whom challenge it directly or indirectly. After eighteen years in seminary education, I came to the following conclusion about seminaries:

> Seminaries should become open theological schools for the preparation of men and women in the diocese for a variety of ministries. All the faithful should have equal access to theological and professional studies limited only by their abilities and academic background. From such fertile ground, competent, specialized, and relevant ordained and nonordained ministries will grow and flourish, and this without losing the value of specialization.[76]

Is ordination a necessary prerequisite for presiding at the Eucharist in a Holarchical Church? As was discussed previously there are three prerequisites for any leadership ministry: (1)the inner *call*; (2) the necessary *competence* to carry out the particular ministry; and (3) the *consent* or affirmation of the community by which the leadership of the individual is confirmed by the community. All these are necessary as well for sacramental leadership, and some public manifestation of affirmation is necessary for the authenticity of ministry. Because of the sacramental leadership of presiding at the Eucharist and all this entails within a sacramental community, it is very fitting that this consent or affirmation be given through a sacramental ritual.

Using the word *ordination* or the phrase *sacrament of orders* to describe this ritual is not appropriate in the new paradigm because it implies that there are different orders and two categories of persons differing in rank within the church. We can too easily slip back into the clergy/laity distinction. The word *affirmation* might be used to describe the sacrament that ritualizes a sacramental leadership role within a sacramental community, but affirmation is almost too generic to be helpful. Perhaps in the future a suitable word, such as *commissioning,* might be found, but, for the present, we will use ordination and define it, not as an entrance into a higher rank or into

---

[76]Wessels, Cletus, "Separate and Unequal: Seminary as Hothouse" in *National Catholic Reporter,* March 25, 1988.

the clerical state, but as a sacramental ritual affirming a sacramental role in a sacramental community.

What about the possibility of celebrating the Eucharist within a small faith community or within a small retreat group without the presence of an ordained minister? There is a two-fold answer to this question. First, it is important to remember that the Eucharist is the celebration of a local community that is the embodiment of the church in a particular place. A local community, the parish or the diocese, is more than simply a worshiping community; it is one that shares in the vision of the reign of God manifested in reconciliation, healing, and liberation. A local community is not an ad hoc group but a stable community that worships together, shares its faith together, and ministers to others through evangelization and pastoral outreach. A Christian community participates in a larger web of relationships and is in "communion" with the broader Christian church. It is within such a community that the Eucharist is most fittingly celebrated. Second, the Eucharist is not the only way for small groups to celebrate and share their faith at a deep level. There are beautiful peace services, healing rituals, word services, and celebrations of nature that may be more appropriate in such circumstances.

How then does this concept of ministry relate to the distinction between the "common priesthood of the faithful" and the "ministerial priesthood of the ordained?" Can such a distinction be maintained in a Holarchical Church without clergy and laity? This distinction is confusing because the "common priesthood" is found in all the baptized, including those "ordained," and those who exercise the ministerial priesthood of the ordained (the sacramental leaders in the new paradigm) are still part of the common priesthood. Moreover, the use of the term *ministerial priesthood* is confusing because there are many ministries in the church that flow in various ways from the priesthood of Jesus Christ. Thus our traditional language always assumes the distinction between the clergy and laity, and in a Holarchical Church some new terminology will develop as these ideas are clarified.

Meanwhile I prefer to speak of the "common ministry of the baptized" when referring to the priesthood shared by all the baptized, and the "ministry of the ordained" when referring to the specific priesthood of those affirmed for sacramental leadership. With these cautions about the use of language, we can deal with the relationship between the common priesthood and the ministerial priesthood described in Vatican II.

> Though they differ from one another in essence and not only in degree, the common priesthood of the faithful and the ministerial or hierarchical priesthood are nonetheless interrelated. Each of them in its own special way is a participation in the one priesthood of Christ. (*Lumen Gentium*, #10)

In a Holarchical Church the common ministry of all the baptized is the fundamental, the first, and the foremost participation in the priesthood of

Christ. The ministry of the ordained or affirmed or commissioned is not a higher (or lower) degree of priesthood, but it is an essentially different way of servant leadership within the community. The ministry of the ordained is a sacramental and ritual leadership called to serve the priesthood of the faithful. A recent Vatican document states, "It must be noted with great satisfaction that in many particular churches the collaboration of the *nonordained faithful* in the pastoral ministry of the *clergy* has developed in a very positive fashion"[77] (emphasis added). A Holarchical Church would reverse the terms and state: It must be noted with great satisfaction that in many particular churches the collaboration of the *ordained* or the *affirmed* in the pastoral ministry of the *baptized faithful* has developed in a very positive fashion. Thus the test of the authenticity of the ministry of the ordained is its effectiveness in service to and collaboration with the common priesthood of the faithful with its interrelated web of ministries.

The community of the baptized, as a self-organizing system, is the inner source of the many offices and ministries that have emerged throughout its history and perhaps will emerge in its future. This calls for an organizational structure in which there are constant interactions between the community and its leaders. This relationship between leadership and the community can be clarified by returning to the theory of holons. Every holon is both a whole and a part. Within a holarchical vision of the church, each member of a local church is a whole Christian believer and also part of the parish. The parish, which is a whole, is also part of a diocese. Where do parish sacramental servant leaders—such as a pastor—or diocesan sacramental servant leaders—such as a bishop—fit into this picture? Is the leader of the community a whole in relationship to the community or is the leader a part of the community? Is the pastor the whole relative to the parish, or the bishop the whole relative to the diocese?

To answer this question it is important to note that each believer is an individual holon, whereas a parish or diocese is a social holon. Individuals can be parts of a social holon, but an individual can never be a whole in a social holon. Thus the pastor or the bishop is a part of the parish or the diocese with a specific ministerial function within the whole complex of ministries in the service of the community. The parish sacramental leader or the diocesan sacramental leader exercises a leadership role within a web of relationships to other ministries and the community as a whole. This style of leadership seems to be part of the structure of the early church.

At the beginning of this transitional period [the postapostolic period] the church's ministry was in no way detached from the community or so to speak set above it; ministry is clearly incorporated into the totality of all kinds of services which are necessary for the community ([see] Eph. 4:11). The peculiarity of the ministerial cha-

---

[77] "Some Questions Regarding Collaboration of Nonordained Faithful in Priests' Sacred Ministry," in *Origins*, November 27, 1997, p. 399.

risma is that the ministers and the whole of the community have the responsibility for keeping the community in its apostolicity or apostolic origin and orientation: the gospel of Jesus the Christ.[78]

The Christian church is always subject to inner conflicts and divisions as well as rebellion from within and persecution from without. As a human organization the church is limited and will find itself in chaos and darkness. But it has within itself the resources both to maintain its identity and vision (self-preservation) while interacting with its environment (self-adaptation) in order to continually renew itself (self-transcendence). These resources are found in the dynamic interaction between the community and its leaders and in the presence of God as the Creator Spirit manifested in the psyche and in the self-organizing principle. The Holarchical Church can look to the future with great faith and hope and love because the apostolic vision of the reign of God will continue to guide the community and its various leaders through death into resurrection.

We can now turn to the final characteristic of the new paradigm of the church, the Church of the World, which deals more deeply with the issues surrounding the emergence of the church from local cultures and the communion among local churches throughout the world.

---

[78]Schillebeeckx, *Ministry,* p. 13.

6

CHURCH OF THE WORLD

In the Gospel stories Jesus often describes the reign of God using parables about seeds—the very small mustard seed that becomes a sheltering tree, the seed sown in good ground that yields a hundredfold, the seed that must die in order to germinate and grow. These parables embody the most basic dimension of the creation story—the unfolding of the latent power and presence of God as manifested in the flashing forth of the universe, the formation of our solar system, the blossoming of the earth planet in all its beauty, and the earth becoming conscious in the human.

In a new paradigm, the Church of the World concerns itself with the cultural and social reality within which the seed of the reign of God can grow and develop. The Church of the World describes how *the church unfolds and emerges from the local culture* in which it lives. The local culture is the womb within which the church is nourished and from which it will eventually be born. The Church of the World describes the need for a global dimension of the church and how such a universal church relates to the local churches. Throughout history there has existed *a tension between the local church and the universal church.* We will discuss the ways in which this tension has developed in the last two centuries, and how the theory of holons can throw some light on this tension. Central to this tension is *the primacy of the bishop of Rome* in the church, and how that primacy can be reinterpreted in a holarchical system. Finally, two specific concerns relative to the Church of the World will be treated: *the meaning of infallibility* and *the future of ecumenism.*

THE CHURCH EMERGING FROM LOCAL CULTURE

Many in the West have not yet come to terms with the idea that the center of Catholicism is shifting now to Asia and the Third World, and that the future world church will not be dominated by Western nations but will be predominantly nonwhite, a coalition and mixture of many races and cultures.[1]

---

[1] Weakland, Archbishop Rembert, "Church of Many Cultures, World of Globalization," in *Origins*, November 12, 1998, p. 392.

In the late 1950s, while studying in Rome, I was very impressed by seeing on the streets so many young seminarians from the African College, a seminary for students from Africa, in their distinctive and colorful cassocks. I thought: What a wonderful opportunity for these young men to study philosophy and theology in Rome. Some years later I discovered that, in fact, many of these young men returned to Africa and were often unable to reintegrate themselves into their local culture. European theology based on Western culture often separated them from their people, and, after Vatican II, these same seminarians often opposed any efforts to develop native African liturgies and culturally based theologies. They brought an image of the church from the outside in, rather than being able to nourish a local church from the inside out.

Our Dominican province had a mission in Latin America for many years. Whenever young Bolivians entered the Order, they eventually were sent to the United States for their study of theology. This was necessary, so we thought, in order that they would know the ethos of our province and become acquainted with their peers in North America. The outcome was that, being nourished outside of their native culture, many of these men either never returned to Bolivia or left the Order once they returned. Later the province founded a novitiate and a house of studies in Bolivia, a substantial number of young men entered the Order, and a vibrant community of native Dominicans emerged with its own indigenous leadership ready to nourish the emerging local church of Bolivia.

This issue of the emergence of the local church from its cultural roots permeated the Synod of Asia held in April and May of 1998. Archbishop Ikenaga from Japan, speaking in the context of evangelization, stated that despite the number of missionaries to East Asia the faith has never flowered there, baptisms are few, and the message of the gospel has never taken root in Asian society.[2] He then explained that it is essential in evangelization to "use Asian ways of expression if our message is to take hold as we respond to the need to proclaim the kingdom of God."[3] The same concern was expressed by Bishop Bastes from the Philippines.

> There are still strong indications that Asian realities have not yet been taken seriously enough in the present practice of the church's pastoral mission in general and in the formation of religious in particular. The church's mission in Asia had been approached from the perspective of a Euro-centered church which was deeply conditioned by the European colonialism of the times. This influence is still clear even in postcolonial times.[4]

---

[2] Ikenaga, Archbishop Leo Jun, "Asian Ways of Expression," in *Origins*, May 7, 1998, p. 769.

[3] Ikenaga, "Asian Ways of Expression," p. 770.

[4] Bastes, Bishop Arturo, "Asian Formation for Consecrated Life," in *Origins*, May 7, 1998, p. 775.

Archbishop Ikenaga illustrated the problem facing local churches in terms of the ways in which Western culture tends to image God and our relationship to creation.

> The God of Christianity is limitless and possesses both fatherly and motherly elements. However, the Christianity that came from Europe tends to overstress the former. In the East we need to give greater expression to the feminine aspects of God: God who permeates the universe, lives in us through faith, receives all people in his embrace, the God of universal love, infinite tenderness, always ready to forgive, Christ atoning for all the sins of mankind on the cross. If our theology, art, preaching and evangelization move along these lines, then Christianity will take on a gentler, more approachable face for the Asian people.[5]

These strong statements were either muted or ignored in the final document that came out of the synod. In the closing homily, Pope John Paul II moved away from the more immanent, Asian way of imaging God and stressed the importance of the transcendence of God.

> If it is true that God is in the world and that he has a certain degree of immanence, it is above all true that he is transcendent, "above" the world, and that he cannot be identified in the world alone. One must not only look for him in the world, as if he were just the most profound mystery of all visible things. On the contrary, one must first of all look for him "on high": He is the Lord of heaven and earth. In virtue of this absolute transcendence, the Son of God descended to the earth.[6]

Nevertheless the synod did express a respect for and an acknowledgment of the spiritual values of the great religions of Asia.

> We respectfully greet all our sisters and brothers in Asia who have put their confidence in other religious traditions. We gladly acknowledge the spiritual values of the great religions of Asia such as Hinduism, Buddhism, Judaism, Islam. . . . We esteem the ethical values in the customs and practices found in the teachings of the great philosophers of Asia, which promote natural virtues and pious devotion to ancestors. We also respect the beliefs and religious practices of indigenous/tribal people, whose reverence for all creation manifests their closeness to the Creator.[7]

Vincent Donovan in his book *Christianity Rediscovered* provides a very moving vision of how the church can emerge from a local culture and of the

---

[5] Ikenaga, "Asian Ways of Expression," p. 770.

[6] John Paul II, "New Chapter in the History of Salvation," in *Origins*, May 28, 1998, p 23.

[7] Synod of Asia, "Message to the People of God," in *Origins*, May 28, 1998, p. 19.

tremendous value of watching the seed of Christianity blossom in the seemingly unfertile soil of East Africa. He was sent to the mission of Loliondo among the Masai in Tanzania in 1965. One year later he wrote a letter to the bishop in which he describes the four well-run, well-maintained, and expensive schools attached to the mission. There is a small chapel and a hospital bringing in some mission revenue. He tells about the frequent visits of the priests to the villages (*kraals*). They attend the important events in Masai life, share in their milk and honey beer, and even sleep in Masai kraals. But then he gives his appraisal of the state of this Christian mission.

> But never, or almost never, is religion mentioned in any of these visits. The best way to describe realistically the state of this Christian mission is the number zero. As of this month, in the seventh year of this mission's existence, there are no adult Masai practicing Christians from Loliondo mission. . . . That zero is a real number, because up until this date no Catholic child, on leaving school, has continued to practice his religion, and there is no indication that any of the present students will do so.[8]

The attempt to build the church among the Masai seemed doomed despite the good will and hard work of the priests and the missionaries. So Donovan proposed that he cast aside all theories and discussions, cut himself off from the schools and the hospital, and just go and talk to the people about God and the Christian message. "Outside of this, I have no theory, no plan, no strategy, no gimmicks—no idea of what will come. I feel rather naked. I will begin as soon as possible."[9]

So Donovan set out on this strange mission. He chose six villages and visited each village once each week. When the people of the village were gathered together he told them he had come to talk about and deal only with God. He would not ask their children to go to the mission school or give them medical care. He wanted nothing from them and the Masai should expect nothing from him except the message of Jesus. He told them that they already knew about God, and that they were a devout and pious people in the face of God. This would be a mutual learning process and they would have to listen to one another.

Donovan discovered that it was difficult to express the message of Jesus because of a lack of language to express Christian concepts. The Masai had no word in their language for *person, creation, grace, freedom, spirit,* or *immortality,* but they had a deep experience of the reality beneath these words. For example, the word that the missionary used to convey *faith* meant literally *to agree to.* One of the elders said that this word was weak and unsatisfactory. It did not convey the full meaning of faith, so the elder went on to describe his sense of faith.

---

[8] Donovan, Vincent J., *Christianity Rediscovered,* Maryknoll, NY, Orbis Books, 1978, p. 15.

[9] Donovan, *Christianity Rediscovered,* pp. 15–16.

He [the Masai elder] said for a man really to believe is like a lion going after its prey. His nose and eyes and ears pick up the prey. His legs give him the speed to catch it. All the power of his body is involved in the terrible death leap and single blow to the neck with the front paw, the blow that actually kills. And as the animal goes down the lion envelops it in his arms (Africans refer to the front legs of an animal as its arms), pulls it to himself, and makes it part of himself. This is the way a lion kills. This is the way a man believes. This is what faith is.

I looked at the elder in silence and amazement. Faith understood like that would explain why, when my own was gone, I ached in every fiber of my being. But my wise old teacher was not finished yet.

"We did not search you out, Padri," he said to me. "We did not even want you to come to us. You searched us out. You followed us away from your house into the bush, into the plains, into the steppes where our cattle are, into the hills where we take our cattle for water, into our villages, into our homes. You told us of the High God, how we must search for him, even leave our land and our people to find him. But we have not done this. We have not left our land. We have not searched for him. He has searched for us. He has searched *us* out and found us. All the time we think we are the lion. In the end the lion is God."

The lion is God. Of course. Goodness and kindness and holiness and grace and divine presence and creating power and salvation were here before I got here. Even the fuller understanding of God's revelation to man, of the gospel, of the salvific act that had been accomplished once and for all for the human race was here before I got here. . . . Only that part of [my message] would be made use of which fit into the immeasurably greater plan of the relentless, pursuing God whose will on the world would not be thwarted. The lion is God.[10]

The missionary does not bring faith to the pagan peoples. The missionary only discovers and learns from the God and the faith already embedded within the local culture. The missionary can bring the Christian message of a God who loves all people, of a God who sent Jesus to preach the good news of the reign of God and the need for reconciliation, healing, and liberation for all peoples, tribes, and nations. If he preaches this message of Christianity, the church that results may not be the church he had in mind. The missionary brings the message of Christ, and the church emerges from the local culture, whatever form it may take.

As Donovan continued to speak about God and about the Christian message he began to look forward to the possibility of baptism for the peo-

---

[10] Donovan, *Christianity Rediscovered*, pp. 63–64.

ple from the villages. After about one year of being with these communities, he told them that he had finished imparting the Christian message, and now it was up to them. They could accept it or reject it. If they did accept it, they would begin preparations for a public baptism. So he went away for a week and gave them the opportunity to make their judgment. This was the culmination of his efforts to share the message of Jesus. Would they accept it and be baptized? So he went to the old man Ndangoya's community to prepare them for the final step.

He stood in front of the assembled community and began by saying that the old man sitting nearby had missed too many of the instruction meetings, and he would not be baptized with the rest. The two standing on the side, as well as a young mother, will be baptized because they always attended each gathering, and understood very well what was talked about. But the man in the back has obviously not understood the instructions, and that lady there has scarcely believed the gospel message. They cannot be baptized. And this warrior has not shown enough effort . . .

> The old man, Ndangoya, stopped me politely but firmly, "Padri, why are you trying to break us up and separate us? During this whole year that you have been teaching us, we have talked about these things when you were not here, at night around the fire. Yes, there have been lazy ones in this community. But they have been helped by those with much energy. There are stupid ones in the community, but they have been helped by those who are intelligent. Yes, there are ones with little faith in this village, but they have been helped by those with much faith. Would you turn out and drive off the lazy ones and the ones with little faith and the stupid ones? From the first day I have spoken for these people. And I speak for them now. Now, on this day one year later, I can declare for them and for all this community, that we have reached the step in our lives where we can say, 'We believe.'"
>
> *We believe.* Communal faith. Until that day I had never heard of such a concept, certainly had never been taught it in a classroom. . . . I looked at the old man Ndangoya. "Excuse me, old man," I said. "Sometimes, my head is hard and I learn slowly. 'We believe,' you said. Of course you do. Everyone in the community will be baptized."[11]

The whole community was baptized! It was truly a baptism of water and the Holy Spirit, but, beyond this, the community enhanced this ritual in their own way. They developed their own symbols out of their own cultural sense of liturgy. On that day they became a true local Christian community. To repeat, the missionary brings the Christian message, and the church emerges from the local culture. What would happen to this and the other

---

[11]Donovan, *Christianity Rediscovered*, pp. 91–92.

fledgling Christian communities in Africa that have become the church through baptism?

> These people [the Masai] considered baptism everything. If I was entrusting them with baptism, in their minds, I was entrusting them with the church, the total responsibility of the church.
>
> They asked me, "What does it mean that we are baptized? Just that, that water was poured on our heads by you? Or does it not mean that we ourselves can now baptize? What does it mean that we are baptized? That we can receive eucharist from your hands any time you choose to come to visit us? Or does it not mean that we are a eucharistic people?" Implying, of course, that they should be able to confect the eucharist without me.
>
> They were right, certainly. And I had to admit to them that they were right. It was not scripture or theology which prevented them from doing what they thought they had a right to do, but simply the history of a church imbedded in a single culture, with its own ideas, coming from that culture, as to what number of years of seminary training were needed to lead a community in the simple act of celebrating the Lord's Supper, as he told us to do. Any command of his to undergo academic training before attempting to break bread together is strikingly missing from scripture.
>
> What these people were suggesting was that the church which sent me should have insured that its bishop (whom they found no difficulty in accepting as head of a larger Christian community) should have come to them to declare that they were, in fact, a fully-fledged, eucharistic, Christian community, just like every other community in the church. Surely that is essentially what ordination means.[12]

Donovan's evangelization of the Masai people provides us with a clear example of the *possibility* of building the church from within the culture of the local community. But what has happened to these missionary endeavors in the years following the birth of these local churches? Have they been able to reach their potential and take their own rightful place in the life of the larger church community? With a certain sense of sadness, Donovan describes the outcome of the efforts to birth a local church out of an indigenous culture.

> Despite some impressive indigenization carried out in certain areas, the African church, in order to be seen as respectable in the eyes of the Western church, has incorporated some of the Western church's worst habits. The need for buildings and institutions is inherited from the missionaries. The clericalization of the church, as regards bishops and priests, is intense in some cases. And the fear on the

---

[12]Donovan, *Christianity Rediscovered*, pp. 122–123.

part of many educated, sophisticated African priests regarding the possibility of a different kind of priest, married and less educated, is almost paranoid. By and large, the official African church still wears a European face.[13]

The African church has, at times, become afflicted with Western respectability, a desire for buildings and institutions, the virus of clericalism, and fear of new structures. In many ways, it has donned the business suit in place of its colorful native robes. Nevertheless, there are some profound lessons in this African experience for those of us in the established churches of Western culture.

First, we must be fully aware of the culture in which we live and the culture that has formed the basis of our churches. The Christian church in North America emerged from a biblical creation story and a Western patriarchal culture that is now inadequate to our contemporary cultural experience. We live in a society that is racked by consumerism and conspicuous consumption, a society overwhelmed by celebrity worship and a growing gap between the rich and the poor, a society saturated by sex and the pleasure principle, and a society becoming more and more multicultural. I do not have the academic background, nor is it within the scope of this book, to treat each of these broad sociological concerns. I want only to make the point that we must discern carefully which dimensions of our local culture must be challenged and which might provide us with fertile ground for the emergence of a local Christian church in North America.

Second, it is one kind of challenge to midwife a church emerging from a culture that has never heard the Christian message, and another, more difficult challenge for a culturally based church to be reborn out of an already established church. In our situation we must not only discern the fertile cultural soil for the Christian message, but we need to discern those elements in the established churches that are no longer viable as well as those that will guide it in the rebirthing process. This process will lead us, once again, to the death and resurrection theme that is central to the Christian message. Just as the early Jewish Christians gradually let go of their cultural and ritual roots in Judaism in order to be able to share their newfound faith throughout the Gentile world, so contemporary Christians are being called to the death of some of their cultural and ritual roots in order that resurrection and new life will be found in a new paradigm of the church. Some things in the established church must die in order that a new church can arise from its cultural roots.

Third, both North American society and the churches within it are becoming more and more culturally diverse. There are people with Native American roots, the many different early immigrants from Europe; the African American population plagued by the evils of slavery and seeking recog-

---

[13] Donovan, *Christianity Rediscovered*, pp. 176–177.

nition of their rights and their dignity; the various Hispanic immigrants from Mexico, the Caribbean, and Latin America; the Asian people, some of whom came as refugees; plus Arab peoples from the Middle East, and Native Africans. And this is not an exhaustive list. What then can be the cultural basis for local churches in North America? Should we look forward to many different local and culturally based churches, or can we move toward more uniform multicultural churches? How can we as Christian churches deal constructively with such complex ethnic, social, and religious questions?

If authentic Christian churches can only emerge from the local culture, as everything in the new creation story and the self-organizing principle indicates, the following guidelines can assist us in this unfolding process:

1. The message of Christ must be presented to each and every local community within its own ethnic and social diversity in terms of the reign of God that is already present, either overtly or covertly, and this reign of God will be found manifested in reconciliation, healing, and liberation.
2. The established churches will have to undergo continuous personal and institutional conversion, rooting out anything opposed to the reign of God and challenging everything within those churches that is divisive or destructive, that is wounded or paralyzed, that is oppressive or domineering.
3. The leadership in the church will have to trust in the reality that the local church is a self-organizing system similar to a bioregion of the earth. It has within itself the ability to educate, to heal, and to reorganize itself in the context of new environments. Even in such extreme climatic events such as the ice ages, the bioregion brings forth new life, new geologies, and new communities of species. Likewise, the church has within itself the Holy Spirit, and even in the midst of the turmoil of the present age it is able to bring forth new life within the established churches.

Vincent Donovan gives us a final word of advice:

A young person in an American university, reflecting on the line of thought presented in this book [*Christianity Rediscovered*], offered some advice: "In working with young people in America, do not try to call them back to where they were, and do not try to call them to where you are as beautiful as that place might seem to you. You must have the courage to go with them to a place that neither you nor they have ever been before."

When the gospel reaches a people where they are, their response to that gospel is the church in a new place, and the song they will sing is that new, unsung song, that unwritten melody that haunts all of us. What we have to be involved in is not the revival of the church or the reform of the church. It has to be nothing less than what Paul and the Fathers of the Council of Jerusalem were involved in for their time—the refounding of the Catholic church for our age.[14]

This refounding of the Christian church will be rooted in the local eucharistic community, but the local community participates in a complex web of relationships with other communities and ultimately with the universal church. This calls for a closer examination of the relations between the local church and the universal church.

THE TENSION BETWEEN THE LOCAL CHURCH AND THE UNIVERSAL CHURCH

The key, then, to the relationship between the Church of Rome and the local Churches is the avoidance of domination by either party. Otherwise, the necessary and fruitful tension will be replaced by authoritarianism or anarchic rigidity. This tension should not and cannot be resolved once and for all; indeed it must be cherished as a sign of ecclesial health evidencing mutual respect of the Church of Rome and the local Churches in their continuing attempt to attune their relationship to the manifold gifts of the Spirit.[15]

If the local church emerges from the local culture, what is its relationship to the universal church? That question certainly emerged from the experience of the evangelization of the Masai, and it has dogged the church off and on throughout its history. In more recent times this relationship has become a serious source of tension, particularly in the Roman Catholic Church, because of Rome's attempts to increase its authority over local churches and the various bishops' conferences. We cannot trace the history of these tensions as they have been played out in the long history of the church, but we can explore the ways in which the new paradigm in terms of the holy web theory and the theory of holons can make a significant contribution to this discussion.

Before beginning to deal with these tensions, it is important to clarify the meaning of the words *divine institution* as they are used in various church documents relating to the foundation and structure of the church. Sometimes *divine institution* carries the sense that during his public ministry Jesus himself established the foundational dimensions of the church, and these are considered to be of divine institution. This is not very helpful because it is very difficult to determine exactly what Jesus said and taught about the church during his lifetime, and what would thus be of divine institution. Perhaps a more helpful sense of divine institution would be grounded in the ongoing presence of the Holy Spirit in the life of the church. This meaning of divine institution fits in well with the new creation story that sees the unfolding of the latent potential of the universe as the result of

---

[14] Donovan, *Christianity Rediscovered,* p. vii.

[15] Granfield, Patrick, *The Limits of the Papacy,* New York, Crossroad, 1987, p. 133.

CHURCH OF THE WORLD

divine institution. Just as the earth and all its creatures result from the inner presence of God, so the latent potential of the church emerges from the inner presence of God's Spirit in the church.

There is, however, a difference between the unfolding of the universe and the emergence of a human organization such as the church. When the wonderful diversity of the flora and fauna unfold, it is clear that this is due to the presence of God, and we can say the reign of God is found there. When a particular church structure emerges in the early church, or at any time throughout the history of the church, we cannot be sure that it is the unfolding of the reign of God. Individuals and communities are capable of acting in ways that are contrary to the reign of God. As we have often said in the course of this work, chaos, darkness, and the shadow side are always hidden within every dimension of creation, including the human. Who would say now that the Crusades or the Inquisition or the selling of indulgences emerged from God's presence in the church? It is always difficult to judge any individual event or organizational structure within the church, but we must be aware that not everything that has emerged in the church flows from the inner presence of God.

Very often in church documents the words divine institution carry the sense of something that is permanent and unchangeable. Our experience of the story of the universe tells us that this is not always true. Stars that emerge within galaxies eventually burn themselves out and die. Our own sun is destined to sacrifice itself in providing light and heat for the earth. The dinosaurs emerged in the course of evolution by divine institution, and yet they no longer exist. In the same way all church structures are open to change even if they are of divine institution. Church structures that emerged within a particular culture or historical moment could well be a manifestation of the presence of God in those circumstances, but those same church structures may become useless or even destructive at another time in history.

How then can we determine at any point in history which church structures are authentic and are the unfolding of God's presence within the church? In terms of organizational structure, Margaret Wheatley and Myron Kellner-Rogers point out that:

> *Life is intent on finding what works, not what's "right."* It is the ability to keep finding solutions that is important; any one solution is temporary. There are no permanently right answers [in an organization]. The capacity to keep changing, to find what works now, is what keeps any organization alive.[16]

In the new paradigm the basic principle is not "this is the way it has always been," but this is the way that works and really makes a difference in the life of the community. It is a search for the structures that can help the

---

[16]Wheatley, Margaret J., and Myron Kellner-Rogers, *A Simpler Way,* San Francisco, Berrett-Koehler Publishers, 1996, p. 13 (emphasis original).

community of disciples discover the presence of God within itself, foster that presence and challenge the obstacles to God's presence.

This does not mean that everything needs to be changed. There are many wonderful dimensions of the Christian church that have guided, and continue to guide, the community in its pilgrim journey. It does mean that all church structures are susceptible to evaluation and possible revision based on the apostolic vision of the church. We don't know what the outcome of this evaluation process will be—it will emerge from within a self-organizing system—but we can examine some possibilities for a new web of relationships within the believing community. As Pope Paul VI said in his opening allocution at the second session of Vatican II, "The Church is a mystery. It is a reality imbued with the divine presence, and for that reason it is always open to new and deeper exploration."[17] Our exploration of the tension between the local church and universal church will treat the following: (1) the mystery of the church and the church as the people of God; (2) communion among local churches; and (3) the primacy of Rome.

THE MYSTERY OF THE CHURCH AND THE CHURCH AS THE PEOPLE OF GOD

The Church
A gathering of people who will work and pray with laughter,
To reach for stars that seem too distant to be touched,
or too dim to be worth the effort.
We will try to be friends with persons in need,
and to celebrate life with people who believe
That the struggle to follow Jesus in building a world
more justly loving is worth the gift of their lives.[18]

The first chapter of the Dogmatic Constitution on the Church of Vatican II is entitled "The Mystery of the Church." The word *mystery* carries with it a twofold meaning. It involves the hidden presence of God that is beyond human comprehension and human words, and yet this same presence of God can be manifested externally in rituals and symbols. Christ, himself, in his words and deeds manifests the hidden presence of God within his very being, and he has been called the sacrament of God. Vatican II also describes the church as a sacrament. "By her relationship with Christ, the Church is a kind of sacrament or sign of intimate union with God, and of the unity of all mankind. She is also an instrument for the achievement of such union and unity" (*Lumen Gentium*, #1).

The Christian church, therefore, is a sacramental community, and its rituals and symbols are central to the very life of the community. Moreover,

---

[17] Vatican II, *Council Daybook*, Washington, DC, National Catholic Welfare Council, 1965, p. 146.
[18] A description of the church by the Quixote Center, P.O. Box 5206, Hyattsville, MD 20782.

the council indicates that all the baptized, by the anointing of the Holy Spirit, are consecrated into a spiritual house and a holy priesthood. The Christian community has an inner life and a communal memory, and through its symbolic rituals and sacraments the community can articulate its inner life and the mystery of God's presence within the community.[19]

> Like the sacraments, like the incarnation, the Church unites two dimensions, the spiritual and the material into a single reality, a mystery which cannot be fully expressed conceptually, sociologically, or juridically, but is best expressed sacramentally. The whole mission of the Church as sacrament is to bring human beings into intimate union with God and to participation in God's divine life.[20]

Vatican II in its second chapter describes this sacramental community as a new people of God, rooted in the history and covenant of the Jewish people, and now ratified in a new covenant through Christ. This recalls the words of Jeremiah, the prophet.

> The days are coming, says the Lord, when I will make a new covenant with the house of Israel and the house of Judah. This is the covenant I will make with the house of Israel after those days, says the Lord. I will place my law within them, and write it upon their hearts; I will be their God, and they shall be my people.   (Jer. 31:31, 33)

The goal of the new people of God is the reign of God, which, as we have seen, has been present in the entire unfolding of the universe and is the guiding vision of the church. All humankind are, in one way or another, part of God's people and are called to share in the reconciling, healing, and liberating presence of the reign of God.

> This characteristic of universality which adorns the People of God is a gift from the Lord himself. . . . In virtue of this catholicity each individual part of the Church contributes through its special gifts to the good of the other parts and of the whole Church. Thus through the common sharing of gifts and through the common effort to attain fullness in unity, the whole and each of the parts receive increase. (*Lumen Gentium*, #13)

The roots of all that the Christian community embodies and the source of all that has emerged or will emerge in the life of the church are found in its character as a sacramental community and the universal people of God. The pilgrim people functions as a self-organizing system guided by the Holy Spirit in its journey through history, always manifesting the presence of the reign of God within the diversity of cultures.

------

[19] See the section on "Rituals, Symbols, and Sacraments" in Chapter 4.

[20] Nichols, Terence, *That All May Be One: Hierarchy and Participation in the Church*, Collegeville, MN, The Liturgical Press, 1997, p. 241.

COMMUNION AMONG LOCAL CHURCHES

> We live in a universe which seeks organization. When simple relationships are created, patterns of organization emerge. Networks, living or not, have the capacity to self-organize. Global order arises from local connections.[21]

In its most simple reality a local church is a gathering of the people of God with their sacramental leader who celebrate the Eucharist and who become servants of one another and all people in need. Patrick Granfield says that "the local Church is that community of Christians called together by the Holy Spirit; under the leadership of the bishop, priests, and other ministers, it preaches the Word, celebrates the eucharist and other sacraments, and manifests the redemptive work of Christ in the world."[22] Using this general definition, the local or particular church can be found in dioceses and in parishes, in schools and hospitals, in religious orders and congregations, and in other small Christian communities. In the history of the church, however, following the early Christian experience, the eucharistic community with its bishop—the diocese—became the primary embodiment of the local church.

This concept of a local church is analogous to a bioregion as we have discussed it in Chapter 5. A bioregion is a relatively autonomous geographic area of interacting life systems that is self-sustaining in the ever-renewing process of nature. It includes the diversity of life functions within a community of species, while retaining a mutual dependency with the broader earth community. We can compare this concept of a bioregion with Granfield's description of the local church.

> The local Church is to some extent self-regulating. As a specific concretization of the Body of Christ, it controls its own destiny to a large degree. But the local Church remains a relational reality, only partially autonomous and always in contact with the shared faith of the universal Church and with the Church of Rome.[23]

According to the eucharistic ecclesiology of the Orthodox Church, the inner unity of the local church is founded on a eucharistic community experienced as the Body of Christ. In this ecclesiology "the local church is autonomous and independent, because the Church of God in Christ indwells it in perfect fullness. . . . Every local church manifests all the fullness of the Church of God, because it is the Church of God and not just one part of it."[24] Many Catholics tend to imagine the reality of the church as the universal church made up of many smaller parts or units with the pope

---

[21] Wheatley and Kellner-Rogers, *A Simpler Way*, p. 32.

[22] Granfield, *The Limits of the Papacy*, p. 110.

[23] Granfield, *The Limits of the Papacy*, p. 114.

[24] Afaanassieff, Nicolas, "The Church which Presides in Love," in *The Primacy of Peter*, London, Faith Press, 1963, p. 75.

handing over the administration of these units to the local bishops, priests, and ministers.

Vatican II, however, teaches that the bishop is not the vicar of the Roman pontiff but a vicar of Christ who exercises leadership in Christ's name, and the diocese is not just a part of the church but is the embodiment of the Church of Christ in its wholeness. "The Church of Christ is truly present in all legitimate local congregations of the faithful which, united with their pastors, are themselves called churches in the New Testament" (*Lumen Gentium*, #26). This same teaching is found also in the Decree on the Bishops' Pastoral Office in the Church (*Christus Dominus*).

> A diocese is that portion of God's people which is entrusted to a bishop to be shepherded by him with the cooperation of the presbytery. Adhering thus to its pastor and gathered together by him in the Holy Spirit through the gospel and the Eucharist, this portion constitutes a particular church in which the one, holy, catholic, and apostolic Church of Christ is truly present and operative.
>
> (*Christus Dominus*, #11)

The local church is a relatively autonomous embodiment of the Christian church but always in communion with other churches. The use of the word "communion" to express the relationship among local churches has become very common among theologians since Vatican II. The following are some examples:

> The vision of the Church developed at Vatican II represented a decisive move away from an excessively institutional view of the Church and toward an ecclesiology grounded in the concept of communion, which . . . has its roots in the biblical notion of *koinonia*. . . .Vatican II recovered an ancient theology of the local Church that viewed the universal Church not as an institutional superstructure but as the *communio ecclesiarum*, the communion of local churches.[25]

> It [the shift in emphasis] concerns the movement from an ecclesiology starting with the idea of the universal Church divided into portions called dioceses, to an ecclesiology which understands the Church as the communion of all the local churches: the universal Church arises from the communion of churches.[26]

> One of the achievements of the council was the rediscovery of the universal church as the sum and communion of the local churches

---

[25] Gaillardetz, Richard, *Teaching with Authority*, Collegeville, MN, The Liturgical Press, 1997, p. xii.

[26] Tillard, J. M. R., *The Bishop of Rome*, Wilmington, DE, Michael Glazier, Inc., 1983, p. 37.

. . . and the rediscovery of the universal church in the local church.[27]

It [the universal Church] is not a mere collection or external union of many local Churches, but the communion of local Churches. The universal Church comes to be out of the mutual reception and communion of local Churches united in faith and the Holy Spirit. The universal Church is the communion of local churches.[28]

The root for the word *communion,* from the Greek *koinonia,* goes back to the earliest Christian community. The Letter to the Galatians speaks of the dispute within the community over the issue of the necessity of circumcision for Gentile converts. Paul went to Jerusalem, and he shared with them the gospel he preached. Paul says,

James and Cephas and John, who were reputed to be pillars of the church, gave me and Barnabas their right hand in partnership [*koinonia*], that we should go to the Gentiles and they to the circumcised.

(Gal. 2:9)

Jerome Hamer comments on this use of the idea of partnership or fellowship or communion.

When "those who were reputed to be the main support of the Church" held out their hands to Paul and Barnabas "in fellowship," this was a good deal more than a gesture concluding a difficult bit of negotiation and setting the seal on an acceptable agreement. It involved the unity of God's people.[29]

In the early centuries of the church, eucharistic communion became the sign of this partnership or communion. First of all communion *within* each local community was founded on a sharing in the community celebration of the Eucharist, and later the communion *among* local communities was founded on mutual recognition of the authenticity of the faith and of the eucharistic celebration within diverse communities. At this time there were heretical churches and sometimes major disputes arose among bishops and between bishops and other church leaders, and it was very important to know how and when churches were in communion with one another.

How was any given bishop's membership of the communion to be established? The test could lie either in his links with the episcopate as a whole or in his relationship with the oldest Churches. Now Rome held the first place in the list of Churches. A Church which

---

[27] Grillmeier, Aloys, "Commentary on *Lumen Gentium,*" Chap. 2, in *Commentary on the Documents of Vatican II,* H. Vorgrimler, ed., New York, Herder and Herder, 1967, Vol. 1, p. 167.

[28] Granfield, *The Limits of the Papacy,* pp. 112–113.

[29] Hamer, Jerome, *The Church Is a Communion,* New York, Sheed and Ward, 1964, p. 164.

was in communion with Rome was, by that very fact, in communion with the whole Church. The idea that Rome was the head of the communion was one of long standing.[30]

Vatican II does not refer explicitly to a communion among local churches, but the council does contain the reality of communion in its description of the college of bishops.

> The individual bishops, who are placed in charge of particular churches, exercise their pastoral government over the portion of the People of God committed to their care, and not over other churches nor over the universal church. But each of them, as a member of the episcopal college and a legitimate successor of the apostles, is obliged by Christ's decree and command to be solicitous for the whole Church.
>
> This solicitude, though it is not exercised by an act of jurisdiction, contributes immensely to the welfare of the universal Church. . . . It is a sacred reality that by governing well their own church as a portion of the universal Church, they themselves are effectively contributing to the welfare of the whole Mystical Body, which is also the body of the churches. (*Lumen Gentium*, #23)

Collegiality rests on the idea of communion. The church is a people united in faith who proclaim their union with Christ and with one another through the sacramental celebration of the Eucharist. The bishops, sacramental leaders, are installed in their proper ministry through a sacramental ritual expressing the consent and affirmation of the community, and this sacrament is the source of the bishops' threefold participation in the web of relationships, which is the church. "In being ordained a bishop, one is united to the community one represents, to the college of bishops, and to its head, the bishop of Rome."[31] Vatican II teaches that the head of the college of bishops is the pope, the bishop of Rome, and without its head the body of bishops has no authority. The body is incomplete without a head, and the head is incomplete without the body.

This dynamic interaction and mysterious web of relationships among local churches is well described by an Eastern Orthodox theologian. Although he does not use the word *communion*, he articulates a vision that is both reminiscent of the mysticism of the Eastern church and the internal causality of the new creation story. It truly foreshadows the mystery of the church found in Vatican II.

> The multitude of local churches was *not* dispersed, it was united. The union was something absolutely *sui generis*: the unity was not the result of separate parts reuniting, but it was the unity of one

---

[30] Hamer, *The Church Is a Communion,* p. 166.

[31] Nichols, *That All May Be One,* p. 242.

and the same Church. Each local church united in itself all the local churches because it possessed all the fullness of the Church of God, and all the local churches together were united, because they were always this same Church of God. Though a local church did contain everything it needed within itself, it could not live apart from the other churches. It could not shut itself in or refuse to be acquainted with happenings in other churches: for anything that happened in other churches as well as its own, happened in the Church of God, the one and only Church. All the multitude of local churches forms one union founded on concord and love.[32]

THE PRIMACY OF ROME

In this Church of Christ the Roman Pontiff is the successor of Peter, to whom Christ entrusted the feeding of his sheep and lambs. Hence by divine institution he enjoys supreme, full, immediate, and universal authority over the care of souls. (*Christus Dominus*, #2)

Among the faithful within the Roman Catholic Church, there is an almost unconscious mythology that describes the origin of the primacy of the Roman pontiff in the church. It is based to some extent on certain passages in Scripture, on the definitions of the First Vatican Council, and on people's experience of papal power as exercised during the last one hundred years.[33] This story can be summarized this way. In some real sense Jesus established the church, gathered the disciples, chose those who would exercise leadership, and selected Peter as the head of the band of apostles. Peter exercised this leadership role in biblical times, and then he went to Rome and established his leadership there. As a result Rome became the center of Catholic unity, and Rome began to exercise its primacy in the church. Then the successors of Peter, in an unbroken line, carried on this leadership and this primacy.

On the other hand, Protestant theologian Oscar Cullmann shows the weaknesses of the evidence for this historical continuity while still taking a positive attitude toward the role of Peter in the life of the early church.[34] His basic thesis is that Peter exercised leadership over the Jerusalem church for a while, and then turned his leadership over to the other apostles, and went out to serve as a missionary. According to Cullmann we cannot prove whether Peter came to Rome or not. Although he accepts the leadership role of Peter in the primitive church, he concludes that the principle of historical

---

[32] Afaanassieff, "The Church which Presides in Love," p. 78.

[33] For a more extensive treatment of this issue see: Tillard, *The Bishop of Rome*, and Granfield, *The Limits of the Papacy*.

[34] Cullmann, Oscar, *Peter: Disciple, Apostle, Martyr*, Philadelphia, Westminster Press, 1962, p. 157. See also his treatment of "The Leadership of the Church," pp. 228–242.

succession cannot be justified either from Scripture or from the history of the ancient church.

We may ask: Does it make any difference whether we can show a historical succession? Have we, perhaps, been approaching the question of the primacy from the wrong perspective? A new possibility appears by an analogy to the use of prophetic texts in the Christian Scriptures.

One way of interpreting the prophetic texts in the Old Testament is to proceed as if the prophetic literature in Jewish Scriptures foresaw, at least in broad general categories, certain things about the life of Jesus, and Jesus then fulfilled those prophecies. This suggests a linear and historical continuity between prophecy and fulfillment. However, there is another way of interpreting the Jewish prophetic literature. In this view the early Christians had a deep experience of the person, life, and work of Jesus, and it was an experience that they had to express in some language and some set of symbols. They looked backed to the religious and social background of their Jewish ancestors, and then used the language and concepts of the Hebrew Scriptures, such as the suffering servant from Isaiah and the Son of Man in Daniel, to express their experience of Jesus. They reinterpreted, idealized, and applied these ideas to the life, death, and resurrection of Jesus. The early Christians used the prophetic language of the ancient literature to express their contemporary experience. Their methodology was more proleptic than linear.

Dominic Crossan describes this process in the following way:

> The past was used to ground the present and found the future, but in the process Jesus became incomparably greater than any predecessor on which he was being modeled. That similarity in general procedure was not coincidental but represented divergent examples of an even earlier Christian tradition, that of searching the scriptures as foundational, and not just apologetic or polemical, texts to understand Jesus, his movement, his destiny, and the lives and hopes of his first followers.[35]

Crossan applies this methodology to the virginity of Mary in what he calls retrojection.

> Clearly somebody went seeking in the Old Testament for a text that could be interpreted as prophesying a virginal conception, even if such was never its original meaning. Somebody had already decided on the transcendental importance of the adult Jesus and sought to retroject that significance onto the conception and birth itself.[36]

---

[35] Crossan, John Dominic, *Jesus: A Revolutionary Biography*, New York, HarperCollins, 1995, p. 16.

[36] Crossan, *Jesus*, p. 18

Crossan uses the word *retroject* to describe this process because the early Christians "looked back" and searched the Scriptures to articulate their faith, and I use the word *proleptic* because I see the early Christians "throwing forward" what is found in the Jewish Scriptures in order to explain their current beliefs. We are both describing the same phenomenon.

A similar process happened within the early church. By the third century the Church of Rome had in fact become the center of the communion among the various churches and was exercising some form of primacy. The foundation for this primacy was a belief that both Peter and Paul were martyred in Rome as well as the historical reality of Rome as the center of the empire at the time. How could the church explain and describe the growth of the primacy of Rome? What language could they use? They reached back into their inspired literature, and they saw in the person of Peter, and in the leadership functions he performed, a way of interpreting and understanding what had developed in the life of the church. They took a contemporary experience and articulated it in terms of their understanding of Peter in the New Testament. Their methodology was also more proleptic than linear. John Meyendorff, an Eastern Orthodox theologian, summarizes this process that gradually became part of the life of the early church.

> The reason why the Roman Church had been accorded an incontestable precedence over all other apostolic churches was that its Petrine and Pauline "apostolicity" was in fact added to the city's position as the capital city, and only the conjunction of both these elements gave the Bishop of Rome the right to occupy the place of a primate in the Christian world with the consensus of all the churches.[37]

It might have been expected that Jerusalem would be the first of the apostolic churches. It was the geographic focus of the most significant events in the life of Jesus. Jerusalem was the church consulted in the major decisions affecting the life of the apostolic church (see Gal. 2:1–10; Acts 6:1–6; 15:1–11). The fact that primacy within the communion of local churches instead emerged at Rome was a decisive event, and it helps to clarify the apostolic basis for that primacy.

> The hierarchy of the Churches was thus determined in relation not to the story of Jesus, but to the apostolic mission and witness. . . . The local church at Rome is first among the churches because the martyrdom of Peter and Paul there made it the supreme place of apostolic witness.[38]

---

[37] Meyendorff, John, "St. Peter in Byzantine Theology," in *The Primacy of Peter,* Afaanassieff et al., London, Faith Press, 1963, p. 8.

[38] Tillard, *The Bishop of Rome,* pp. 74–75.

It is important to notice that in the early church the primacy, which Rome possessed, was not tied to the person of the bishop but to the apostolic significance that the church at Rome had within the communion of local churches. Nevertheless, the one who occupied the See of that city gradually assumed a personal primacy in the church. Over the centuries, the primacy of the bishop of Rome increased in scope and in power in such a way that its origins in a local church and its interdependent relationship within the communion of churches was weakened and at times lost altogether. We can see the shift of power from the church at Rome to the bishop of Rome in the actual words of three popes, one from the late sixth century, one from the eleventh century, and one from the late thirteenth century.[39]

Gregory the Great (590–604) wrote a letter to the patriarch of Alexandria who had addressed him as the universal pope. Gregory writes, "Here at the head of your letter I find the proud title of universal pope, which I have refused. I pray your most beloved Holiness not to do it again, because what is exaggeratedly attributed to another is taken away from you." Gregory the Great does not wish to be seen as a universal pope.

Gregory VII (1073–1085) gave a list of 27 papal prerogatives in his work entitled *Dictates Papae*. Below are several examples that show both the growth of his universal power and the inerrancy of his teaching.

> Only the Roman pontiff deserves to be called universal.
> No canonical text exists without his authority.
> He may not be judged by anyone.
> The Roman Church has never erred and, as Scripture shows, can
>   never err.
> He may depose and absolve bishops outside any synodal assembly.

The broad power of the papacy over salvation is clearly stated by Boniface VIII (1294–1303) in the papal bull, *Unam Sanctam*, "We declare, state and define that it is absolutely necessary to salvation for every human creature to be subject to the Roman pontiff."

This historical process, which increased the power of the pope, reached its climax in the words of the Dogmatic Constitution of the First Vatican Council (1870):

> If, then, any one shall say that the Roman Pontiff has the office merely of inspection or direction but not the full and supreme power and jurisdiction over the Universal Church, not only in things pertaining to faith and morals, but also in those things that relate to the discipline and government of the Church spread throughout the world; or that he possesses merely the principal part, and not all the fullness of this supreme power; or that this power which he enjoys is not ordinary and immediate, both over

---

[39] For the sources of these texts see Tillard, *The Bishop of Rome*, pp. 53–55.

each and all the Churches, and all the pastors and the faithful: let him be anathema.[40]

The primacy of the Roman Church had become the primacy of the Roman pontiff.

A century later the Second Vatican Council, in some ways, modified this emphasis on the primacy of the Roman pontiff by reaffirming that the Church of Christ is truly present in the local churches and by developing a theology of the college of bishops with the bishop of Rome as its head. A new insight of Vatican II as compared with Vatican I is "the movement from an ecclesiology starting with the idea of the universal Church divided into portions called dioceses, to an ecclesiology that understands the Church as the communion of all the local churches: the universal Church arises from the communion of churches."[41] These developments gave some hope for a new synthesis and a reduction of the tensions between the local churches and the universal church, between the communion among the churches and the primacy of Rome.

What has happened, however, is that the tensions have been increasing rather than decreasing in the years since Vatican II. There are several reasons for the increase in tension:

1. Vatican II failed to clarify the relationship between the supreme authority of the pope as head of the church and the supreme authority of the college of bishops under the leadership of the pope. Both can be understood to be supreme in the council documents.
2. The Synod of Bishops has not fulfilled its hoped-for function of demonstrating that all the bishops in hierarchical communion share in the responsibility for the universal church. Rather, it has become a consultative body and not a deliberative body, a forum without power.
3. The Conference of Bishops, which has shown its value and usefulness in many ways, has also become a body dependent on the approval, and often on the disapproval, of the Roman authorities.
4. The efforts of the pope and Vatican authorities to maintain a tight control on theology and the boundaries of dissent further accentuated the centralization of power.
5. The personality and charism of Pope John Paul II and his many pastoral visits have given him the aura of a universal pope and have made him an embodiment of supreme power over all the church.

Is it possible at this point in history to find a way of articulating the tradition of the church that will maintain the values of a communion among local churches and a primacy of the Church of Rome? Can we develop a new theology and a church structure that will enable the church to emerge

---

[40] Denzinger-Schonmetzer, 3064.

[41] Tillard, *The Bishop of Rome,* p. 37.

from local churches and to preach the good news of salvation and the reign of God more effectively? There is a way to live out the vision of the church and provide servant leaders who will be truly in touch with the pressing needs of this new age. It can be found in the new universe story and the holy web based on holarchical theory.

CHURCH AND THE NEW UNIVERSE STORY

As we begin this holarchical description of the church, we will briefly review the concept of holons, the difference between an individual holon and a social holon, and the place of leadership in a social holon. Then we will amplify these concepts, broaden them, and apply them to the church.

The general idea of a holon as a whole/part is found in the words of Ken Wilbur:

> Whole atoms are parts of molecules; whole molecules are parts of cells; whole cells are parts of organisms, and so on. Each *whole* is simulaneously a *part*, a whole/part, a holon. And reality is composed, not of things nor processes nor wholes nor parts, but of whole/parts, of holons.[42]

An *individual holon* is a whole/part that is found in the very physical make-up of the universe, such as a molecule, a living cell, a dog, or a human. A *social holon* is a whole/part that comes into being by the interaction and the decision of individuals and social groups, such as a marriage, a church, a city, or the United Nations. An individual holon can never be a whole in relationship to a social holon. Thus the one who exercises a *leadership role in a social holon* is a part of that social holon.

As we have seen, the most fundamental reality of the mystery of the church is the people of God. The people of God are the church. Each member of a parish is an individual holon, a whole person who is also a part of a parish.[43] The parish is a social holon, and the parish community is a part of the diocese. As with all holons the whole is greater than its parts, and yet is dependent on its parts. Without atoms there would be no molecules, and without molecules there would be no cells; similarly, without members there would be no parish, and without parishes there would be no dioceses.[44]

---

[42] Wilber, Ken, *Sex, Ecology, Spirituality: The Spirit of Evolution*, Boston, Shambhala, 1995, p viii.

[43] For the sake of simplicity we will use the term "parish," not in its juridical sense, but in its broadest sense to include communities that gather regularly to celebrate the Eucharist, such as, communities of women and men religious, hospitals, autonomous schools, and intentional communities.

[44] Historically, up to the sixth century the diocese and the parish were identical, and it was only during the Middle Ages at the Council of Trent that the parish became a juridical entity forming a part of a diocese. See Sabbas J. Kilian, *Theological Models for the Parish,* New York, Alba House, 1977, pp. 3–39.

Thus holons emerge from atoms to molecules to cells to organisms, and the church emerges from members to parishes to dioceses.

We should look now at two related qualities of holons: their *depth* and their *span*. The number of levels that a holarchy incorporates determines its depth. For example, a cell has greater depth than subatomic particles because it is a whole that incorporates a greater number of levels, such as, molecules, atoms, and subatomic particles. The span of a holon, on the other hand, is determined by the number of holons at any particular level. Because holons of greater span are the components of deeper holons, the number of holons at the lower level is greater than the number of holons of more depth. In the human body, for example, there are a greater number of atoms than molecules, and more molecules than cells. Thus the greater the depth the less the span, and the greater the span the less the depth.

This understanding helps clarify the distinction between what is more *fundamental* and what is more *significant* in reality. The greater the span of a holon the more fundamental it is because it is the component of so many other holons. Atoms are more fundamental than cells because they have a greater span and are the necessary part of not only cells but a multitude of other holons. Without atoms much of the beauty and depth of the earth would not exist, including the cells of the human body.

On the other hand, the greater the depth of a holon the more *significant* that holon is because it possesses a greater wholeness. A living body is more significant than an atom because the body contains not only atoms but molecules and cells, and organs, and so on. Thus we can say that the greater the depth of a holon, the lesser its span, and the more significant it is; the greater the span of a holon, the lesser its depth, and the more fundamental it is.

These characteristics of holons can also be applied to the local churches in which there are various levels of depth and of span. The parish is a whole whose parts are its individual members, and the diocese is a whole whose parts are the parishes. As we saw above, in any holon the greater the depth the lesser the span, and the greater the span the lesser the depth. There are more members than parishes, and more parishes than dioceses, so the members have a greater span than the dioceses. On the other hand, there is greater depth in dioceses as compared to parishes and members precisely because the diocese is a whole combining both members and parishes. This is illustrated in the diagram on the opposite page.

Thus it also follows that there is a holarchy among the various dimensions of the church. Dioceses have greater depth than parishes and hence are more *significant,* whereas the parishes have greater span than dioceses and hence are more *fundamental.* In the life of the church, there is a mutual interdependence because of this relationship. The more fundamental (the parish) governs the *possibilities* of the more significant (the diocese), and the more significant (the diocese) governs the *probabilities* of the more fundamental (the parish).

QUALITIES OF HOLONS
DEPTH OR SPAN: FUNDAMENTAL OR SIGNIFICANT

The greater the depth, the less the span

Depth

The greater the depth, the more significant

Global Church

(Communion among local churches)

Dioceses Dioceses Dioceses

Parishes Parishes Parishes Parishes

Members Members Members Members Members Members Members

Span

The greater the span, the less the depth

The greater the span, the more fundamental

For example, in one North American diocese, the diocesan authorities sent out a proposed list of parish clusters with the request that each of these clusters begin to meet and plan how they would move toward institutional collaboration. Many of the parishes found that there was little or no potential for clustering in their area. They met once or twice, and the plan at the diocesan level evaporated. Thus the parishes, the more fundamental holons, were able in this instance to govern the possibility of the diocese, the more significant holon.

Likewise, the more significant governs the probabilities of the more fundamental. A local intentional community without diocesan affiliation has a certain indeterminancy in terms of the directions it might go and how it might operate, but once such an intentional community becomes part of a diocese, there will be less indeterminancy and certain patterns will become more probable as relates to diocesan policies. In this way the diocese, the more significant, governs the probabilities of the intentional community, the more fundamental.

The question might arise: Are we not slipping back into the "great chain of being" and the traditional hierarchical structure of the church by saying that the diocese is a deeper holon and, as such, is more significant? If the diocese is more significant than a parish, and the parish is more significant than its members, are we not making a value judgment that places dioceses above parishes and parishes above its members?

In reality, holarchy involves something more radical. In holarchy, the movement of being has its center in God and flows out into a mutually dependant dynamic web of relationships among holons with various levels of depth and span and with varying fundamental and significant roles to play.

In any configuration, holons with greater depth are more significant because they have greater wholeness and embrace greater diversity than holons with lesser depth. Likewise, in any configuration holons with greater span are more fundamental because they are the origins and source of those holons with greater depth. *But the flow of being in a holarchy is from the inside out and not from the top down.*

In a Holarchical Church the power, authority, and holiness flow from God as its center out into a mutually dependent dynamic web of relationships among the members, the parishes and the dioceses with various levels of depth and span and with varying fundamental and significant roles. Dioceses are, indeed, more significant than parishes because of their greater wholeness and the greater diversity that they embrace. Parishes, however, are more fundamental because they are the origin and source of dioceses because dioceses depend on parishes and parishes depend on members. *Once again, the flow of power, authority, and holiness is from the inside out* (sensus fidelium) *and not from the top down.*

Moreover, in the traditional hierarchical structure of the church, the bishop is seen as the head over the diocese with the fullness of power to teach, to sanctify, and to govern within the dioceses. In holarchy, however, as pointed out above, there is a difference between *individual* holons and *social* holons. Individual holons can be part of a social holon, but an individual holon cannot be a social holon. Thus the pastor of a parish is a member and a part of the parish with a particular sacramental leadership ministry among the many other ministries within the parish. Likewise, the bishop of a diocese is a member of a diocesan parish. Because of his membership in the local parish, the bishop can exercise a sacramental leadership ministry within the diocese among the many other ministries within diocese. The same thing is true for the pope because, as Granfield says, "One enters the Church only through a local Church; every Christian, including the Pope, belongs to some local Church. The Pope is the Bishop of Rome and head of the universal Church, but he is also a member of the local Church of Rome."[45]

Sacramental leadership affirmed by the community within a sacramental church, whether a parish or a diocese, is central and essential to the life of the community, but this leadership function is dependent for its full realization on all the other ministries within the parish or the diocese and the mutual accountability between the leader and the community. "The Holy Spirit does not just speak to the community through its bishop; it may also speak to the bishop through the community." [46]

There is another very important dimension of the relationship between individual holons and social holons. Even though an individual holon, such as a member of a parish, exists inseparably from its social environment, such as a parish, and is dependent on this environment, it retains its own in-

---

[45] Granfield, *The Limits of the Papacy,* p. 112.

[46] Nichols, *That All May Be One,* pp. 243–244.

dividuality and subjectivity within the environment. There is a temptation to describe a social holon, such as a diocese, as a superorganism, which has priority over the individual holons that are its parts. Ken Wilbur argues "that the essence of pathological social hierarchies is precisely the attempt to turn them [social holons] into individual holons (*L'etat c'est moi*) and treat citizens as mere components in a 'more holistic system.'"[47] There is a temptation to function as if the parish is the pastor and the diocese is the bishop. However, the diocese and the parish, as social holons, are accountable to the members, and they must respect the subjectivity and rights of their members. The purpose of the diocese and the parish is to foster, guide, and protect the interests of its member holons who are the people of God.

Is the communion among diocesan churches described above a new and deeper holon than the individual dioceses? Does the communion among local churches constitute a new social holon, which can be called the universal church? Sometimes the universal church seems to function as if it were primary and the diocese is simply a dependent administrative unit of the universal church. In this way of understanding the universal church, the bishop becomes the vicar of the Roman pontiff and not the vicar of Christ. This is contrary to the teaching of Vatican II.

> These faith assemblies [the diocesan churches] are not simply administrative units of the universal Church, but are concrete realizations, admittedly in varying degrees, of the entire mystery of the Body of Christ which is one. The local Church is the Church, because it possesses the entire promise of the Gospel, the full reality of the faith, and the grace of the Triune God. The local Church is the Church, because in it Christ is wholly present.[48]

In a Holarchical Church the communion among local churches would be a new and deeper social holon. Therefore, I prefer to use the phrase "global church" in place of "universal church." The phrase "universal church" carries with it the connotation of a worldwide organization with a uniform liturgy and a uniform legal structure. A "global church" seems to catch the sense of a dynamic communion among relatively autonomous churches around the entire globe, and it describes more accurately the holarchical nature of the church.

In the church, as it currently functions, the most basic structure is the diocese "in which the one, holy, catholic and apostolic Church of Christ is truly present and operative" (*Christus Dominus*, #11). The dioceses, however, as members of the global church, are not totally autonomous. If we see the communion among dioceses in terms of quantum particles and waves, the particle dimension of the diocesan holon is what determines its identity and its capacity for self-preservation, and the wave dimension of the dioce-

---

[47] Wilber, *Sex, Ecology, Spirituality,* p. 65.

[48] Granfield, *The Limits of the Papacy,* p. 112. See *Lumen Gentium,* #27.

san holon enables it to relate to other diocesan churches through its capacity for self-adaptation. This is what Wilber calls "a network of relationships with other holons at the *same level of organization.*"[49]

The global church, however, is a new and different holon at a level with more depth than the dioceses. This image can help us grasp more readily the internal relationships among dioceses called the communion among churches. It can illustrate how a diocese can be both a whole in which the one, holy, catholic, and apostolic Church of Christ is truly present and operative and, at the same time, a member of a global church within a broader web of relationships. A friend of mine describes this holarchical structure in the following way:

> A parish or congregation achieves holon status when it achieves a size that is stable. Similarly, dioceses represent a group of congregations that is, in itself, stable. A church achieves universality when, as a congregation of dioceses, it achieves stability. A congregation to achieve holonhood must have diversity. One thousand people all alike do not make a stable and new entity. Similarly, to be a valuable higher-level social holon, a diocese must be diverse, bringing together congregations that are very different, one from the other so that something new and richer is created in the existence of the diocese. If this is true then the universal [global] church gains its right to exist from its very diversity. Only in the body of the universal [global] church do people from all corners of the globe unite and become something larger than the sum of the parts.[50]

This communion among local churches involves a same-level relational exchange that is symbolized in the celebration of the Eucharist, which is the sacramental bond among local churches.

> Each local community bonded into itself by the Eucharist finds that by that very fact it is "in full unity" with the other local communities, wherever they may be in the world: not "by virtue of a superimposed external structure, but by virtue of the whole Christ who is present in each one of them."[51]

Because the concept of a college of bishops in Vatican II is based on this reality of the communion among local churches, in the new paradigm we can more accurately describe this collegiality. Vatican II says: "The collegial nature and meaning of the episcopal order found expression in the very ancient practice by which bishops appointed the world over were linked with one another and with the Bishop of Rome by the bonds of unity, charity and peace" (*Lumen Gentium*, #22).

[49] Wilber, *Sex, Ecology, Spirituality,* pp. 66–67 (emphasis original).

[50] A comment from Bob Veitch, a member of the First Friday Group.

[51] Tillard, *The Bishop of Rome,* p. 151.

According to the new paradigm, each bishop, including the bishop of Rome, is a member of a local church and exercises a specific servant leadership ministry within the diocese as a result of the sacramental ritual of ordination or affirmation. Because of the communion among diocesan churches, each bishop becomes a member of the college of bishops with care and concern for the whole church. The college is a way of naming the mutual relationships among dioceses and the responsibilities that flow from that relationship. Each bishop, including the bishop of Rome, is part of the college because of the bishop's relationship to a local church, and the bishop of Rome is the head of the college of bishops because of the primacy of the church of Rome, as explained above. As the head of the college the bishop of Rome has a servant leadership role as the first among equals, the *primus inter pares*.

In terms of the new paradigm based on holons, neither the church at Rome nor the pope, who is the bishop of the Roman church, stands outside of or above the communion among local churches or the college of bishops. In *Lumen Gentium*, #22, Vatican II says, "The college or body of bishops has no authority unless it is simultaneously conceived in terms of its head, the Roman Pontiff" and, according to the new paradigm, the pope as the bishop of Rome has no authority unless it is simultaneously conceived in terms of the body of bishops. In the tradition of the Roman Catholic Church, the election of a pope and the enthronement of the pope are not considered to be a sacrament in the same way as that of consecration of a bishop in a sacrament. Thus the office of the pope does not give the pope an authority in isolation from the college of bishops, but it does give the pope a primacy based on his role as bishop of the primatial See of Rome. Tillard describes this ecclesiology:

> The ecclesiology of the Church as a communion of local churches entrusted to the *episkope* of the bishops in communion with each other should be considered in close connection with another major theme of *Lumen Gentium*: the fact that episcopal authority and its juridical institution is founded upon a sacrament—the episcopate.[52]

> The full weight of this assertion from *Lumen Gentium* needs to be brought to bear on the theology of the papacy. For it is clear that whatever is founded upon a sacrament must have priority within the Church of God: the Church comes about by faith and sacraments and all its essential marks are to be found within the osmosis of faith and sacraments. To deny this would be to forsake the Great Tradition, that of the Church still undivided which takes precedence over the divided Churches. For the election of a pope has never been reckoned a sacrament. What is more, neither the elec-

---

[52] Vatican II, *Lumen Gentium*, #26: "[The bishop is] marked with the fullness of the sacrament of orders."

tion nor the enthronement of a pope conveys any "indelible character"; when a pope resigns he simply ceases to be pope.

Putting the supreme pontiff above the bishops in a sort of
pseudo-sacramental halo which makes him transcend the episcopal
order in "dignity" makes him beyond all doubt something *more
than* and *different from a pope.*[53]

This ecclesiology, as well as the new paradigm, seems to limit the power
of the pope. How can this be justified as Vatican II says that the Roman
pontiff enjoys supreme, full, immediate, and universal authority within the
church? The only guideline issuing from the council itself is found in the re-
fusal of the assembled bishops in July 1964 to accept an amendment that
Pope Paul VI wanted to include. The amendment was to be attached at the
end of *Lumen Gentium* saying that the Roman pontiff ought certainly to
take account of the collegial power of the bishops, but that the pope was accountable to God alone. The commission replied: "The Roman pontiff is
bound to abide by Revelation itself, the basic structure of the Church, the
sacraments, the definitions of the first Councils, etc. It is impossible to list
them all."[54]

Patrick Granfield in his book *The Limits of the Papacy* states the question in this way.

> The expansion of papal power may be understandable in view of
> historical circumstances, but to many it seems far removed from the
> scriptural ideal of authority as humble service within and for the
> People of God. Catholics and non-Catholics inevitably ask about
> the limits of papal authority. What are the boundaries that deter-
> mine the legitimate exercise of papal authority?[55]

In terms of the new paradigm the following limitations can be suggested:

1. *The intrinsic limits:* The overarching and guiding vision of the church
is the reign of God manifested in healing, reconciliation, and liberation.
This vision of the church is the specific purpose that determines and deline-
ates papal authority. The mandate of the bishop of Rome, therefore, is to
maintain and safeguard the visible unity of the church in accordance with
the vision of the reign of God and to show care and concern for all the local
churches that belong to the *communio.* Any action that violates this man-

---

[53] Tillard, *The Bishop of Rome,* pp. 38–39 (emphasis original). See Archbishop Rembert
Weakland, "Church of Many Cultures, World of Globalization," in *Origins,* November 12,
1998, p. 396. "Somehow we must arrive at the stage where it is clear in law and in practice
that the Holy Father, for the ordinary governance of the church, is acting within the college of
bishops and not separated from it."

[54] See Tillard, *The Bishop of Rome,* p. 41.

[55] Granfield, *The Limits of the Papacy,* p. 51.

date or runs contrary to the vision of the reign of God is blameworthy and may even be invalid.

2. *The limits of natural law:* Popes, like the rest of humanity, are bound by the fundamental norms that have their source in human reason; they must act according to the precepts of natural law. The pope is bound by the laws of nature, and he is neither above them, exempt from them, nor in control of them.[56]

3. *The limits of revelation:* The pope, like all Christians, must follow and live out the revelation of God found within the universe, within the Word of God in Scripture, and within the traditions of the Christian church. It is always difficult to delineate the contents of revelation, but the search for the meaning of revelation sets definite parameters for the church, and even for the pope. "The magisterium is not above the Word of God, but serves it, teaching only what has been handed on" (*Dei verbum,* #10).

4. *The limits of holarchy:* The authority of the pope is limited because it flows from his position as the bishop of Rome and from the primacy of that See, and that authority is exercised within the college of bishops and the communion among the churches. Moreover, within a holarchical model, the more fundamental holons, such as the members and the parishes, set the possibilities of the more significant holons, such as the dioceses. Thus the faith and the faith experiences of church members and parishes can and do determine the possibilities of the papal authority.

5. *The limits of the* sensus fidei: The abstract concept of the more fundamental determining the possibilities of the more significant is concretized in the *sensus fidei,* that is a graced sensitivity given to all believers enabling them to perceive the truth of faith. This sensitivity creates a climate and a communal instinct that enables believers to grasp the truth because Christian truth exists only in the living faith of people. If the Holy Spirit is present within all believers, then the faithful play a fundamental role in the discernment and reception of the faith. Reception involves the entire church, and thus limits the possibilities of papal authority.

These are some of the limits of the authority of the bishop of Rome. It is equally important that we stress some of the unique contributions that can be made by the servant leadership ministry of the bishop of Rome at the level of the global church, which is sometimes called the *Petrine ministry.* The story of the "Council of Jerusalem" (Acts 15:1–33) describes how some of the early leaders in the church, the "pillars" of the community, exercised a Petrine ministry for and in the name of the whole church. After extensive discussion the decision was made by "the apostles and presbyters in agreement with the whole church" (vs. 22). The resulting letter states clearly that "it is the decision of the Holy Spirit and of us not to place on you any bur-

---

[56]See Granfield, *The Limits of the Papacy,* pp. 63–64.

den beyond the necessities" (vs. 28). In a Holarchical Church and in a media society, there is an even greater need for a Petrine ministry for and in the name of the whole church because of the global reach and the interconnectedness possible in the technological age.

In a self-organizing system, such as the Christian church, it is not possible to predict what will emerge in the future, but we can suggest some of the dimensions of the Petrine ministry of the bishop of Rome within a new paradigm of the church.

1. *The service of unity:* "[Vatican I and Vatican II] are careful to give this service of unity as the essential mission of the local church at Rome and her bishop."[57] Because of the high visibility of the bishop of Rome, made possible by the media and by extensive travels, the pope can be a credible and visible witness of Christian unity and a visible foundation for the unity of faith. This is possible only if the pope is able to facilitate the cooperation, communication, and consultation necessary for consensus within the whole church. In this service to the church, it is important to remember, the bishop of Rome does not create unity—that comes from the inner presence of the Holy Spirit—but helps to discover, foster, and preserve that unity that comes from the Spirit.

2. *The service of communion:* The church at every level is a dynamic web of relationships found in the reality of communion that exists at every level from the parish to the diocese to the global communion among local churches. "The charism of the bishop of Rome is to be a facilitator of consensus and a center of unity among the episcopal college."[58] The functions of the bishop of Rome in the service of communion are to support the various churches in their confession of the apostolic faith, to ensure respect for the privileges proper to each of the churches, and to energize the churches in their mutual efforts to preach the good news of the reign of God among the people of diverse cultures. The pope can work to safeguard the cultural identity of each local church, while encouraging and strengthening the web of relationships among and within the churches.

3. *Corporate personality:* The concept of "corporate personality" is both a biblical term and a sociological term. It describes a phenomenon in which the life of a group becomes concentrated and focused in one of its members who in every respect is like the other members but becomes the symbol of the entire group. For example, in the Jewish Scriptures the "suffering servant" of Isaiah refers sometimes to an individual and sometimes to the nation. The bishop of Rome, even though he is only a bishop, performs actions and has functions in which the entire episcopate is caught up and symbolized. "He [the Pope] plays a sacramental and symbolic role as the

---

[57] Tillard, *The Bishop of Rome*, p. 126.

[58] Nichols, *That All May Be One*, p. 325.

center of the *communio* of the Churches. The Pope is an effective and a ju-
ridically empowered symbol."[59]

There is a real danger, however, that this symbolic person can become a
self-directed, charismatic, and authoritarian leader. Nevertheless, within a
community that is essentially sacramental, it is not surprising that the
bishop who exercises a leadership role within the communion of churches
would be experienced as a corporate personality and as a symbol of the
whole church. If the bishop of Rome searches out the heart of the believing
community, functions within the college of bishops, serves the whole people
of God in their search for the reign of God in this world, then the pope, as a
corporate person, can fulfill a useful, powerful, and sacramental role in
service to the people of God.

4. *Solidarity with all humanity:* "The papal ministry can offer love,
hope, truth, and compassion to people who are longing for a renewed sense
of spiritual values. By demonstrating his solidarity with all humanity, the
Pope, through his unique role as head of a large, international, and influential religious organization, is able to communicate effectively the saving
message of the Gospel."[60] The primacy of the church at Rome had as its reason for being, at least partially, the position of the city of Rome in the empire. Similarly today there is a responsibility for the bishop of Rome to look
beyond the boundaries of the Christian church. Given the high visibility of
the pope in this global society, the bishop of Rome can be very influential insofar as he recognizes and respects the spiritual values and the religious
authenticity of the many cultures of the world.

In 1987 before the papal visit to the United States, I was working with a
group in Washington D.C. called Catholics Speak Out. The purpose of the
group was to encourage Catholics to speak out on issues within the church.
We decided to send a petition, signed by over two thousand people, to
Rome asking that the pope during his visit would reduce by half the number
of talks he would give and use the other half of his visit as a time to listen to
the voices of the people. We did not receive an answer to this request, but
we did hold a series of listening sessions throughout the United States in
which people were asked to share those things that they would have liked to
say to the pope on his visit.

I believe that the success of any Petrine ministry in the church will depend on the willingness of the bishop of Rome to listen to the voices of the
people—the voice of the poor and suffering people around the globe, the
voice of politically powerful of the world, the (often unheard) voice of
women, the voice of theologians, the voice of the local churches. "Ecclesial
communion is not welded together without the Roman see, but that see only

---

[59] Granfield, *The Limits of the Papacy,* p. 60.

[60] Granfield, *The Limits of the Papacy,* p. 177.

welds together what it 'receives' from the churches. The true function of the Roman see is to be found precisely in that reception."[61]

CONCERNS

The Church of the World emerges from the local culture that provides the womb and the nourishment in which the message of Christ can be heard and lived out. The Church of the World as a communion of local churches is global in its outlook, and it ministers in service to all cultures and all nations, and, indeed, the whole of humanity. There are two realities, however, that may the impede the church from fulfilling its mission to the world. (1) The infallibility of the pope, in the way it has been exercised during the last one hundred years, has been at times oppressive within the church itself and an obstacle to relationships beyond the church. This situation calls for an attempt to rediscover the meaning of infallibility in a Holarchical Church. (2) The long-standing schism between the Eastern and Western churches and the divisions among the Western churches call for a discussion of the future of ecumenism in the new paradigm.

THE MEANING OF INFALLIBILITY

> *Life organizes around identity.* Every living thing acts to develop and preserve itself. Identity is the filter that every organism or system uses to make sense of the world. New information, new relationships, changing environments—all are interpreted through a sense of self. This tendency toward self-creation is so strong that it creates a seeming paradox. An organism will change to maintain its identity.[62]

In the summer of 1971 I began a sabbatical with the purpose of studying the meaning of infallibility in the church. Several people asked me, "Since people no longer accept the infallibility of the pope, why do you want to study infallibility?" In reply I often said, "It is not helpful to challenge something unless we know the reason it originally emerged in the life of the church. Before reinterpreting infallibility, I want to discover the meaning of infallibility and why this doctrine was defined at the First Vatican Council." Another reason for the urgency of reviewing this Catholic teaching was my experience that the church had come to interpret the infallibility of the pope in such broad and absolute terms that it had become an oppressive and divisive force within the Christian community. As a result of my study of Christian tradition and its relationship to the holarchical nature of the church, I have found richness in the reality expressed by the word *infallibility*. The word itself, however, carries many negative connotations and may have to be replaced, but the reality underlying the word can be a dynamic force in the life of the Christian community.

---

[61] Tillard, *The Bishop of Rome*, p. 189.

[62] Wheatley and Kellner-Rogers, *A Simpler Way*, p. 14.

We will first explore, in a very brief overview, the story of Vatican I, and then integrate that story with Vatican II and a new paradigm of the church. In the historical background of Vatican I there were three major currents that were swirling around Europe and the Vatican: (1) the church and nationalism; (2) faith and rationalism; and (3) authority and liberalism.[63]

One of the pressing problems in Europe during the nineteenth century was the rise of nationalism and the attempt by national leaders to control the life of the church and even to set up national churches. For example, Joseph II of Austria assumed control over the nomination of bishops, the training of priests, parish and diocesan boundaries, and the administration of church property. In France the state claimed the right to establish seminaries and approve catechisms and liturgical practices. A basic principle of the Christian faith was at stake in these political intrigues. Christian faith is a gift of God and its growth and development can never be subject to state control, nor can the Christian church be so subservient to nationalism that it can no longer bring critical judgment to bear on the policies of the state. The pope in the nineteenth century became the symbol of the freedom and universality of the Christian faith.

There were also many sources of intellectual foment in Europe during the nineteenth century, such as rationalism, historicism, and fideism, and they produced widespread confusion and apprehension within the church. The church responded by appealing to authority as the one safe means of arriving at certitude in religious matters. Against fideism, which exalted sheer faith at the expense of reason, Rome defended the validity of human reason in attaining some knowledge of God, and against rationalism Rome taught clearly that faith is something beyond pure reason. Thus the intellectual revolution of the nineteenth century turned the eyes of the Catholic clergy and people toward Rome for the defense of the basic principle that faith is neither identical with nor subject to human reason.

The third major conflict affecting the church in the nineteenth century grew out of the French Revolution (1789). Liberalism was in the air and every major European nation was locked in a struggle between those who stood for the legitimate monarch and those who were pressing for a liberal reform. The struggle between liberalism and the church became a struggle between liberalism and authority. The clergy and the people began to feel that their liberties were endangered more by the new popular governments than by the papacy, and they turned more and more to Rome. The papacy led the counterattack. The conflict, however, raised basic questions for Christianity. Is the church necessarily a monarchy? Can the Christian community operate as a democracy? Should the church be governed by a popular sovereignty? The bishops at the First Vatican Council felt it incumbent upon them to answer these questions by reaffirming the authority and primacy of the bishop of Rome.

---

[63] See Wessels, Cletus, "The Adequacy of Vatican I," in *Listening,* Spring-Autumn, 1972, pp. 94–117.

In their various ways Rationalists, Nationalists, Liberals and the rest were laying claims to men's allegiance that were new and the Pope—most notably in the Syllabus of Errors—was condemning these claims in the sense that he was rejecting the notion that their doctrines offered an alternative means of salvation to that offered by the church.[64]

By emphasizing papal primacy and authority, the First Vatican Council reaffirmed against nationalism that the Christian community can never be ultimately subject to state control, against rationalism that the Christian community can never be ultimately subject to the control of human reason, against liberalism that the Christian community can never be ultimately subject to popular sovereignty.

Into this political and intellectual context stepped the great figure of Pius IX. Tillard provides us with a concise description of this pope who knew how to parlay the political and spiritual forces surrounding him with his own magnetic personality.

> For many believers of the time he [Pius IX] became a symbol compounded from his winning ways, his obvious and easy piety, his charming gestures, his noble bearing, like a disarmed monarch, and his contact with the pilgrims whom the railway brought to Rome. He seemed to be, as it were, . . . "a refuge at once profoundly human and doggedly faithful" when the Christian ideal was under judgment, a point of stability and hope at the moment when so many civil societies were breaking up. . . . The ideal of the papacy was thus defined around the image of a pope "super pope," as was the "devotion to the pope" which developed. The life of the Catholic Church ever since has been deeply disturbed by it.[65]

The First Vatican Council was really left with no other option than to define the primacy and the infallibility of the pope. The definition satisfied the need for stability in a very turbulent time, it protected the people from the onslaught of nationalism, rationalism, and liberalism, and it provided a basis for the absolute truth demanded by the contemporary Cartesian search for certitude.

Even though the definition of the infallibility of the pope seemed inevitable, there was extensive discussion of the actual text. The minority made its voice heard in a way that impacted and mollified the definition. In a letter to Montalembert in 1853 Archbishop Sibour of Paris noted the dangers in this movement. He pointed out that there may be times when the pope can place himself above the rules and when his power is as wide as the necessities of the church, just as there may be times when a civil ruler may suspend the usual principles of law. There is a danger, however, that the excep-

---

[64] Hales, E. E. Y., *Pio Nono*, London, Eyre & Spottiswoode, 1954, p. 325.

[65] Tillard, *The Bishop of Rome*, pp. 19–20.

tion may become the rule.[66] In time of siege it is justifiable to declare martial law, but it is not justifiable to make martial law the norm of civil society. In the nineteenth century it seemed justifiable to grant to the pope extensive powers over the church, and the majority carried the day. The final text of the council document reads:

> We teach and define that it is a dogma divinely revealed: that the Roman Pontiff, when he speaks *ex cathedra*, that is, when, acting in the office of shepherd and teacher of all Christians, he defines, by virtue of his supreme apostolic authority, doctrine concerning faith or morals to be held by the universal Church, possesses through the divine assistance promised him in the person of St. Peter, the infallibility with which the divine Redeemer willed his Church to be endowed in defining doctrine concerning faith or morals; and that such definitions of the Roman Pontiff are therefore irreformable because of their nature, but not because of the agreement of the Church.[67]

Thus, the word *infallibility* became enshrined in the life and theology of the Catholic Church.

We now live in a different political and religious context, and it is necessary to reread and revisit this definition in the light of Vatican II and a new paradigm. In order to understand the deeper meaning of infallibility it is essential to remember that Christian truth is not abstract or philosophical truth, but it exists only in the living faith of the people. The deeper dimension of infallibility is not directly related to theological truth or to the effort to settle theological disputes, rather it relates to the living truth and the relationship of that truth to the apostolic faith that lives in the hearts of the people of God and guides them in the living out that faith. "The *sensus fidei,* a function of the entire Church, creates a climate, a communal instinct that enables Christians to grasp the truth that saves."[68]

The truth that saves emerges from the law of the gospel, the law written on the heart, which is grace of the Holy Spirit given to those who believe in Christ.[69] Thus individual Christians who act out of the law written on their hearts, the *sensus fidei*, will inevitably live out the truth that saves. This discernment is grounded in and circulates within the entire self-organizing system that is the church itself. The deeper sense of infallibility, better called "communal discernment," is the infallibility with which the divine Re-

---

[66] See a letter in 1853 to Montalembert in Lecanuet, Montalembert, Paris, c. Poressielque, Vol. 3, 1902, pp. 104–106.

[67] *The Church Teaches: Documents of the Church in English Translation,* St. Louis, B. Herder Book Co., 1955, p. 102.

[68] Granfield, *The Limits of the Papacy,* p. 135.

[69] See Thomas Aquinas, *Summa Theologiae,* I–II, q. 106, a. 1.

deemer endowed the church, and which is found in the documents of Vatican II.

> The body of the faithful as a whole, anointed as they are by the Holy One (cf. Jn. 2:20–27), cannot err in matters of belief. Thanks to a supernatural sense of the faith which characterizes the People as a whole, it manifests this unerring quality when, "from the bishops down to the last member of the laity," it shows universal agreement in matters of faith and morals. For, by this sense of faith which is aroused and sustained by the Spirit of truth, God's People accepts not a human word but the very Word of God.
>
> (*Lumen Gentium*, #12)

Communal discernment of the living truth requires a community. Individuals can act in a way that contradicts the apostolic faith either out of ignorance or out of malice, and thus they may act contrary to the law written on their hearts. However, individuals can be in touch with this inner law through prayer and contemplation, and in the context of a community they can experience a deep awareness of this inner law. The community can provide mutual support and challenge for all its members, and it can provide the resources for a common search for the living truth found in the memory of the community. This is the community of disciples described in Chapter 3 as a community of hearers and listeners. The disciple is by definition a person who is a learner and a listener, one who is willing to "hear" others, and one who is open to what is new and challenging in life. If individuals, through the *sensus fidei*, can experience the law written on their heart, so much more can a community of disciples, by communal discernment, discover the truth that saves.

Is it not possible for a community of disciples to lose sight of its apostolic faith and vision? There are examples of local communities that have become racist parishes, others that become inbred and selfish without any outreach in mission, and still others that have lost the centrality of the church as a sacramental community. In order to maintain its vision of the reign of God, Christian communities within a diocese must care for, support, and challenge each other, not in a competitive way, but in a collaborative way that will lead to the benefit of the people. The bishop is called to encourage the search for the living truth within the diocese and, when articulating that communal faith, the bishop will guide the community in the communal discernment process based on the *sensus fidei* of the community.

The charism of infallibility or communal discernment is also found within the communion among the diocesan churches as well as the college of bishops, because this brings together the *sensus fidei* of the people of God with the mutual fidelity of the diocesan churches.

> Although the individual bishops do not enjoy the prerogative of infallibility, they can nevertheless proclaim Christ's doctrine infallibly. This is so, even when they are dispersed around the world, pro-

vided that while maintaining the bond of unity among themselves and with Peter's successor, and while teaching authentically on a matter of faith or morals, they concur in a single viewpoint as the one which must be held conclusively. This authority is even more clearly verified when, gathered together in an ecumenical council, they are teachers and judges of faith and morals for the universal Church. (*Lumen Gentium*, #25)

Within the communion among diocesan churches, the church of Rome, as we have already described, has a primacy, and the bishop of Rome exercises this primacy based on a leadership role within the college of bishops. Thus when the bishop of Rome acts as the teacher of all Christians, that is, when acting as the head of the college of bishops, he possesses that infallibility or communal discernment with which the divine Redeemer willed his church to be endowed. The charism of communal discernment is found in a special way in the bishop of Rome when he speaks *ex cathedra* in the name of the entire communion of churches for the welfare of the people of God. Any papal definition of the apostolic faith, which flows radically from the Holy Spirit as manifested in the *sensus fidei* of God's people, will be an articulation of the living truth of the Christian community.

Richard Gaillardetz offers the following interpretation of Vatican II:

In the theology of Vatican II, Jesus Christ, as both the mediator and sum of divine revelation, is God's personal address to not only the whole Church but the whole human race. Firmly rejected is the view that God communicates divine revelation primarily to the hierarchy, who then transmit that revelation to the rest of the Church. Rather, the word of God emerges within the whole Church through a complex set of ecclesial relationships in which all the baptized, professional theologians, and the college of bishops play important roles.[70]

This rereading of Vatican I, based on the principles of holarchy, respects the primacy and infallibility of the bishop of Rome, while seeing the beginning and the purpose of infallibility within the community of disciples, the people of God.

As we explore the tradition of the church over the last few centuries, we come to see that the word "infallibility" may not be the best word to describe this deeper meaning because it focuses on the end product of the search for the living truth as articulated in doctrinal statements. When the focus is on the end product of a doctrinal formulation, gradual stagnation is the inevitable outcome. The written words become lifeless, rigid, and unchanging. Moreover, as Tillard explains, "This [infallible] judgment will always be marked by the conditions of its time and place and moulded by

---

[70] Gaillardetz, *Teaching with Authority*, p. xi.

language which will always be limited."[71] Such doctrines might be expressions of the apostolic faith, but they will remain lifeless and limited unless they continue to be part of a process of communal reinterpretation and discernment.

> When the Church or a council defines a truth of faith, it is doing so through the assistance of the Holy Spirit. Dogmas are irrevocably true. But they give only limited insights into the mystery of divine truth; deeper understanding and development are possible and necessary. Dogmas must be interpreted; they are not isolated, ahistorical events.[72]

The limited character of the written word was seen by Thomas Aquinas when he says it was not fitting for Christ to write down his teaching for posterity. Raymond Nogar explains, "His [Christ's] interpretation of reality, the Divine revelation of the meaning of existence, was too mysterious to be written. It had to be lived, to be acted out, as it were, in the presence of those who could personally understand with love."[73] If the charism of infallibility focuses on the end product of the search for living truth, it will inevitably be caught up in the limits of language and the written word. Written doctrinal statements are inadequate vessels for the living truth, and they are unable to contain the overflowing mystery of God's extravagant love.

Rather, in the Holarchical Church, we focus on the process involved in the search for the living truth. This process does not result in the rejection of the past but in an ongoing, dynamic search for the mystery of God's love as manifested in the story of Jesus and its impact on the Christian community. The search process calls for a more interpersonal dialogue in which the speaker, the listener, and the Word of God are caught up in a drama of human experience. It is our shared human experience under the guidance of the Holy Spirit that enables us to explore the living truth at the depths of creation, of human society, and of the believing community. This exploration opens for us the deeper meaning of infallibility because it is only in this living process that the truth will prevail. Christian truth is not found in doctrinal formulations. Christian truth is not an abstraction but exists only in the living faith of people.

The word "infallibility" defined as doctrinal statements that are infallibly true and unchanging is no longer appropriate language in a continuously unfolding and changing universe and a self-organizing system. Perhaps the word infallibility may be one more Gordian knot that must be cut in order to free the church to become a dynamic web of relationships that can explore new life forms flowing from its vision of the reign of God. Per-

---

[71] Tillard, *The Bishop of Rome,* p. 173.

[72] Granfield, *The Limits of the Papacy,* p. 70.

[73] Nogar, Raymond J., *The Lord of the Absurd,* New York, Herder and Herder, 1972, pp. 23–24.

haps a better way of describing the deeper sense of infallibility can be found in the phrase "communal discernment" that involves the dynamic presence of the Holy Spirit within a web of relationships. This communal discernment will guarantee that the living truth will prevail in the church, and that "the gates of hell shall not prevail against it" (Matt. 16:18).

THE FUTURE OF ECUMENISM

> The mission of the Christian Church is to be a sign and an agent of the integration of all creatures in Christ. This entails both vertical and horizontal communion, as well as communion in time. But if the Church is to be a sacramental sign of the reconciliation of all things in Christ, it must itself be united. Fragmented into competing denominations, it cannot image the integration of the Mystical Body. But also it cannot be artificially united by a command hierarchy which suppresses legitimate diversity. Thus I suggest that it be united according to the principles of participatory hierarchy and holarchy.[74]

As the word has been used in the ecumenical circles during the last fifty years, "unity" is often seen as a structural or governmental union among churches. This view is well stated by Lewis Mudge, who says, "When churches come together, there must be agreement that henceforth they will live under some particular system of church government. Otherwise there is not visible unity."[75] Those of us who grew up Catholic think of unity in terms of a unified government, a unified church structure, and a unified sacramental system. The Consultation on Church Unity (COCU) also searched for ways to form a Uniting Church, which the COCU conceives as a search for structural and governmental unity among the churches involved. Mergers between Protestant denominations have usually resulted in the formation of a new unified church body, for example, the United Church of Christ and the United Methodist Church. In my opinion, if the future of ecumenism is conceived of in these terms, we will never find Christian unity.

The biblical concept of unity, however, says nothing about unity of structure or government. The word "unity" seldom appears in the New Testament. It is found, however, in the Letter to the Ephesians:

> I, then, a prisoner of the Lord, urge you to live in a manner worthy of the call you have received, with all humility and gentleness, with patience, bearing with one another through love, striving to preserve the unity of the spirit through the bond of peace: one body and one Spirit, as you were also called to the one hope of your call; one Lord, one faith, one baptism; one God and Father of all, who is over all and through all and in all.   (Eph. 4:1–6)

---

[74] Nichols, *That All May Be One*, pp. 331–332.

[75] Mudge, Lewis S., *One Church: Catholic and Reformed*, Philadelphia, Westminster Press, 1963, p. 95.

Unity of the Spirit, yes; unity of faith, yes; but there is no demand for uniformity in terms of structure, government, worship, or doctrine. The biblical concept of unity is crucial in the life of the church and in the development of true ecumenism, but as Cardinal Augustin Bea has written: "Unity, for example, must not be mistaken for uniformity. It is not necessary to burden the children of God with unnecessary restriction on their legitimate freedom or to try to abolish unexceptionable customs inherent in the various churches."[76]

If not organic church unity then what vehicle is there for manifesting our Christian unity? Some see the future of Christian unity in a federation of all churches with each retaining its autonomy in doctrine, in government, in ministry, and in worship. An example of federation can be found in the World Council of Churches, in which churches throughout the world have come together to form a council while members maintain their freedom and autonomy. There is no common creed that binds all of its members; there is no common sacramental system. The council offers an opportunity for discussion among churches, various charitable and service ministries, theological discussion, and joint missionary efforts. Each church can retain its identity, and yet they can share in a common service to one another and to the peoples of the world.

The World Council of Churches has contributed a great deal to the life of the Christian church, but I believe its emphasis on the autonomy of the local church leaves something lacking. Federation says little or nothing about the relationship of the member churches to each other. Yet the Christian church is a reality that, in some way, is profoundly "one" despite all its diverse manifestations. The concept of federation does not really catch the full biblical idea of the church as the body of Christ or the living imagery of the vine and the branches, nor does it deal adequately with the new paradigm and the character of a Holarchical Church.

As we look to the future should we work for church unity that involves unity of structure, liturgy, and doctrine? I believe that path will lead nowhere. Should we then have a loose federation of autonomous churches? No, this path will lead to some important ideological and missiological advances, but it is an inadequate road toward a realization of our profound unity of faith and the Spirit. The future of ecumenism demands that we engage in a common effort to establish a communion among Christian churches, as described earlier in this chapter—a communion that will allow each church to maintain the riches of its own structure, liturgy, and doctrine, while allowing for the handshake of fellowship and communion (see Gal. 2:9).

Within the Roman Catholic Church the opening for such communion among Christian churches is found in the documents of Vatican II. First of

---

[76]Bea, Cardinal Augustin, *The Way to Unity after the Council,* New York, Herder and Herder, 1967, p. 65.

all, Vatican II began to use the word *church* rather than *denominations* or *separated brethren* to describe those communities not seen by the Roman Church as possessing full unity. This may seem like a small linguistic change, but it opens up the possibility of recognizing a real communion among the various churches. Vatican II says, "We can say that in some real way they [other churches or ecclesial communities] are joined with us in the Holy Spirit, for to them also He gives His gifts and graces, and is thereby operative among them with His sanctifying power" (*Lumen Gentium*, #15). There are a number of texts from Vatican II that seem to be "prophetic" as we reread them after thirty years. The following citations from the past read today like a blueprint for the future of ecumenism:

> God has gathered together as one all those who in faith look upon Jesus as the author of salvation and the source of unity and peace, and has established them as the Church, that for each and all she may be the visible sacrament of this saving unity.
>
> (*Lumen Gentium*, #9)

> This characteristic of universality which adorns the People of God is a gift from the Lord himself. . . . In virtue of this catholicity each individual part of the Church contributes through its special gifts to the good of the other parts and of the whole Church. Thus through the common sharing of gifts and through the common effort to attain fullness in unity, the whole and each of the parts receive increase. (*Lumen Gentium*, #13)

> Moreover, within the Church particular churches hold a rightful place. These Churches retain their own traditions without in any way lessening the primacy of the Chair of Peter. This chair presides over the whole assembly of charity and protects legitimate differences, while at the same time it sees that such differences do not hinder unity but rather contribute to it. (*Lumen Gentium*, #13)

> All men are called to be part of this catholic unity of the People of God, a unity which is harbinger of the universal peace it promotes. And there belong to it or are related to it in various ways, the Catholic faithful as well as all who believe in Christ, and indeed the whole of mankind. For all men are called to salvation by the grace of God. (*Lumen Gentium*, #13)

> While preserving unity in essentials, let all members of the Church, according to the office entrusted to each, preserve a proper freedom in the various forms of spiritual life and discipline, in the variety of liturgical rites, and even in the theological elaborations of revealed truth. (*Unitatis Redintegratio*, #4)

If these "prophecies" are to be fulfilled by achieving full communion among the churches, we need to pursue with prayer, diligence, and dialogue the following five goals:

1. *The mutual acceptance of sacred Scripture,* the Word of God, as the fundamental witness to Christian life and mission. This goal is generally accepted by the Christian churches.

2. *A mutually acceptable, though not necessarily uniform, expression of the unity of faith and of the Spirit.* Doctrine and theology have always been important in the life of the Christian community, and the expression of doctrine cannot be left to each individual Christian. A common creed or a uniform theology is not always necessary, but it is essential that the official doctrinal positions of the churches be seen as authentic expressions of our common faith. We have made great strides in this area, but we have not yet reached mutually acceptable theological articulations of our Christian faith.

3. *A mutual recognition of the authenticity of Christian ministry in the various churches.* Communion is impossible until we can accept the reality and validity of one another's ministry. Over the last twenty years, progress has been made, many of the bilateral dialogues have reached substantial agreement, and many of the theological obstacles have been removed. But we have not yet fulfilled this goal for communion.

4. *Mutual recognition of the authentic worship life of local communities with the possibility of shared Eucharist as the fullest manifestation of communion.* This is also an aspect of our ecumenical life in which there has been growth and development. Ecumenical dialogues have come to a broad consensus on the theological meaning of worship and the sacraments. In many individual cases groups have shared worship and even the Eucharist, but official and public endorsement of this practice will probably come only with the establishment of full communion among our various churches.

5. *A common acceptance of primacy among the local churches,* and the need for leadership in the global church that manifests and encourages communion among the churches. Granfield says that more and more Christians "are beginning to recognize that a global ministry of unity is necessary for a united Church. This openness to some form of primacy within the Church demands a better understanding of the nature and limits of the primatial office."[77] In this chapter we have explored a holarchical vision of the primacy of the church at Rome that might be the basis of further dialogues. All of us must face this issue of primacy very directly in both structural and theological terms in order to see its place in the life and mission of the Christian church.

---

[77] Granfield, *The Limits of the Papacy,* p. 171.

We are at a turning point in the life of the Christian church. Visible communion was shattered at the time of the Great Schism and of the Reformation; suspicion and hatred have often erupted among us. Now we are beginning to move toward a new stage in our journey. People in the divided churches are discovering in each other a profound unity of faith and the Spirit. What remains is to find ways to establish communion among Christian churches that will respect both the unique character of each local church and the newly discovered reality of our interrelationship.

In the new paradigm we can see clearly the possibility of visible communion using the analogy of the quantum reality of particles and waves. The particle dimension of the local church enables it to maintain its identity and its capacity for self-preservation, while its wave dimension enables it to relate in communion with other churches and exercise its capacity for self-adaptation. Each church must build on the presently existing communion, not by living at the level of the least common denominator, but by living the Christian life to the fullest as contained in our various traditions.

If we wish to reach the goal of manifesting visibly our unity of faith and of the Spirit, the first requirement is to be, as deeply as possible, the church of Christ in our own local culture and in our own local church. As we do that we will discover that we can join hands in communion. And once Christians join hands in a communion of love and service, we can reach out and join hands in communion, or partial communion, with all those expressions of truth that might appear outside of the Christian church, whether non-Christian religions, or in secular movements. "In our exploration of what's possible, we are led to search for new and different partners. Who we become together will always be different than who we were alone. Our range of creative expression increases as we join with others. New relationships create new capacities."[78]

What a marvelous worldwide holy web embracing all humanity is awaiting us!

SUMMARY AND CONCLUSION

Some years ago, after I explained this general outline of the church and the new universe story, someone asked me if the four characteristics of the new paradigm had any relationship to the four traditional marks of the church. My response was that I had never considered that possibility. The more I thought about it, however, the more it became clear that there was a profound, yet surprising relationship. I will summarize the major conclusions of this book in terms of the one, holy, catholic, and apostolic church.

The Church Is One.   The oneness of the Church of the Earth is expressed in recognizing the presence of God in the inner unfolding of the earth, the Wisdom within the universe, and the reality of the human becom-

---

[78]Wheatley and Kellner-Rogers, *A Simpler Way*, p. 18.

ing the consciousness of the earth. The Church of the Earth challenges fragmentation and divisiveness at every level and is a profound symbol of the
unity of our planet and the unity of the human race. It is a dynamic web of
relationships based on wholeness and relationality within the universe, the
earth, the human community, and the church.

The Church Is Holy.   The Church of Deeper Consciousness is a web of
relationships that is deeply spiritual, ministerial, and sacramental. Its holiness is manifested in a community that helps people to find images, rituals,
and symbols that express their self-awareness, their awareness of God
within, and their awareness of Jesus, who embodies the reality of God with
us. The Church of Deeper Consciousness has the richness of two thousand
years of tradition, but it also now has a new creation story, unknown and
unheard of before in history. As a community of disciples the church has the
responsibility to enter into this cosmic journey and to help people discover
the holy web within the universe. The church brings to all people the good
news of God's holiness, God's extravagant love, and God's powerful presence within the whole universe, and the church is called to celebrate that holiness, love, and presence in life-giving rituals.

The Church Is Catholic.   The Church of the World emerges out of the
local culture that is its womb and its source of nourishment, and the universality or catholicity of the church means that the message of Christ can take
root and grow in any culture. The Church of the World is focused on a
global communion among local churches with an openness to a primacy of
servant leadership within this communion. The Church of the World is a
web of relationships binding together all Christian churches based on mutual acceptance of one another's authenticity, and at least a partial communion with non-Christian religions and secular movements.

The Church Is Apostolic.   The Holarchical Church is a self-organizing
system guided by the Holy Spirit in its journey through history, always
manifesting the presence of the reign of God in reconciliation, healing, and
liberation. It provides a deeper insight into the meaning of apostolicity insofar as the foundation for apostolic succession is the community of faith itself
as made visible in a succession of servant leaders. In a Holarchical Church
there are multiple ministries, all of which flow from the common priesthood
celebrated sacramentally in baptism, and a sacramental leadership unfolding from within a sacramental community.

The universe flashes forth fifteen billion years ago. In that powerful and
spectacular event the presence and love of God unfolds from within: *the inauguration of the Holy Web and the reign of God in the universe.* The Wisdom of God, Sophia, unfolds in the galaxies, the stars, our sun with its planets, and our earth with all of its beauty and richness.

In the human the earth becomes conscious and the spirituality of the
universe becomes visible. The human becomes aware of the reign of God in

the universe and begins to live in harmony with the earth. Now our child-hood as a human race is over, and our brief adolescence reaches its crisis point. Will we as humans continue the divine unfolding process or will we abort the process in a fit of helpless self-destruction?

I believe in the Creator God, the source of all goodness, truth, and holi-ness. I believe in the guidance of Sophia and the Word made flesh in Jesus. I believe in the power and presence of God in the Holy Spirit. I believe in the beauty of all creation and the holy web within the universe. I believe in the willingness of the human race to make the giant leap into adulthood in tune with the community of species. I believe that the Christian church will be a powerful force for reconciliation, healing, and liberation as it discovers and lives out the dynamic web of relationships both within itself and as part of a larger web with and among all peoples. I believe that out of the chaos and darkness will come a new heaven and a new earth, a new creation and a new church. The dream of God will continue to unfold in the universe.

BIBLIOGRAPHY

BOOKS

Afaanassieff, Nicolas, et al., *The Primacy of Peter,* London, Faith Press, 1963.

Bea, Cardinal Augustin, *The Way to Unity after the Council,* New York, Herder and Herder, 1967.

Berry, Thomas, *The Dream of the Earth,* San Francisco, Sierra Club Books, 1988.

Bertalanffy, L. von, *General System Theory,* New York, Braziller, 1969.

Bohm, David, *Wholeness and the Implicate Order*, New York, Routledge & Kegan Paul, 1980.

Borg, Marcus J., *Meeting Jesus again for the First Time,* San Francisco, HarperSanFrancisco, 1994.

Bozarth-Campbell, Alla, *Womanpriest: A Personal Odyssey,* New York, Paulist Press, 1978.

Bronowski, Jacob, *The Ascent of Man,* Boston, Little, Brown, 1973.

Brueggemann, Walter, *The Prophetic Imagination,* Philadelphia, Fortress Press, 1978.

Capra, Fritjof, *The Turning Point,* New York, Bantam Books, 1983.

Chittister, Joan, O.S.B., *Heart of Flesh: A Feminist Spirituality for Women and Men,* Grand Rapids, MI, William B. Eerdman's Publishing Company, 1998.

The Church Teaches: Documents of the Church in English Translation, St. Louis, B. Herder Book Co., 1955.

Crossan, John Dominic, *Jesus: A Revolutionary Biography,* New York, HarperCollins, 1995.

Cullmann, Oscar, *Peter: Disciple, Apostle, Martyr,* Philadelphia, Westminster Press, 1962.

Donovan, Vincent J., *Christianity Rediscovered,* Maryknoll, NY, Orbis Books, 1978.

Driver, Tom, *The Magic of Ritual,* San Francisco, HarperSanFrancisco, 1991.

Dulles, Avery, *A Church to Believe In: Discipleship and the Dynamics of Freedom,* New York, Crossroad, 1985.

Edwards, Denis, *Jesus the Wisdom of God: An Ecological Theology,* Maryknoll, NY, Orbis Books, 1995.

Faivre, Alexandre, *The Emergence of the Laity in the Early Church,* New York, Paulist Press, 1990.

Ferguson, Marilyn, *The Aquarian Conspiracy,* New York, St. Martin's Press, 1980.

Gaillardetz, Richard, *Teaching with Authority,* Collegeville, MN, The Liturgical Press, 1997.

Goergen, Donald J., *The Mission and Ministry of Jesus,* Wilmington, DE, Michael Glazier, 1985.

Granfield, Patrick, *The Limits of the Papacy,* New York, Crossroad, 1987.

Granfield, Patrick, *The Papacy in Transition,* New York, Doubleday, 1980.

Greenleaf, Robert K., *Servant Leadership,* New York, Paulist Press, 1977.

Hales, E. E. Y., *Pio Nono,* London, Eyre & Spottiswoode, 1954.

Hall, Douglas John, *God and Human Suffering,* Minneapolis, MN, Augsburg Publishing House, 1986.

Hamer, Jerome, *The Church Is a Communion,* New York, Sheed and Ward, 1964.

Hamilton, Virginia, *In the Beginning: Creation Stories from around the World,* New York, Harcourt Brace Jovanovich, 1988.

Harris, John C., *Stress, Power, and Ministry,* The Silvan Institute, 1977.

Haughton, Rosemary, *The Passionate God,* New York, Paulist Press, 1981.

Hilkert, Mary Catherine, *Naming Grace: Preaching and the Sacramental Imagination,* New York, Continuum, 1997.

Jaworski, Joseph, *Synchronicity: The Inner Path of Leadership,* San Francisco, Berrett-Koehler Publishers, 1996.

John Paul II, "*Redemptor Hominis,*"in *Origins,* March 4, 1979, Washington, DC, U.S. Catholic Conference, 1979, No. 21.

Johnson, Elizabeth, *She Who Is: The Mystery of God in Feminist Discourse,* New York, Crossroad, 1994.

Johnson, Elizabeth, *Women, Earth, and Creator Spirit,* New York, Paulist Press, 1993.

Johnson, Robert A., *We: Understanding the Psychology of Romantic Love,* San Francisco, Harper & Row, 1983.

Joseph, Lawrence E., *Gaia: The Growth of an Idea,* New York, St. Martin's Press, 1990.

Keck, L. Robert, *Sacred Eyes,* Boulder, CO, Synergy Associates, 1992.

Keen, Sam, *The Passionate Life: Stages of Loving,* San Francisco, Harper & Row, 1983.

Kilian, Sabbas J., *Theological Models for the Parish,* New York, Alba House, 1977.

Kingsolver, Barbara, *Animal Dreams,* New York, Harper Perennial, 1991.

Kingsolver, Barbara, *High Tide in Tucson,* New York, Harper Perennial, 1995.

Kuhn, Thomas S., *The Structure of Scientific Revolutions,* Chicago, University of Chicago Press, 1970.

Lawler, Michael G., *Symbol and Sacrament: A Contemporary Sacramental Theology,* New York, Paulist Press, 1987.

Ludwig, Robert A., *Reconstructing Catholicism: For a New Generation,* New York, Crossroad, 1995.

McFague, Sallie, *Super, Natural Christians,* Minneapolis, MN, Fortress Press, 1997.

Mudge, Lewis S., *One Church: Catholic and Reformed,* Philadelphia, Westminster Press, 1963.

Murray, John Courtney, *The Problem of God,* New Haven, CT, Yale University Press, 1964.

Naisbitt, John, *Global Paradox,* New York, William Morrow and Co., 1994.

Nichols, Terence, *That All May Be One: Hierarchy and Participation in the Church,* Collegeville, MN, The Liturgical Press, 1997.

Nogar, Raymond J., *The Lord of the Absurd,* New York, Herder and Herder, 1972.

Nolan, Albert, *Jesus before Christianity,* Maryknoll, NY, Orbis Books, 1992.

O'Meara, Thomas Franklin, O.P., *Theology of Ministry,* New York, Paulist Press, 1983.

O'Murchu, Diarmuid, *Quantum Theology,* New York, Crossroad, 1997.

O'Murchu, Diarmuid, *Reclaiming Spirituality,* New York, Crossroad, 1998.

Parent, Remi, *A Church of the Baptized: Overcoming the Tension between the Clergy and the Laity,* New York, Paulist Press, 1989.

Prigogine, Ilya, and Isabelle Stengers, *Order Out of Chaos: Man's New Dialogue with Nature,* New York, Bantam Books, 1984.

Progoff, Ira, *Depth Psychology and Modern Man,* New York, McGraw-Hill, 1959.

Progoff, Ira, *The Symbolic and the Real,* New York, McGraw-Hill, 1973.

Quinn, Daniel, *Ishmael: An Adventure of the Mind and Spirit,* New York, Bantam Turner, 1992.

Rahner, Karl, *Shape of the Church to Come,* New York, Seabury Press, 1974.

Raymo, Chet, *Skeptics and True Believers: The Exhilarating Connection between Science and Religion,* New York, Walker and Company, 1998.

Ruether, Rosemary Radford, *Gaia and God: An Ecofeminist Theology of Earth Healing,* San Francisco, HarperSanFrancisco, 1992.

Schillebeeckx, Edward, *The Church with a Human Face,* New York, Crossroad, 1990.

Schillebeeckx, Edward, *Ministry: Leadership in the Community of Jesus Christ,* New York, Crossroad, 1981.

Schweizer, Eduard, *The Holy Spirit,* Philadelphia, Fortress Press, 1980.

Shea, John, *Stories of God,* Chicago, Thomas More Press, 1978.

Sobrino, Jon, *Christology at the Crossroads,* Maryknoll, NY, Orbis Books, 1978.

Swimme, Brian, *The Hidden Heart of the Cosmos,* Maryknoll, NY, Orbis Books, 1996.

Swimme, Brian, *The Universe Is a Green Dragon,* Santa Fe, NM, Bear & Company, 1985.

Swimme, Brian, and Thomas Berry, *The Universe Story,* San Francisco, HarperSanFrancisco, 1992.

Thomas, Gordon, and Max Morgan-Witts, *Pontiff,* Garden City, NY, Doubleday, 1983.

Tillard, J. M. R., *The Bishop of Rome,* Wilmington, DE, Michael Glazier, Inc., 1983.

Tillard, J. M. R., *Church of Churches: The Ecclesiology of Communion,* Collegeville, MN, Liturgical Press, 1992.

Vatican II, *Council Daybook,* Washington, DC, National Catholic Welfare Council, 1956.

Vatican II, *Lumen Gentium, Gaudium et Spes, Unitatis Redintegratio, Christus Dominus,* Walter Abbott, S.J., editor, New York, Guild Press, 1966.

Welch, John, O. Carm., *Spiritual Pilgrims,* New York, Paulist Press, 1982.

Wheatley, Margaret J., *Leadership and the New Science,* San Francisco, Berrett-Koehler Publishers, 1994.

Wheatley, Margaret J., and Myron Kellner-Rogers, *A Simpler Way,* San Francisco, Berrett-Koehler Publishers, 1996.

Whitehead, Evelyn Eaton, and James D., *Christian Life Patterns,* Garden City, NY, Doubleday, 1979.

Wilber, Ken, ed., *The Holographic Paradigm and Other Paradoxes,* Boulder, CO, The New Science Library, 1982.

Wilber, Ken, *Sex, Ecology, Spirituality: The Spirit of Evolution,* Boston, Shambhala, 1995.

Woods, Richard, *Mysterion: An Approach to Mystical Spirituality,* Chicago, Thomas More Press, 1981.

Zohar, Danah, *The Quantum Self: Human Nature and Consciousness Defined by the New Physics,* New York, Quill/William Morrow, 1990.

Zohar, Danah, and Ian Marshall, *The Quantum Society: Mind, Physics, and a New Social Vision,* New York, Quill/William Morrow, 1994.

ARTICLES

Afaanassieff, Nicolas, "The Church which Presides in Love," in *The Primacy of Peter*, London, Faith Press, 1963.

Bastes, Bishop Arturo, "Asian Formation for Consecrated Life," in *Origins*, May 7, 1998.

Beifuss, Joan Turner, "Feminists Are Clarifying Old Values," in *National Catholic Reporter*, December 23, 1983.

Berry, Thomas, C.P., "Contemplation and World Order," in *The Whole Earth Papers*, Vol. 1, No. 10, 1978.

Berry, Thomas, C.P., "The Spirituality of the Earth," in *The Whole Earth Papers*, No. 16, 1982.

Chittister, Joan, O.S.B., "Heart of Flesh: A Feminist Spirituality for Women and Men," in *Spirituality Justice Reprint*, Call To Action, January, 1998.

Chittister, Joan, O.S.B., "Pentecost Papacy Would Listen to Women," in *National Catholic Reporter*, October 10, 1997.

Clifford, Anne, "Creation," in *Systematic Theology: Roman Catholic Perspectives*, Minneapolis, MN, Augsburg Press, 1991.

Grillmeier, Aloys, "Commentary on *Lumen Gentium*," Chap. 2, in *Commentary on the Documents of Vatican II*, Vol. 1., H. Vorgrimler, ed., New York, Herder and Herder, 1967.

Hadisumarta, Bishop Francis, "Enhanced Role for Bishops' Conferences," in *Origins*, May 7, 1998.

Heilig, Gabriel Saul, "Spirituality and Manhood," in *Tenderness Is Strength*, Harold Lyons Jr., New York, Harper & Row, 1977.

Ikenaga, Archbishop Leo Jun, "Asian Ways of Expression," in *Origins*, May 7, 1998.

John Paul II, "New Chapter in the History of Salvation," in *Origins*, May 28, 1998.

John Paul II, "*Redemptor Hominis*," in *Origins*, March 4, 1979.

Meyendorff, John, "St. Peter in Byzantine Theology," in *The Primacy of Peter*, Nicholas Afaanassieff et al., London, Faith Press, 1963.

Mische, Patricia, "Towards a Global Spirituality," in *The Whole Earth Papers*, No. 16, 1982.

Pius X, "*Vehementer Nos*," No. 8, February 11, 1906, in *The Papal Encyclicals 1903–1939*, McGrath Publishing Company, 1981.

Senge, Peter, "Introduction," in *Synchronicity: The Inner Path of Leadership*, Joseph Jaworski, ed., San Francisco, Berrett-Koehler Publishers, 1996.

"Some Questions Regarding Collaboration of Nonordained Faithful in Priests' Sacred Ministry," in *Origins*, November 27, 1997.

Synod of Asia, "Message to the People of God," in *Origins*, May 28, 1998.

Toffler, Alvin, "Forward: Science and Change," in *Order Out of Chaos*, Ilya Prigogine and Isabelle Stengers, eds., New York, Bantam Books, 1984.

Weakland, Archbishop Rembert, "Church of Many Cultures, World of Globalization," in *Origins*, November 12, 1998.

Weber, Renee, "The Enfolding-Unfolding Universe: A Conversation with David Bohm," in *The Holographic Paradigm and Other Paradoxes*, Ken Wilber, ed., Boulder, CO, The New Science Library, 1982.

Weber, Renee, "The Physicist and the Mystic: Is a Dialogue between Them Possible? A Conversation with David Bohm," in *The Holographic Paradigm and Other Paradoxes*, Ken Wilber, ed., Boulder, CO, The New Science Library, 1982.

Wessels, Cletus, O.P., "The Adequacy of Vatican I," in *Listening*, Spring-Autumn, 1972.

Wessels, Cletus, O.P., "Coping with Conspiracy of Silence, Climate of Fear," in *National Catholic Reporter*, January 29, 1988.

Wessels, Cletus, O.P., "Separate and Unequal: Seminary as Hothouse" in *National Catholic Reporter*, March 25, 1988.

Wilson, Edward O., "The Biological Basis of Morality," in *Atlantic Monthly*, April, 1998.

INDEX